Military Vehicles
of the World

CHRISTOPHER F. FOSS

Charles Scribner's Sons
NEW YORK

Contents

Printed in Great Britain
Library of Congress Catalog Card Number 75-46380
ISBN 0-684-14678-9

To Robert Joy (The Parachute Regiment)

Introduction

The aim of *'Military Vehicles of the World'* is to cover, in some detail, the majority of cargo type vehicles, both tracked and wheeled, to be found in Army service throughout the world.

This book, together with my previously published books *'Armoured Fighting Vehicles of the World'* and *'Artillery of the World'* with the forthcoming book *'Infantry Weapons of the World'* will enable the reader to obtain a complete set of volumes to cover all current military equipment.

Only vehicles at present in service or at a very advanced stage of development are included. Indeed, the development of military vehicles is so rapid that some vehicles in this volume may have had their development stopped or be phased out of service by the time this book is published. There are also quite a few vehicles of World War II vintage still in service, these have however, been omitted.

In these days of economic difficulties many nations are purchasing vehicles for Army use that are little more than civilian vehicles with bigger tyres and a coat of Army paint. It remains to be seen if this trend is continued or whether future vehicles for Army use will be designed specifically for the use of the military but using, wherever possible, existing civilian components. The new German range of high mobility vehicles is a good example of the use of standard commercial components in military vehicles.

The majority of vehicles found in front-line use with Armies will be found in this book. There is insufficient room to include all of the other vehicles used for general Army work such as buses, fire-engines, as well as the highly specialised engineer equipment, to cover these as well would require several more volumes. All data is metric. Wherever possible full technical details are supplied. This includes length (overall), width, height (with and without rear covers), track (front and rear), wheelbase (for 6×6 vehicles this has been taken from the centre of the 1st wheel to the centre of the 2nd wheel, and then from the centre of the 2nd wheel to the centre of the 3rd wheel), weights (loaded and empty), load area (inside dimensions of the rear cargo area), engine details, crew, speed, range, fuel (without additional fuel tanks), gradient, turning radius, fording and size of tyres.

The material for this volume has been supplied by numerous governments, manufacturers and individuals all over the world and the author would like to express his thanks to all those who have assisted in the preparation of this volume. Special thanks are due to Robert Forsyth, John F. Milsom and Geoffrey Tillotson for their most valuable assistance.

Additional material, including photographs, for future editions of 'Military Vehicles of the World' should be forwarded to Ian Allan Limited, Terminal House, Shepperton, TW17 8AS, England.

1975   **Christopher F. Foss**

Abbreviations

AFV	Armoured Fighting Vehicle	m	Metre(s)
APC	Armoured Personnel Carrier	mm	Millimetre(s)
ATGW	Anti-Tank Guided Weapon	max	Maximum
BHP	Brake Horse Power	min	Minimum
c/c	Cross country	o/a	Overall
f	Front	OHV	Overhead Valve
F	Forward	prep	Prepared
FGR	Federal German Republic	PTO	Power Take Off
GDR	German Democratic Republic	r	rear
GVW	Gross Vehicle Weight	rpm	Revolutions per minute
G/CLEARANCE	Ground Clearance	R	Reverse
G/PRESSURE	Ground Pressure	RHD	Right Hand Drive
HP	Horse Power	ROF	Royal Ordnance Factory
inc	Including	SAM	Surface to Air Missile
kg	Kilogramme(s)	SWB	Short Wheelbase
kg/cm²	Kilogrammes per square centimetre	T/RADIUS	Turning Radius
		V/OBSTACLE	Vertical Obstacle
km	Kilometre(s)	WB	Wheelbase
km/ph	Kilometres per hour	w/o	Without
LHD	Left Hand Drive	W/W	With Winch
LWB	Long Wheel Base	WO/W	Without Winch
MBT	Main Battle Tank		
MVEE	Military Vehicle and Engineering Establishment, M.o.D. (UK)		

Acknowledgements

The author would like to thank the following companies for their most valuable assistance during the preparation of this book.

Aérospatiale (France)
Alvis (Great Britain)
AM General (United States)
Australian Army
Austrian Army
Auto-Union (Germany)
Berliet (France)
Bolinder-Munktell (Sweden)
British Leyland (Great Britain)
British Ministry of Defence (Army)
Canadair (Canada)
Caterpillar (United States)
Citroen (France)
Crane Fruehauf (Great Britain)
DAF (Netherlands)
Engesa (Brazil)
Faun-Werk (Germany)
Fiat (Italy)
Finnish Army
FMC (United States)
FN (Belgium)
Foden (Great Britain)
Ford (Germany and United States)
German Army
Indian Army
International Harvestor (Australia)
Italian Army
Japanese Self Defence Force
Laird (Great Britain)
Lockheed Aircraft Service Company (United States)
Magirus-Deutz (Germany)

Pegaso (Spain)
Reynolds Boughton (Great Britain)
Rover (Great Britain)
Saviem (France)
Scania-Vabis (Sweden)
Scammel (Great Britain)
Sisu (Finland)
Steyr-Daimler-Puch (Austria)
United States Army
United States Marine Corps
Valmet (Finland)
Vauxhall (Great Britain)
Volkswagen (Germany)
Volvo (Sweden)

International (4 x 4) 2 ½ -Ton Truck   Australia

Length: 6.375m
Width: 2.438m
Height: 2.896m (canopy)
2.616m (cab)
G/Clearance: .343m
Track: 1.854m
Wheelbase: 3.683m
Weight: 8,032kg (loaded)
5537kg (empty)
Load Area: 4.367m × 2.134m
Engine: International Model AGD-282, 6-cyclinder in-line petrol engine developing 148HP at 3,800rpm.
Crew: 1 + 1
Speed: 80km/hr
Range: 480km
Fuel: 200 litres
Gradient: 60%
Angle Approach: 44°
Angle Departure: 37°
T/Radius: 9.14m
Fording: 1.981m (prep)
1.092m (w/o prep)
Tyres: 12.00 × 20

Development

The full designation of the vehicle is Truck, Cargo, 2½-ton, GS, there are various marks. The design of the vehicle started in the 1950s and by 1966 over 1,500 had been built by International Harvester Company of Australia. The majority of the components are of Australian design and construction.

It is provided with an open type, drop side body which has a canopy, there are eight swing up seats either side of the cargo body. The canopy, bows, seats and sides can be quickly removed to leave a flat type body. The gearbox has 5F and 1R gears, the 2nd, 3rd, 4th and 5th being synchromesh. The two speed transfer case is mounted behind the gearbox.

It can tow a trailer, gross vehicle weight (with trailer) being 12,568kg (road) and 10,753km (cross-country). Some models are fitted with a winch with a capacity of 5000kg and 61m of rope. The latest models are the Mk. 3s which have fibre-glass mudguards and the Mk. 4 which have steel mudguards. The cab of the vehicle is the same as that used for the International 6 × 6 5-ton truck, as are some other components.

Variants

There is one model in service with the British designed and built Class 30 portable roadway system mounted on the rear of the vehicle.

Employment

Australia

Note: *The Australian Army also uses the standard Ford 2½-ton truck slightly modified for military purposes. It was announced in 1972 that the Australian Army was to replace its fleet of ¾-ton vehicles by 1-ton vehicles. Contracts for the development of this vehicle were awarded to the Ford Motor Company and the International Harvester Company. By 1971/72 each company had built four prototypes and these were being tested.*

Above: *Australian International (4 × 4) 2½ Ton Truck laying portable roadway system.*

7

Truck, Cargo (6 x 6) 5-Ton GS, F1 (With Winch)   Australia

Length: 6.908m
Width: 2.438m
Height: 3.022m (canopy)
2.616m (cab)
Ground Clearance: .33m
Track: 1.854m
Wheelbase: 3.784m
Weight: 13,600kg (loaded)
11,350kg (loaded c/c)
6,780kg (empty)
Engine: International AGD-283, 6-cyclinder, in-line petrol engine, OHV.
Crew: 1 + 1
Speed: 72km/hr
Range: 483km
Fuel: 191 litres
Gradient: 60%
Angle Approach: 44°
Angle Departure: 40°
Fording: 1.981m (prep)
.914m (w/o prep)
Tyres: 12.00 × 20

Development

Development of the vehicle was started by the International Harvester Company in 1958 and the first two prototype vehicles were completed in 1960, production commenced in 1966. It has a similar cab to the 4 × 4 International 2 ½-ton truck and the 4 × 2 truck/tractor which has also been built by International Harvester.

The gearbox has 5 forward and 1 reverse gears, the 2nd, 3rd, 4th and 5th are constant mesh gears, with 1st and reverse sliding. The two speed transfer case is mounted behind the gearbox. The front axle suspension consists of semi-elliptical springs, tele-

scopic shock absorbers and rubber bump stops. Inverted semi-elliptical springs are fitted to the rear bogie. All wheels have hydraulic brakes and these are operated from a two-line compressed air system, with rear couplings for trailer braking. Two air take-off valves are fitted, one for tyre inflation and the other for deep wading and pressurising the transmission.

The winch is mounted behind the transfer case and provides front and rear winching facilities with controls in the cab, the engine is automatically switched off when overheating occurs.

The cargo body has drop down sides and tailgate, swing-up bench-type seats are provided. Its towed load is 8,165kg on roads or 5,900kg cross country.

Variants

The dump truck model is designated Truck, Dump, 5 cu yards, GS, F1, with winch. A front mounted, three stage telescopic hoist is used for tipping the body of the dump truck and this is controlled from the cab. The dump truck can also be converted to a troop carrying role by the provision of bench type seats. There is also a recovery model whose designation is Truck, Wrecker, Medium, 5-ton, GS, 6 × 6 (F5) and has twin booms at the rear and a full range of tools and equipment. The basic cargo version can also be used to carry containers.

Employment
Australian Army

Below: *Australian Truck, Wrecker, Medium, 5-Ton (6 × 6), General Service (F5).*

Other vehicles used by the Australian Army.

Above right: *2½-Ton Ford (4 × 2) CL (Truck, Cargo, 2½-Ton CL)*

Centre right: *Semi-Trailer, Tank Transport, 60-Ton, 20 Wheeled Aust. No. 1 Mk. 1 coupled to a Diamond T Tractor. This is used for carrying Centurion Main Battle Tanks of the Australian Army.*

Below: *Diamond Reo and semi-trailer of the Australian Army (Truck, Tractor, GS & S/T, Cargo, 20-Ton). Many other armies use the Diamond Reo.*

Steyr-Puch 700 AP Haflinger   Austria

Length: 2.83m
Width: 1.35m
Height: 1.74m (o/a)
1.36m (reduced)
Ground Clearance: .24m
Wheelbase: 1.5m
Track: 1.13m
Weight: 1,150kg (loaded)
580kg (empty)
Load Area: 1.54m × 1.275m
Engine: Model 700 AP, 2-cylinder, air-cooled petrol engine developing 24hp at 4,500rpm. From 1967 vehicles were fitted with a 27hp (at 4,800rpm) engine.
Crew: 1 + 3
Speed: 64km/hr
Range: 400km
Fuel: 20 litres
Gradient: 33°
T/Radius: 3.8m
Fording: .4m
Tyres: 5.20 × 12

Development/Variants

This 4 × 4 vehicle can carry 400kg of cargo. It is built by Steyr-Puch and has been in production for some 15 years. The chassis is of tubular construction with the engine and transmission at the rear. If required, a winch with a capacity of 1,500kg can be fitted. A differential locking system is provided. Its transmission has 4F and 1R gears, vehicles built since 1966 have a transmission with 5F and 1R gears. A LWB model with a wheelbase of 1.8m has also been produced. There are a number of variants in service with the Austrian Army, these include a radio vehicle and a command vehicle. Prototypes have been built of a number of anti-tank vehicles including the following: fitted with the Swedish 90mm recoilless rifle; fitted with Swedish Bantam (six at the front and eight at the rear) ATGW; fitted with four Mosquito ATGWs ready to fire with a further four in reserve. As far as it is known, none of these have entered service.

Employment

Australia, Austria, Indonesia, Italy, Great Britain, Netherlands, Nigeria, Switzerland and South Africa.

The 700 AP Haflinger without hood and doors, note the windscreen folded down.

The 700 AP Haflinger with hood erected and doors fitted.

Steyr-Puch 710 Pinzgauer (4 x 4) 1-Ton Truck   Austria

Length: 4.2m
Width: 1.76m
Height: 2.1m
Wheelbase: 2.2m
Weight: 2,950kg (loaded)
1,950kg (empty)
Engine: Steyr-Puch 4-cylinder petrol engine developing 92hp (early models had a 87hp engine).
Crew: 1 + 1
Speed: 100km
Range: 500km
Fording: .6m

Development/Variants
This vehicle has been developed by Steyr-Puch and is essentially a larger model of the Haflinger. The first prototype was completed in 1965 with production starting in 1971, it entered service with the Austrian Army in 1973. It is available in both fully enclosed personnel carrier (the 710M) or as a cargo model, the latter has bench type seats for a total of eight men. A 6 × 6 model has also been built and tested.

Employment
In service with the Austrian Army.

Above: *The Pinzgauer (4 × 4) Personnel Carrier*

Below: *The (6 × 6) Pinzgauer Cargo Truck*

Husar HA 2-90 (4 x 4) 1 ½ -Ton Truck

Austria

Length: 5.65m
Width: 2.13m
Height: 2.84m
Wheelbase: 3.4m
Weight: 3,750kg (empty)
6,700kg (loaded, road)
Engine: Model D-0834 M8, 4-cylinder diesel developing 90 bhp at 2,500 rpm. (4.7 litres).
Crew: 1 + 1
Speed: 85km/hr
Range: 500km
Gradient: 60%
Fording: .8m
Tyres: 9.00 × 20

Development/Variants/Employment

This is a 4 × 4 truck specifically developed for the Austrian Army by O.A.F., the first prototype was completed in 1966, production commenced in 1968 and the vehicle entered service in 1969. It can carry 3,000kg of cargo on roads or 1,500kg of cargo across country. It can also be fitted with a winch with a capacity of 3,500kg.

Above left: Husar HA 2-90 Truck of the Austrian Army

Steyr 480 (4 x 2) 4-Ton Cargo Truck

Austria

Length: 6.84m
Width: 2.4m
Height: 2.8m
Wheelbase: 3.71m
Weight: 3,850kg (empty)
7,850kg (loaded)
Engine: Steyr Model WD 413, 4-cylinder diesel developing 95hp. (5.322 litres).
Crew: 1 + 1
Speed: 78km/hr
Range: 300km
Gradient: 30%
Fording: .9m

Development/Variants/Employment

This is a 4 × 2 general purpose cargo truck with limited cross country mobility, its maximum cargo capacity being approximately 4,000kg. It is in service only with the Austrian Army. The Steyr 580g is similar in appearance to the Steyr 480. The 580g is a 4 × 4 truck which is capable of carrying 3,000kg of cargo across country or 5,000kg of cargo on roads. Its towed load being approximately 8,000kg. It is powered by a 4-cylinder diesel developing 95bhp, a later model, the Steyr 586g had a more powerful 6-cylinder diesel engine developing 120bhp.

Above right: Steyr 480 (4 × 2) Truck of the Austrian Army

Steyr 680 M (4 x 2) 2½-Ton Truck

Austria

Length: 6.57m
Width: 2.4m
Height: 2.85m (canvas cover)
2.63m (cab)
G/Clearance: .3m
Track: 1.81m(f) 1.67(r)
Wheelbase: 3.7m
Weight: 12,000kg (loaded)
5,430kg (empty)
Load Area: 4.06m × 2.232m
Engine: Steyr Model WD 610.23, 6-cylinder in-line water-cooled diesel developing 120hp at 2,800 rpm.
Crew: 1 + 1
Speed: 80km/hr
Range: 450km
Fuel: 165 litres
Gradient: 59%
Angle Approach: 28°
Angle Departure: 28°
T/Radius: 7.5m
Fording: .5m
Tyres: 9.00 × 20

Development/Variants

The Steyr 680M is a nominal 2½-ton truck although its maximum stated cross country load is 4,570kg, maximum road load being 6,570kg. Towed load is 8,000kg on roads and 4,000kg cross country. A winch with a capacity of 4,500kg is fitted and this is provided with 90m of cable, the empty weight of the vehicle with winch is 5,830kg. The cab is of the forward control type and is of all steel construction, a heater is fitted and there is a hatch in the roof of the cab. The rear body is provided with a tailgate, drop sides, bows and a tarpaulin, if required seats for approximately 20 men can be provided in the rear.

The gearbox has 5F and 1R gears and a two-speed transfer case. The maximum gradient of 59% is for when the vehicle weighs 10,500kg (GVW) and 1st gear (low range) is being used. The rear wheels have dual tyres, hydraulic brakes are fitted and the steering is power-assisted.

Variants

None, although the Steyr 680 M3 (6 × 6) truck is based on the 4 × 4 Steyr 680M.

Employment

Austrian Army; some are also used by the Swiss Army.

13

*The Steyr 680M (4 × 4)
2½-Ton Truck being used
to carry infantrymen*

Steyr 680 M3 (6 x 6) 3 ½ -Ton Truck   Austria

Length: 6.73m
Width: 2.4m
Height: 2.85m (canvas cover)
2.63m (cab)
G/Clearance: .3m
Track: 1.81m(f) 1.72m(r)
Wheelbase: 2.76m + 1.2m
Weight: 13,200kg (loaded)
6,500kg (empty)
Load Area: 4.06m × 2.198m
Engine: Steyr 6-cylinder, in-line, OHV, water-cooled diesel (with supercharger) developing 165hp at 2,800rpm.
Crew: 1 + 1
Speed: 79.7km/hr
Range: 500km
Fuel: 180 litres
Gradient: 74%
Angle Approach: 28°
Angle Departure: 32°
T/Radius: 7.25m
Fording: .5m
Tyres: 9.00 × 20

Development
The Steyr 680 M3 is basically the Steyr 680 M with a more powerful engine, bigger fuel tank and six wheels. Its maximum load cross country is 3,500kg, maximum road load being 6,500kg. It can tow a trailer with a maximum weight of 4,000kg (cross-country) or 8,000kg (road). The cab is of the forward control type and is of all steel construction, a heater is fitted and there is a hatch in the roof of the cab. The rear body is provided with a tailgate, drop sides, bows and a tarpaulin, if required seats can be fitted. A winch with a capacity of 4,500kg and 90m of cab is provided.

The gearbox has 5F and 1R gears and a two speed transfer case, the maximum gradient of 74% is for when the vehicle weighs 10,500kg (GVW) and 1st gear (low range) is being used. The front suspension consists of horizontally positioned semi-elliptical springs with additional rubber hollow springs and telescopic shock absorbers, the rear suspension consists of horizontal positioned semi-elliptical springs, reverse mounted, with reversible spring hangers positioned in the middle of the rear axles. The rear wheels have dual tyres, hydraulic brakes are fitted and the steering is power-assisted.

Variants
A dump truck model is in service, as is a fuel-tanker.

Employment
Austrian Army.

*The Steyr 680 M3 (6 × 6)
2½-Ton Truck*

Gräf and Stift Trucks

Austria

	LAVT-9F/2H	ZAVT-9F/1	ZA-200/1A
Length:	6.55m	6.49m	8.6m
Width:	2.4m	2.4m	2.4m
Height:	2.9m	3m	2.9m
Weight:	8,300kg	7,200kg	10,650kg
Speed:	75km/hr	75km/hr	70km/hr
Range:	500km	400km	350km
Gradient:	60%	60%	72%
Wheelbase:	3.86m	3.86m	4.32m

LAVT-9F/2H 6 TON CARGO TRUCK

This 4 × 4 vehicle is powered by a Gräf and Stift Model 6 VT-145 6-cylinder diesel engine developing 75hp. It is provided with a gear box with 5F and 1R gears and a two-speed transfer case. The rear body is provided with a tailgate, removable bows and a tarpaulin. Other models in service include a pontoon boat carrying model, which also tows a trailer with another boat. Some cargo models have a HIAB crane.

ZAFT-9F/1 6 TON CARGO TRUCK

This 4 × 4 vehicle is basically the LAVT-9F/2H with a larger cab. It is provided with the same engine and transmission as the above model. A winch is provided, this vehicle is often used to tow artillery.

ZA-200/1A 8 TON CARGO TRUCK

This 6 × 6 cargo truck is powered by a Gräf and Stift Model 6 VT-200, 6-cylinder diesel engine which developes 200bhp at 2,000rpm (10.809 litres). The gearbox is provided with 6F and 1R gears and a two speed transfer case. The rear body is provided with drop sides, tailgate and a HIAB crane. A winch, with a capacity of 4,500kg leads out through the front of the vehicle.

There are a number of variants in service with the Austrian Forces including an extended cab model which has seats for five men (instead of the normal two seats). The ZAFD-210/36 is basically the extended cab model with a 15 ton crane mounted on the rear. The ZA-210/3 also has an extended cab and this is used as a prime mover for towing trailers carrying tanks (i.e. Austrian M-47s and M-60A1s) or heavy engineer equipment. The air force has an aircraft refuelling model which uses the chassis of the ZA-200/1A.

Employment

All of these vehicles are used only by the Austrian Armed Forces.

*The Gräf and Stift
LAVT-9F/2H (4 × 4)
Truck*

FN AS 24 Airborne Vehicle Belgium

Length: 1.89m
Width: 1.64m
Height: .89m
Track: 1.306m(r)
Wheelbase: 1.27m
Weight: 564kg (loaded)
224kg (empty)
Engine: Type FN 24, 2-cylinder, 2-stroke petrol engine developing 15hp at 5,300rpm.
Crew: 1 + 3
Speed: 57.2km/hr
Range: 200km
Fuel: 10.5 litres
Gradient: 60%
T/Radius: 1.75m
Tyres: 22.00 × 12

Development

This very interesting vehicle was designed by the famous British engineer Nicholas Straussler, who also developed the Duplex drive system which was used so successfully on Allied tanks in World War II. Production was however, undertaken by FN of Herstal, Belgium.

A total of four men can be carried on the front bench type seat, maximum cargo capacity is 330kg and it can also tow a trailer with a maximum load of 250kg.

The chassis is of all welded steel construction. The side members are made in two parts which slide together and allow the vehicle to be collapsed and extended. It takes approximately one minute to prepare the vehicle for operations after it has been air-dropped or one and a half minute to retract it again. When the vehicle is retracted the seat goes to the rear. It is normally air-dropped on a 1.8m × 2m pallet.

The gearbox has 4F but no reverse gear. The steering colum is hinged on a cardan joint and is telescopic to allow for easy retraction.

Variants

The following variants were proposed by FN and most of them were built as prototypes, for normal use it is usually found carrying men and ammunition: carrying stores such as fuel, ammunition or mines, evacuation of wounded, fire-fighting vehicle, guided missile vehicle with three anti-tank guided weapons, laying telephone cables, machine gun carrier mounting a 7.62mm FN machine gun or mortar carrier, two AS 24s can carry a complete mortar, ammunition and crew.

Employment

Belgium, France.

The FN AS 24 Airborne Vehicle carrying four men

FN 4RM/62 Ardennes (4 x 4) 1 ½-Ton Truck Belgium

Length: 4.306m
Width: 2.13m
Height: 2.252m (overall)
G/Clearance: .34m (axles)
Track: 1.616m(f)
1.62m(r)
Wheelbase: 2.35m
Weight: 4,930kg (loaded)
3,430kg (empty)
Load Area: 2.4m × 1.98m
Engine: FN 652 6-cylinder in-line, OHV petrol engine developing 130hp at 3,500rpm.

Crew: 1 + 1
Speed: 105km/hr
Range: 500km
Fuel: 95 litres
Gradient: 40%
Angle Approach: 48°
Angle Departure: 36°
T/Radius: 6m
Fording: 1.5m (with kit)
Tyres: 9.00 × 20

Development
The FN 4RM/62 Ardennes truck was designed and built by the Fabrique Nationale D'Armes De Guerre of Herstal, Belgium. The prototype was completed in the early 1950s with production starting in the late 1950s. Production has now been completed.

The vehicle can carry a maximum of 1500kg of cargo on both roads and cross country and can also tow a trailer with a maximum weight of 500/1,000kg. The cab is of the forward control type and is of all steel construction, both the engine and the gearbox are under the cab. The cab is provided with a detachable waterproof canvas roof and this enables the overall height of the vehicle to be reduced. The rear cargo body is provided with a tailgate, bows and a tarpaulin cover.

The gearbox has 4F and 1R gears and a two-speed transfer case. The suspension consists of heavy-duty springs and double-acting hydraulic shock absorbers, front and rear. If required a winch can be fitted.

Variants
Components of this vehicle were also used in the FN 4RM/62F AB 4 × 4 armoured car which is used by the Belgian Gendarmerie. Other versions of the Ardennes truck in service include a personnel carrier for the police and a fire truck for the Air Force.

Employment
Belgian Police, Army and Air Force.

Above: *The Belgian FN 4RM/62 Ardennes (4 × 4) 1½-Ton Truck*

FN 4RM/652 3M (4 x 4) 3-Ton Truck   Belgium

Length: 5.925m
Width: 2.24m
Height: 2.83m (overall)
2.47m (cab roof)
G/Clearance: .32m
Track: 1.605m(f) 1.65m(r)
Wheelbase: 3m
Weight: 7,600kg (loaded)
4,450kg (empty)
Load Area: 4.28m × 2.14m
Engine: FN 652, 6-cylinder in-line OHV petrol engine developing 130hp at 3,500rpm.
Crew: 1 + 1
Speed: 90km/hr
Range: 500km
Fuel: 125 litres
Gradient: 40%
Angle Approach: 45°
Angle Departure: 35°

T/Radius: 7.45m
Fording: 1.5m (with kit)
Tyres: 11.00 × 20

Development
The FN 4 RM/652 3M truck was designed to a NATO specification by the Fabrique Nationale D'Armes De Guerre of Herstal, Belgium. The prototype was built in the 1950s with production being completed in the early 1960s.

It is a 4 × 4 vehicle that has been designed to carry 3,000/3,500kg of cargo on both road and cross country and can also tow a trailer with a maximum weight of 3,000kg. In place of the cargo, twenty fully equipped troops can be carried in the rear. The cargo body is provided with a tailgate, bows and a tarpaulin cover. The cab is of the forward control type and has a detachable cover and folding windshield, this facilitates the loading of the vehicle into aircraft.

The gearbox has 4F and 1R gears and a two-speed transfer case. A winch with 60m of 13mm cable is fitted as standard equipment. The suspension consists of double acting hydraulic shock absorbers and heavy duty leaf-springs, front and rear.

Variants
There are no variants known to be in service. There may also be some FN/Brossel/Miesse 4RM/62C

(4 × 4) 4½-ton cargo trucks in service. Belgium has also built Land Rovers under licence, these being known as the Minerva/Land Rover.

Employment
Belgian Army.

Above: The FN 4 RM/652 3M (4 × 4) 3-Ton Truck

Engesa EE-15 (4 x 4) 1 ½-Ton Truck　　　Brazil

Length: 5.335m
Width: 2.105m
Height: 2.29m (with cover)
2.12m (w/o cover)
G/Clearance: .31m
Track: 1.618m
Wheelbase: 3.26m
Weight: 6,420kg (loaded)
2,820kg (empty)
Load Area: 2.2m × 1.6m
Engine: Chevrolet 2067-6100, 6-cylinder, in-line petrol engine developing 149hp at 3,800rpm (data above relates to this model) OR Perkins 6357, 6-cylinder, in-line diesel engine developing 140hp at 3,000rpm.
Crew: 1 + 2
Speed: 90km/hr
Range: 600km
Fuel: 120 litres
Gradient: 65%
Angle Approach: 46°
Angle Departure: 43°
T/Radius: 8m
Fording: .7m
Tyres: 9.00 × 20

Development/Variants
This vehicle has been designed and built by Engesa of Sao Paulo, Brazil. Its normal cross-country

payload is three men and 1,500kg of cargo, when travelling on roads it can carry 3,000kg of cargo and three men. The cab is of all steel construction and is provided with a vinyl top, doors and a windscreen that can be folded flat on the bonnet if required. The rear body is provided with a tarpaulin cover and bows, two retractable seats are provided and these seat a total of ten men. The gearbox has 4F and 1R gears and a two-speed transfer case. The suspension consists of semi-elliptical springs front and rear with double acting shock absorbers on the front wheels. Hydraulic brakes are fitted and the steering is of the worm type.

If required the vehicle can be fitted with a central winch with a capacity of 7,500kg, this is mounted behind the cab with two side spools, one acting to the front and the other to the rear, each one having 100m of cable. Or a front mounted winch with a capacity of 3,000kg, this being provided with 50m of cable.

Other bodies could be fitted including dump truck.

Employment
Reported to be in production for Brazilian Armed Forces.

Other Engesa vehicles include 6 × 6 armoured cars and armoured personnel carriers, and various 4 × 4 and 6 × 6 2½-ton cargo trucks, some of which are based on American and German vehicles.

XM-571 Dynatrac High Mobility Vehicle   Canada

Length: 6.019m
Width: 1.625m
Height: 1.593m (steering wheel)
1.231m (hull top)
G/Clearance: .304m
Weight: 3878kg (loaded)
2,790kg (empty)
Track Width: .457m
Vertical Obstacle: .457m
Ground Pressure: .16kg/cm²
Engine: Chevrolet Corvair Model HD 164 air-cooled flat-6 engine developing 70bhp at 3,600rpm.
Crew: 1 + 3
Speed: 48.28km/hr
Range: 482km
Fuel: 246 litres
Gradient: 60%
Angle Approach: 64°
Angle Departure: 67°
T/Radius: 8.38m
Fording: Amphibious

Development

In the early 1950s the Canadair Company developed a small articulated vehicle called the RAT, a total of 37 RATs were built for trials purposes from 1957 to 1958. These proved the basic concept and Canadair then developed a further vehicle called the Dynatrac. The first prototype was completed in 1959 and extensive trials were carried out by Canada, Britain and the United States. Although the Dynatrac has been made Standard 'A' by the United States Army it is not yet in large scale use, the Canadian Armed Forces have purchased some but Britain purchased the Bv. 202 from Norway instead.

The Dynatrac consists of two fully tracked units connected together. The front unit contains the engine, transmission, driver and three passengers.

The rear unit has additional fuel and can carry a total of eight men or a total load of 680kg. If required the front unit can be operated on its own, and if required a third unit can be attached to the second unit. The Dynatrac is fully amphibious being propelled in the water by its tracks at a speed of 4.83km/hr.

Note: *In 1968 Canadair acquired the tracked vehicle assets of Flex-Trac Equipment Limited and Robin-Nodwell Manufacturing Limited. This new company took over the Dynatrac project.*

Variants

The following kits have been developed for the Dynatrac: General purpose enclosure kit, austere enclosure kit, arctic kit, tropical kit, ambulance kit, radio vehicle kit, armour kit, windshield kit with wiper, 7.62mm M-60 machine gun kit, 81mm mortar mounting, M-40A1 106mm recoilless-rifle kit. The vehicle could also be adopted as a fire fighting vehicle, recovery vehicle, missile-carrying vehicle, mine-detector vehicle and so on.

The Squad Support Vehicle (SSV) was essentially the front unit of a Dynatrac with an additional road wheel either side, the prototype was built in 1967. The XM-571A1 has a Wankel engine and the XM-571A2 has a torquematic automatic transmission.

Employment

In limited use with Canadian and United States Armed Forces.

Note: *There are no Canadian designed military vehicles as such. Canada has built US pattern 4 × 4 and 6 × 6 vehicles and these are identical to their American counterparts.*

Left: *The Engesa EE-15 (4 × 4) 1 ½ - Ton Cargo Truck*

Right: *A XM-571 Dynatrac of the United States Army with general purpose cab*

Tatra 805 (4 x 4) 1 ½ -Ton Truck   Czechoslovakia

Length: 4.72m
Width: 2.04m
Height: 2.92m (canvas cover)
2.42m (cab)
G/Clearance: .4m
Weight: 4,250kg (loaded)
2,750kg (empty)
Engine: Tatra 603, 8-cylinder air-cooled petrol engine developing 75hp at 4,200rpm.
Crew: 1 + 1
Speed: 77.5km/hr
Range: 600km (estimate)
Gradient: 33.5°
Wheelbase: 2.7m
Fording: .65m
Tyres: 10.50 × 16

Development
This was introduced in 1953 and is widely used in the Czechoslovakian Army as a personnel carrier, cargo truck and as a prime-mover for various types of artillery, for example 57mm anti-tank gun and the Czech 82mm recoilless-rifle M59. It can carry 1,500kg of cargo across country or 2,250kg on paved roads, its towed load across country is 2,250kg. It has an all-steel cab with an observation hatch in the roof, the normal body is of the drop side type and it is often provided with bows and a tarpaulin. Its gearbox has 4F and 1R gears and a two-speed transfer case and its suspension is of the torsion bar type. The Tatra 805 is also available commercially.

Variants
There are various types of van model of the Tatra 805 in service.

Employment
Czechoslovakia.

A Tatra 805 (4 × 4) 1 ½ - Ton Truck towing a M-1942 (ZIS-3) 76mm gun

Praga V3S (6 x 6) 3-Ton Truck

Czechoslovakia

Length: 6.91m
Width: 2.31m
Height: 2.92m (canvas top)
2.51m (cab)
G/Clearance: .4m
Track: 1.87m(f) 1.755m(r)
Wheelbase: 3.58m + 1.12m
Weight: 8,350kg (loaded)
5,350kg (empty)
Engine: Tatra T-912 6-cylinder in-line, air-cooled diesel developing 98hp at 2,100rpm. Late production models have the Tatra T-912-2 engine as used in the Praga S5T-2, this develops 110hp at 2,200rpm.
Crew: 1 + 1
Speed: 62km/hr
Range: 500km
Fuel: 120 litres
Gradient: 31°
Fording: .8m
Tyres: 8.25 × 20

Development

The Praga V3S dates from the early 1950s and it is widely used by both military and civilian authorities in Czechoslovakia. Initial production was by Praga but in the 1960s production was transferred to the Avia company. Its payload is 3,000kg cross-country,

3,300kg on rough roads and 5,300kg on the highway. its towed load is 5,500kg on the highway and 3,100kg on dirt roads. The gearbox has 4F and 2R gears and a two-speed transfer case. The cab is of all-steel construction with an observation hatch in the roof, the rear body is provided with drop sides, bows and a canvas cover; some vehicles have a winch with a capacity of 3,500kg.

Variants

There are many civilian and military variants of the Praga V3S and these include the Praga V3S THZ special tanker, 3,000 litres fuel tanker, Praga V3S-K rear-tipping dump truck, Praga V3S-A tractor, Praga V3S-K hopper truck, workshop vehicle complete with a jib crane at the front of the vehicle and various crane models of the Praga V3S. The Praga V3S chassis is also used to mount the 130mm (32 round) M-51 Multiple Rocket System and is the basis for the armoured M53/59 twin 30mm anti-aircraft gun system. The Praga S5T (4 × 2) truck uses the same engine as the Praga V3S.

Employment

Used by Bulgaria, Czechoslovakia and numerous other countries. The M-51 multiple rocket system is used by Austria, Bulgaria, China, Czechoslovakia, Egypt and Romania.

*The Praga V3S (6 × 6)
3-Ton Truck*

Tatra 138 Series

Czechoslovakia

Length: 7.215m (8.465m)
Width: 2.438m (2.45m)
Height: 2.44m (2.44m)
G/Clearance: .29m (.29m)
Track: 1.93m(f) 1.764m(r)
Wheelbase: 4.55m (4.26m + 1.32m)
Weight: 13,050kg (20,590kg loaded)
5,850kg (8,740kg empty)

Engine: Tatra 928-12, 8-cylinder air-cooled diesel developing 180hp at 2,000rpm.
Crew: 1 + 2
Speed: 100km/hr (71km/hr)
Range: 500km
Gradient: 23° (25°)
Fording: 1.4m (1.4m)
Tyres: 10.00 × 20 (11.00 × 20)

Data in brackets relates to the Tatra 138 6 × 6

TATRA 138 (4 × 4)

This was known as the Tatra 137 for a short time and is the replacement for the earlier Tatra 128. It is the 4 × 4 model of the Tatra 138. Its gearbox has 5F and 1R gears and a two-speed transfer box is fitted. It has an all-steel cab with an observation hatch in the roof. The vehicle can carry 7,200kg of cargo on roads and has a maximum towed load of 5,800kg. Variants of the basic vehicle include the Tatra 138NT tractor truck for towing semi-trailers and the Tatra 138S1 hopper-type dump truck.

TATRA 138 (6 × 6)

This entered production in 1963 and is the replacement for the Tatra III vehicle. It has the same cab as the 4 × 4 model and can be fitted with a winch if required. The body is normally of the dropside type with bows and a tarpaulin. It has a gearbox with 5F and 1R gears and a two-speed transfer case. It can carry 11,850kg of cargo on paved roads or 8,000kg on dirt roads, its maximum towed load on a paved road is 15,000kg. Some models are powered by the Tatra 928K supercharged engine developing 220hp at 2,000rpm. The Tatra T148 S3 is based on the earlier Tatra 138 (6 × 6). There are many variants of the Tatra 138 (6 × 6) in service including the following: Tatra 138 NT tractor, Tatra 138 S1 and S3 dump trucks, airfield lighting truck, and at least two types of crane truck, the AJ-6 and D-031A (crane/shovel).

Employment

Warsaw Pact Forces, Egypt. Also available on the civilian market.

Right: *Tatra 138 (4 × 4) tanker*

Below: *Tatra 138 trucks with Soviet PMP pontoon units mounted on the rear*

Tatra 813 (8 x 8) 8.38-Ton Truck

Czechoslovakia

Length: 8.88m
Width: 2.52m
Height: 2.69m (cab)
3.15m (canvas top)
G/Clearance: .4m
Track: 2m
Wheelbase: 1.65m + 2.2m + 1.45m
Weight: 14,420kg (empty)

Engine: Tatra 930, V-12, air-cooled diesel developing 270hp at 2,700rpm.
Crew: 1 + 6
Speed: 75km/hr
Range: 1,000km
Trench: 1.6m
V/Obstacle: .6m
Gradient: 35°

Fording: 1.4m
Tyres: 15.00 × 21

Development
The Tatra 813 was designed in the early 1960s and it entered production in 1968, it is also known as the Kolos. The dual-range gearbox has 5F and 1R gears and an overdrive. A winch with a capacity of 22,000kg is fitted as is a tyre pressure regulation system. It can carry 8,380kg of cargo on roads or cross country, its towed load on a dirt road is 12,000kg or a good road a maximum of 65,000kg. A steel cab with four doors is fitted and the body has drop sides, bows and a canvas cover can be fitted if required. The OT-64 (8 × 8) APC uses many components of the Tatra 813.

Variants
There is an engineer vehicle fitted with the BZ-T hydraulically operated dozer blade, it is also used to carry pontoons, a model also exists with the AD 350 crane. A multiple rocket version is designated the M-1972, this has an armoured cab for the crew of six, mounted on the rear is a 122mm 40-barrelled multiple rocket launcher with a rapid loading system, some M-1972s have the BZ-T dozer blade fitted.

The Tatra 813 is also available commercially in both 4 × 4 and 6 × 6 versions, models of the latter include tractors, dump trucks and flat beds. A more recent model of the Tatra 813 is fitted with TMM bridging units on the rear.

Employment
Used by members of the Warsaw Pact Forces including East Germany and Czechoslovakia.

The Tatra 813 (8 × 8) 8-Ton Truck

The Tatra 813 (6 × 6) Prime Mover

Tatra 141 (6 × 6) Prime Mover with enlarged cab

Tatra 111 Series (6 x 6) 10-Ton Truck   Czechoslovakia

Length: 8.3m
Width: 2.5m
Height: 3.05m (canvas top)
2.64m (cab)
G/Clearance: .29m
Track: 2.08m(f) 1.8m(r)
Wheelbase: 4.175m + 1.22m
Weight: 18,840kg (loaded)
8,600kg (empty)
Engine: Tatra 111A, 12-cylinder, air-cooled diesel developing 180hp at 1,800rpm
Crew: 1 + 2
Speed: 61.5km/hr
Range: 500/600km
Gradient: 27°
T/Radius: 11.5m
Fording: .8m
Tyres: 11.00 × 20

Development
The Tatra 111 series of 6 × 6 trucks are widely used by both civil and military authorities in Eastern Europe. It can carry 10,240kg of cargo across rough country and tow a trailer with a maximum weight of 22,000kg. The gearbox has 4F and 1R gears and a two-speed transfer case, the rear differentials can be locked. The rear body is provided with drop down sides and a tailgate, bows and a tarpaulin cover. The vehicle is fitted with air brakes and a winch with a capacity of 6,000kg is fitted to many vehicles.

There was a 4 × 4 model of the Tatra III called the Tatra 128, but this is no longer in production. The Tatra 111 itself is no longer in production its place being taken by the more recent Tatra 138 which is built in both 4 × 4 and 6 × 6 models.

Variants
Variants of the Tatra 111 include the following: Tatra 111R and Tatra 111NR cargo trucks, Tatra 111A tractor truck, Tatra 111C 7000 litre tanker, there are at least three different types of dump truck — Tatra 111S, Tatra 111S-2 (side dump) and DC-5 (rear dump), Tatra 141 and 141B heavy prime movers (some of which have four door cabs), crane trucks (K-32, HSC 4 and HS5 the latter having a folding jib).

Employment
Warsaw Pact Forces including Czechoslovakia. Vietnam.

Sisu A-45 (4 x 4) 3-Ton Truck   Finland

Length: 5.7m
Width: 2.3m
Height: 2.8m (overall)
2.44m (cab top)
G/Clearance: .34m (front axle)
Track: 1.89m
Wheelbase: 3.4m
Weight: 7,500kg (loaded)
5,000kg (empty)
Load Area: 4.28, × 2.16m
Engine: Leyland 6-cylinder diesel developing 165hp at 2,600rpm or a turbo-charged diesel developing 165hp.

Crew: 1 + 2
Speed: 86.2km/hr
Range: 800/1000km
Fuel: 210 litres
Gradient: 60%
Angle Approach: 38°
Angle Departure: 38°
T/Radius: 7.6m
Fording: 1m
Tyres: 14.5 × 20

Development
The Sisu A-45 has been designed and manufactured

by Sisu (Suomen Autoteollisuus AB) of Helsinki. It can carry 4,150kg of cargo on roads or 3,000kg of cargo cross country, in addition it can tow a standard trailer weighing a total of 4,000kg on roads or 2,000kg across country.

The cab, which is of steel and glass-fibre construction, has seats for two men plus the driver. If required the top half of the cab can be removed. The engine projects into the load carrying area for a short distance. The cargo body is of steel and wood construction and is provided with drop sides, tailgate, bows and a fully enclosed cover complete with windows.

The A-45s gearbox has 5F and 1R gears and a two-speed transfer case. The suspension consists of leaf springs with shock absorbers on the front wheels. Air brakes are fitted and power assisted steering is provided. A winch with a capacity of 6,500kg is mounted under the chassis, this can be led out at the front or rear and is provided with 60m of cable. Optional extras include cold starting equipment.

The A-45 can be fitted with a hydraulic mechanism for the operation of Sisu hydraulic motors in a trailer, or gun. This system consists of the basic truck, this has the pump, clutch, fluid tank, valve compound, gauges, pipes and connections to the rear trailer, in the latter are the Sisu hydraulic hub motors (i.e. two for a two wheel trailer) and a pressure reservoir. Thus the trailer's wheels are hydraulically driven when crossing rough country and going up steep gradients.

Variants

The basic truck can also be used as an ambulance, fire vehicle, radio or command vehicle or a workshop. In most of these cases, a fully enclosed cabin would be used.

Employment

Finnish Army.

Below: *Sisu A-45 (4 × 4) 3-Ton Truck of the Finnish Army*

Sisu KB-46 (6 x 6) Prime Mover

Finland

This 6 × 6 vehicle is used to two medium artillery such as the 122m Tampella m/60 field gun or the Soviet M-1946 130mm field gun, both of which are used by the Finnish Army. The engine, which is a British Leyland 6-cylinder diesel, is mounted under the forward control type cab, this can be tilted forwards to gain access to the engine. Behind the cab is a fully enclosed cabin for the rest of the gun crew and there is ample space at the rear for ammunition and stores. If required, it could be fitted with a powered trailer/gun as developed for the Sisu A-45. The Sisu KB-46 is used only by the Finnish Army.

Above: *Sisu KB-46 prime mover towing 122mm Tampella field gun m/60*

Below: *A Sisu standard 4 × 2 truck used by the Finnish Army. Other Sisu trucks used by the Finnish Army include the K-137, 7-ton (4 × 4). Finnish Vanaja 7-ton 4 × 4 and 4 × 2 trucks are also used by the Finnish Army.*

Valmet 865 BM (4 x 4) Cross-Country Vehicle   Finland

Length: 7.06m
Width: 2.37m
Height: 2.62m (inc. cover)
1.91m (w/o cover)
G/Clearance: .66m
Wheelbase: 1.82m
Weight: 10,050kg (loaded)
6,250kg (empty)
Ground Pressure: .8kg/cm²
Engine: Valmet Model 411A, 4-cylinder direct injection diesel developing 90hp at 2,300rpm
Crew: 1 + 8
Speed: 32km/hr
Range: 550km
Fuel: 200 litres
Gradient: 60%
T/Radius: 5.3m
Tyres: 18.4 × 26

Development/Variants

The Valmet 865 BM has been designed and manufactured for the Finnish Army by Valmet Oy of Finland, the vehicle has been designed for the transportation of men and cargo across rough country. The first prototype was completed in 1964, and early models were known as the Model 4-363D, it was in production from 1969 until 1971. This vehicle is not amphibious, although a number of publications have stated that it is.

The Valmet 865 BM basically consists of two units joined together. The front unit contains the engine, cab and seats for the driver and eight men. The rear unit can carry 3,000kg of cargo or 14 men. If required, a tarpaulin cover can be erected over the front unit, this has windows in the sides, the basic vehicle has a windscreen as a permanent fitting. The rear cargo unit is provided with a tailgate to facilitate loading. If required the Valmet 865 BM can tow an additional trailer, or, light artillery.

The vehicle is provded with a gearbox with 8F and 2R gears and the rear differential has an automatic lock-up. Power-assisted steering is provided and all the wheels have disc brakes. A hydraulic winch with a capacity of 6,000kg is mounted at the front of the vehicle.

Employment

Used only by the Finnish Army.

Note: *Valmet 502 and 702 tractors are used by the Finnish Army and Air Force for a variety of roles including towing aircraft and artillery.*

Below: *Valmet 865 BM (4 × 4) cross-country vehicle. Note the winch on the front of the vehicle.*

Right: *Valmet 865 BM (4 × 4) cross-country vehicle towing an additional trailer*

M 201 (4 x 4) Utility Vehicle

France

Length: 3.36m
Width: 1.58m
Height: 1.77m
1.37m (windshield flat)
G/Clearance: .22m
Track: 1.24m
Wheelbase: 2.03m
Weight: 1,520kg (loaded)
1,120kg (empty)
Engine: 4-cylinder, in-line, water-cooled petrol engine developing 61hp at 3,600rpm. (2200cc).
Crew: 1 + 3
Speed: 100km/hr
Tyres: 6.50 × 16

Development
The M 201 VLTT (Véhicule de Liaison Tout Terrain) was built by Hotchkiss from 1953 until 1969 and is almost identical to the World War II Jeep. It can carry a total of 400kg of cargo and tow a maximum load of 500kg. The gearbox has 3F and 1R gears and a two-speed transfer case. The suspension consists of semi-elliptical springs with shock absorbers on all four wheels. A canvas cover can be erected if required and the windscreen folds down flat against the bonnet.

Variants
All models can be fitted with a variety of radio installations and the following models were available — standard, dual control, reinforced suspension and a special desert model. The DTAT/GIAT have fitted, for trials purposes, a M 201 with the 20mm M621 cannon. The French Army has a number of M 201s fitted with recoilless rifles including the American 106mm M-40. There is also a M201 fitted with four ENTAC anti-tank missiles in the ready to fire position at the rear of the vehicle, another three missiles are carried inside the vehicle.

Other models produced by Hotchkiss included the HWL 4 × 4 Jeep. This had a GVW of 1,900kg and could carry a maximum of eight men when being used in the troop-carrying role. It was available with a petrol engine (61hp at 3,600rpm) or a diesel engine. Basic data was length 3.89m, width 1.45m, height 1.99m, wheelbase 2.53m. The JH 102 had a wheelbase of 2.03m and an overall length of 3.39m.

Employment
French Armed Forces, and various African countries.

Below: *The Hotchkiss M 201 (4 × 4) Jeep fitted with ENTAC ATGWs*

Above: *The standard Hotchkiss M 201 (4 × 4) Jeep as used by the French Army*

SUMB (4 x 4) 1.5-Ton MH 600 BS Truck France

Length: 5.1m
Width: 2.1m
Height: 2.88m (overall)
1.94m
G/Clearance: .33m (minimum)
Track: 1.65m
Wheelbase: 2.9m
Weight: 5,300kg (loaded)
3,550kg (empty)
Load Area: 2.95m × 1.97m
Engines: 8-cylinder petrol engine developing 100bhp at 3,000rpm (4184cc) OR 6-cylinder Fiat 8060 diesel developing 100 bhp at 3,000rpm (5184cc).
Crew: 1 + 1
Speed: 85km/hr
Range: 550km
Fuel: 130 litres
Gradient: 60%
Angle Approach: 43°
Angle Departure: 42°
T/Radius: 7.5m
Fording: 1.2m
Tyres: 10.00 × 20

Development/Variants

The SUMB (Simca-Unic Marmon-Bocquet) 1.5-ton truck model MH 600 BS is manufactured by FFSA, Camions UNIC at Suresnes, it was developed in the 1960s and is still in production.

The vehicle can carry, 1,500kg of cargo on road or cross country and a trailer with a total weight of 2,000kg can be towed. If required a winch with 60m of rope can be fitted to the front of the vehicle. The cab is fitted with a waterproof hood and this is fixed on an articulated iron frame that can be folded so that the cab can be either open or closed. The rear of the vehicle is provided with five bows and a canvas cover, seats can be fitted in the rear allowing 14 troops to be carried.

The gearbox has 4F and 1R gears and a two-speed transfer case with differential locking on the rear axle only. The front and rear suspension consists of coil springs and hydraulic shock absorbers. Brakes are hydraulic with air servo-booster.

The SUMB (4 × 4) VLRA is a similar vehicle but can carry 3,000kg of cargo or 22 troops and is powered by a 6-cylinder diesel.

Variants

The French Army has a number of these vehicles fitted with a Poclain light hydraulically powered shovel on the rear. Stabilisers are provided so that the vehicle is stable when the shovel is in use. Some years ago a SUMB (4 × 4) 1½-ton MH 600 BS chassis was fitted with a fully armoured body and used as an APC, this progressed no further than the trials stage.

Employment

In service with the French Army.

Below: *SUMB (4 × 4) 1½-Ton MH 600 BS Truck*

Saviem TP 3 (4 x 4) 1.83-Ton Truck   France

Length: 5.298m
Width: 1.996m
Height: 2.41m (soft cab)
2.4m (metal cab)
G/Clearance: .25m
Track: 1.636m
Wheelbase: 2.64m
Weight: 3,950kg (loaded)
2,120kg (empty)
Load Area: 3m × 1.85m × .45m
Engine: Renault Model 817-04, 4-cylinder petrol engine developing 78hp at 3,600rpm (2.6litres). Diesel engine optional.
Crew: 1 + 1
Speed: 95km/hr
Range: 500km
Fuel: 120 litres
Gradient: 50°
T/Radius: 7.25m
Fording: .5m
Tyres: 9.00 × 16

Development

The TP 3 is based on standard civilian components and is available in two basic models one with a metal cab and the other has a open-type cab with a windshield that can be folded flat against the front of the vehicle. The gearbox has 4F and 1R gears and a two-speed transfer case. The suspension consists of leaf-springs and hydraulic shock absorbers (front and rear), hydraulic brakes are fitted. The total carrying capacity of the vehicle is 1,830kg.

The sides of the rear body can be removed if required and a tailgate is provided. If required the rear body can be fitted with four bows and a tarpaulin. Optional extras include a PTO, benches in the rear, rear towing hook, heater and fire extinguisher.

Variants

The ambulance model has an all-steel body and can carry six stretcher patients or 12 seated patients. The command/radio vehicle has a similar body to the ambulance. A dump truck is also available.

Employment

France.

Above: Saviem TP 3 (4 × 4) Cargo Truck

Berliet 380 K (4 x 4) 2-Ton Truck France

Length: 5.8m (w/o winch)
Width: 2.1m
Height: 2.75m (o/a)
2.65m (cab)
G/Clearance: .3m
Track: 1.73m(f) 1.63m(r)
Wheelbase: 3.055m
Weight: 5,500kg (loaded)
2,850kg (empty)
Engine: Perkins 4-cylinder diesel developing 90hp at 2,800rpm.
Crew: 1 + 2
Speed: 85km/hr
Range: 350km
Fuel: 70 litres
Gradient: 50%
Angle Approach: 42°
Angle Departure: 40°
T/Radius: 7.5m
Fording: 1m
Tyres: 12.5 × 20

Development
The Berliet 380 K (4 × 4) is based on the Berliet commercial 380 (4 × 2) truck suitably modified for military service. The first prototype was completed in 1973 and the vehicle entered production in 1974.

Its normal load is 2,000kg of cargo across country or 3,000kg of cargo on roads. If not carrying cargo it can carry a maximum of 20 fully equipped men.

It has a gearbox with 5F and 1R gears and a two-speed Simpar transfer case. The rear cargo body is provided with drop sides, tailgate, bows and a tarpaulin cover. There are numerous optional extras including a winch with a capacity of 2,000kg or 4,000kg, this is provided with 75m of 9mm cable. A four-door cab with seats for a total of six men, including the driver, is available.

Variants
Projected variants include a tanker truck and a tipper truck.

Employment
France.

Note: *Development of the Berliet 680 T (4 × 4) 3-ton truck was stopped in 1974.*

Below: *Berliet 380 K (4 × 4) 2-Ton Cargo Truck*

VLRA (4 x 4) ALM Type TF-4 20 SM (2.5-Ton)   France

Length: 5.956m
Width: 2.07m
Height: 2.621m (canvas top)
2.076m (top of windhsield)
G/Clearance: .27m (axles)
Track: 1.76m(f) 1.66m(r)
Wheelbase: 3.6m
Weight: 6,750kg (loaded)
4,200kg (empty)
Load Area: 2.7m × 1.836m × .6m
Engine: Ford Model 589E 6-cylinder water-cooled petrol engine developing 125hp at 3,000rpm
Crew: 1 + 2
Speed: 80km/hr
Range: 1,000km
Fuel: 360 litres
Gradient: 50%
Angle Approach: 43°
Angle Departure: 41°
T/Radius: 7m
Fording: .8m
Tyres: 8 × 18

Development/Variants
The VLRA is built by the Ateliers de Construction Mechanique de L'Atlantique at Saint-Nazaire, and it is also available commercially. The VLRA is a light reconnaissance and support vehicle and has been designed for long range patrol work, especially in desert areas. It can carry a maximum of 2,550kg of cargo and can also tow a 105mm M-101 howitzer or a trailer. A winch with a tractive effort of 2,000kg is mounted at the front of the vehicle.

It is fitted with a type 508 E gearbox with 4F and 1R gears and a ALM transfer case. The front and rear suspension consists of springs and hydraulic shock absorbers, sand channels are carried to enable the vehicle to cross ditches or assist it when operating in the desert.

The cab has no side doors and is provided with a canvas roof and a fold-down windscreen. The rear cargo body is provided with removable bows and a canvas cover. A tank holding 200 litres of drinking water is fitted. 4 × 20 litre jerrycans carry an additional 80 litres of fuel. The VRLA is airtransportable in the Nord Atlas 2501 and Transall aircraft.

An experimental model was built and fitted with an Aerospatiale NA1 turret fitted with four SS 11 ATGW.

Employment
Chad, France.

Below: *The VLRA (4 × 4) ALM Type TF-4 20 SM Truck*

SUMB (4 x 4) 3-Ton Truck France

Length: 6.55m
Width: 2.41m
Height: 2.97m (o/a)
G/Clearance: .38m
Track: 1.7m
Wheelbase: 4.1m
Weight: 7,420kg (loaded)
4,220kg (empty)
Load Area: 4.4m × 2.29m
Engine: 6-cylinder diesel engine developing 100hp at 3,000rpm
Crew: 1 + 1
Speed: 82km/hr
Range: 550km
Fuel: 130 litres
Gradient: 50%
Angle Approach: 42°
Angle Departure: 43°
T/Radius: 5.75m
Tyres: 12.50 × 20

Development/Variants
This is built by FFSA — Camions Unic and can carry a maximum of 22 men or 3,000kg of cargo, in addition it can tow a trailer with a maximum weight of 2,000kg.

Its gearbox has 4F and 1R gears and a two-speed transfer case, differential locking on the rear axle only. The front and rear suspension consists of coil springs and hydraulic shock absorbers. Hydraulic brakes are fitted and the system has an air servo-booster.

The cab is provided with a removable roof and the windscreen can be folded down if required. The rear cargo area is provided with a tailgate, bows and a tarpaulin cover, outwards facing benches can be fitted if required. A front mounted winch with a capacity of 1,500/2,000kg can be mounted. It can ford to a depth of .8m without preparation or 1.2m with preparation.

Employment
In service with the French Army.

Below: *The SUMB (4 × 4) 3-Ton Cargo Truck, note that this is almost identical to the SUMB (4 × 4) 1½-Ton Truck*

Simca-Unic F 594 WML (4 x 4) 3-Ton Cargo Truck   France

Length: 6.806m
Width: 2.286m
Height: 3.2m (overall)
2.55m (cab)
Track: 1.7m(f) 1.75m(r)
Wheelbase: 3.655m
Weight: 8,000kg (loaded)
4,800kg (empty)
Engine: SIMCA F6 CWM 8-cylinder petrol engine developing 85bhp at 2,900rpm
Crew: 1 + 1
Speed: 80km/hr
Range: 500km
Gradient: 40%
Angle Approach: 33°
Angle Departure: 25°
T/Radius: 9.75m
Fording: .8m
Tyres: 9.00 × 20 or 10.00 × 20

Development

This was manufactured by FFSA/Camions Unic in the late 1950s and was based on commercial components. It can carry 3,000kg of cargo on both roads and cross-country, or a total of 20 fully equipped men, in addition it could tow a trailer with a maximum weight of 2,000kg.

Its gearbox has 4F and 1R gears and a two-speed transfer case. The front and rear suspension consists of springs and hydraulic shock absorbers. Hydraulic brakes are fitted as standard and if required a winch, leading out through the front of the vehicle, could be fitted, this was provided with 60m of rope. The rear wheels on the vehicle had dual tyres.

The rear cargo body is provided with bows, a tarpaulin cover and a tailgate. The cab is of the forward control type and has a soft roof, the doors also have removable tops; if required the windscreen can be removed or folded down.

Variants

The basic model is the WML (long wheel base), the other model being the WMC (short wheel base), this has a wheelbase of 3.04. Variants of the SWB (WMC) include dump trucks, water tankers and wreckers. Variants of the LWB (WML) are many and include mobile compressor units, office/command post, workshops and some time ago some were fitted with missiles.

Employment

In service with the French Army.

Below: *The Simca-Unic F 594 (4 × 4) 3-Ton Cargo Truck of the French Army*

Citroen FOM (4 x 4) 3/5-Ton Truck   France

Length: 7.01m
Width: 2.48m
Height: 3.09m (canvas top)
2.77m (cab)
Wheelbase: 4.6m
Weight: 12,500kg (loaded)
9,500kg (empty)
T/Radius: 5m
Engine: 6-cylinder petrol engine developing 140hp at 2,800rpm.
Crew: 1 + 1
Speed: 100km/hr
Range: 800km
Fuel: 150 litres
Gradient: 75%
Angle Approach: 57°
Angle Departure: 36°
Fording: .5m
Tyres: 12.00 × 20

Development
The FOM (Forces d'Outre-Mer or Overseas Forces) was designed by Citroen specifically to operate under the most severe weather conditions likely to be encountered in Africa. Production has now been completed.

It is provided with a gearbox with 5F and 1R gears and a two-speed transfer case. The front and rear suspension consists of leaf-springs and hydraulic shock absorbers, the steering is power assisted.

The rear cargo body is provided with a tailgate, bows and a tarpaulin cover. If required the cab roof can be removed and the windscreen folded flat against the bonnet. A winch is provided.

The vehicle was usually fitted with a 6-cylinder petrol engine (as above), but could also be fitted with a 6-cylinder diesel engine developing 85hp at 2,600rpm, there was also a model available with a 97hp petrol engine.

The 3-ton model is provided with single rear wheels (12.00 × 20 tyres) and the 5 metric ton model has dual rear tyres (11.00 × 20).

The standard model has a 150 litre fuel tank with a further 120 litres carried in jerricans, there was also a model with 250 litre fuel tank (plus jerricans) and a special model was developed for use in the Sahara, this had a 500 litres main fuel tank, this gave the vehicle a range of about 1,500km.

Variants
Citroen did propose that the vehicle could be fitted with the following types of body: 3,000 litre water carrier, 3,500 litre fuel carrier, command and radio vehicle, flat truck, recovery vehicle or with a thermally insulated body.

Employment
In service with the Cameroons, Chad, France, Ivory Coast, Mauritania, Senegal, Upper Volta.

Below: *The Citroen FOM (4 × 4) truck with tanker body*

Below: *The Citroen 55U (4 × 2) 5-Ton Cargo Truck has been widely used by the French Armed Forces and is essentially a civilian vehicle with a few modifications to suit it for military service*

Bottom: *The standard Citroen FOM (4 × 4) 3-Ton Truck with single rear wheels.*

Berliet GBC 8 KT (6 x 6) 4-Ton Truck   France

Length: 7.28m
Width: 2.4m
Height: 3.3m (o/a)
2.7m (cab)
G/Clearance: .28m (axles)
Track: 1.86m
Wheelbase: 3.31m + 1.28m
Weight: 13,500kg (loaded)
8,600kg (empty)
Engine: Berliet MK 520 water-cooled, multi-fuel, 5-cylinder engine developing 125hp at 2,100rpm
Crew: 1 + 2
Speed: 80km/hr
Range: 800km
Fuel: 200 litres
Gradient: 50%
Angle Approach: 45°
Angle Departure: 45°
T/Radius: 10.5m
Fording: 1.2m
Tyres: 12.00 × 20

Development

This range of tactical vehicles were developed from the famous Gazelle truck which was built for use in the Sahara in the 1950s. Delivery of the first 300 for the French Army started in 1958 and production continues, to date over 16,000 have been built.

It has a gearbox with 6F and 1R gears and a two-speed transfer box. The front suspension consists of semi-elliptical leaf type springs and hydraulic shock absorbers. The rear suspension consists of leaf-springs on an oscillating pivot. The cab has a removable roof and drop windows, the windscreen can be folded flat if required. The normal cargo body is provided with bows that can be adjusted for road or rail travel, tarpaulin cover, tailgate, dropsides and a central bench seat. A winch with a capacity of 5,000/7,000kg can be fitted if required.

Variants

Variants of the GBC 8 KT (6 × 6) truck include the LWB model which has an overall length of 8.205m, light recovery vehicle with 2-ton crane, winch and tools, tipper truck, 5,000 litre tanker, mobile compressor, tractor truck, medium wrecker truck fitted with hydraulic crane with a traverse of 270° and a telescopic jib. This can lift a maximum of 6,000kg, a full range of tools and cutting equipment is carried. There is also a 4 × 4 model of the GBC, this can carry 4,000kg of cargo across country and its GVW off-the-road is 13,630kg. The GBC 8 KT (6 × 6) and 4 × 4) can also tow guns or trailers up to 155mm in calibre. The GBC 8 MT vehicles have a diesel engine developing 150hp at 2,100rpm.

Employment

Algeria, Austria, China, France, Iraq, Morocco, Portugal.

Below: *Berliet GBC 8 KT (6 × 6) 4-Ton Cargo Truck of the French Army*

Above: *Berliet TBC 8 KT*
(6 × 6) Wrecker

Centre right: *Berliet GBC*
8 KT (6 × 6) Tipper Truck

Below right: *Berliet TBC 8*
(6 × 6) Tractor

Saviem SM8 (4 x 4) 4-Ton Truck

France

Length: 6.434m
Width: 2.19m
Height: 3.085m (canvas top)
2.665m (cab)
G/Clearance: .3m
Track: 1.836m (f) 1.77m (r)
Wheelbase: 3.5m
Weight: 11,200kg (loaded)
4,375kg (empty)
Engine: Saviem 597 6-cylinder petrol engine developing 135hp, at 2,900rpm (5.27 litres)
Crew: 1 + 1
Speed: 90km/hr
Range: 450km
Fuel: 150 litres
Gradient: 45%
Angle Approach: 40°
Angle Departure: 40°
T/Radius: 9m
Tyres: 12.00 × 20

Development/Variants

The Saviem SM8 is a development of a standard commercial vehicle which is available in three different wheelbases — 3.2m, 3.5m and 4m.

The vehicle is available with a fully enclosed metal cab or a cab with a canvas top and a windscreen that can be folded flat against the front of the vehicle, the cab can be tilted forward to gain access to the engine.

The gearbox is the Type 301, this has 5F and 1R gears, 2nd to 5th being synchronised, and a type G300 two speed transfer case (normal 1/1 and low 1/1.72). The chassis consists of pressed side members and cross members welded together. Suspension — variable flexibility through leaf spring 'Evidgom' pads of decreasing flexibility, level type shock absorbers front and rear. The steering is power assisted and pneumatic brakes are fitted. The platform is provided with bows and a tarpaulin, longitudinal benches for 20 men can be fitted if required. Its maximum load carrying capability is 6,825kg and that is for road travel and for cross-country operation 4,000kg. A trailer with a total weight of 4,000kg can be towed.

There are many optional extras including a winch with a capacity of 4,000kg, long range tanks, differential lock and various other types of bodies including dump trucks, ambulances and command vehicles.

Employment
France.

*Saviem SM8 (4 × 4)
Cargo Truck*

*Saviem SM8 (4 × 4)
Cargo Truck with cab
roof, bows and tarpaulin
cover removed*

Berliet GBD (6 x 6) 6-Ton Truck   France

Length: 7.9m
Width: 2.4m
Height: 2.825m (cab)
G/Clearance: .37m
Track: 1.936m(f)
1.938m(r)
Wheelbase: 3.8m + 1.4m
Weight: 15,440kg (loaded)
9,440kg (empty)
Engine: Berliet model MIS 620-30 6-cylinder diesel
developing 227hp at 2,400rpm (8,820cc)
Crew: 1 + 2
Speed: 93km/hr
Range: 500km
Fuel: 200 litres
Gradient: 60%
Angle Approach: 45°
Angle Departure: 40°
T/Radius: 11m
Fording: 1.2m
Tyres: 14.00 × 20

Development
The Berliet GBD (6 × 6) is at present undergoing
trials with the French Army. It has been designed to
carry 6,000kg of cargo across country or 10,000kg of
cargo on roads, its maximum towed load is 4,440kg.
The cab roof can be removed if required and the
windscreen folds flat against the front of the vehicle.
The rear cargo body is provided with drop sides,
tailgate, bows and a tarpaulin. When being used as a
personnel carrier it can carry a maximum of 20 fully
equipped men.

The vehicle is fitted with a Berliet BDSL gearbox
with 6F and 1R gears, in addition a two speed
transfer case is fitted. The steering is power assisted.
Optional extras include a four door cab with six seats
and a winch with a capacity of 5,000/7,000kg, an
additional fuel tank holding 200 litres can be fitted if
required.

Variants
Projected variants include a tipper truck, fuel tanker
and a tractor for hauling semi-trailers.

There is also a 4 × 4 variant of the GBD (6 × 6)
under development, this is simply called the GBD
(4 × 4). It has the same engine as the 6 × 6 vehicle but
without the turbo-charger, this develops 176hp at
2,400rpm, the same gearbox is fitted. Basic data is as
follows: length 6.815m, wheelbase 3.8m, load is
4,000kg across country and 6,000kg road, GVW
(road) is 13,500kg, other data and performance
figures are similar to the 6 × 6 model.

Employment
Development/trials.

Below: *The Berliet GBD (6 × 6) 6-Ton Cargo Truck.*

Right: *The Berliet GBD (4 × 4) 6-Ton Cargo Truck*

Berliet GBU 15 (6 x 6) 6-Ton Truck

France

Length: 7.974m
Width: 2.5m
Height: 3.25m (tarpaulin up)
3m (cab)
Track: 2.04m
Wheelbase: 3.48m + 1.45m
Weight: 24,500kg (loaded)
14,500kg (empty)
Engine: Berliet 6-cylinder, multi-fuel, water-cooled
engine developing 214hp at 1,800rpm
Crew: 1 + 3
Speed: 75km/hr
Range: 800km
Fuel: 400 litres
Gradient: 60%
Angle Approach: 45°
Angle Departure: 45°
T/Radius: 9.2m
Fording: 1m
Tyres: 14.00 × 20

Development

This vehicle was developed in the 1950s and was based on the T-6 (6 × 6) 6-ton vehicle designed by the Rochet-Schneider Company, whom Berliet took over. Production commenced in 1959 and the vehicle is still in production. It has been designed to carry a maximum of 6,000kg of cargo across country or 10,000kg of cargo on roads, and its maximum towed load is 15,000kg.

It is fitted with a gearbox with 5F and 1R gears and a two speed transfer box. The wheel train consists of two tandem axles, operating with a flexible progressive air driven differential locking device, this ensures power transmission of the engine, even when only one wheel remains in contact with the ground. Air brakes are fitted and the steering is power assisted, a winch with a capacity of 8,000kg is fitted at the rear of the vehicle.

The cab is provided with a soft roof which can be removed if required, as can the tops of the doors, the windscreen can be folded flat against the front of the vehicle. The rear cargo body is provided with five bows and a tarpaulin cover, the sides and rear of the body hinge down to facilitate loading.

Variants

Artillery Tractor GBU 15. This tows the French 155mm gun as well as carrying the crew and ammunition.
Tractor TBU 15. This has an empty weight of 13,500kg and tows a semi-trailer with a maximum weight of 22,000kg. This is used to transport engineering equipment and AMX-13 type light tanks.

Tanker GBU 15. This is the tanker model of the basic GBU 15.

Tipper GBU 15. This is the basic chassis fitted with a dump body.

Heavy Wrecker TBU 15 CLD. This is fitted with a hydraulic crane on the rear of the chassis, and this has a maximum capacity of 10,000kg and can be rotated through 270°. The front winch has a capacity of 7,000kg and the rear winch a capacity of 10,000kg. Anchor spades are provided front and rear and a full range of tool and cutting equipment is carried. Performance is similar to the basic vehicle, basic data is as follows: length 8.8m, width 2.5m, and height 3m, weight in travelling order is 21,200kg.

Employment
Abu-Dhabi, Belgium, China, France.

Left and Below: The Berliet GBU 15 (6 × 6) 6-ton truck with canopy in position

Berliet TBO 15 M3 (6 x 4) Tractor, Wheeled, Semi-Trailer   France

Length: 8.23m
Width: 3.07m
Height: 2.95m (cab)
1.65m (5th wheel)
G/Clearance: .5m
Track: 2.1m(f) 2.19m(r)
Wheelbase: 3.74m + 1.52m
Weight: 18,450kg (loaded)
Tyres: 16.00 x 20
Engine: Berliet Model MS 640A, 6-cylinder super-charged diesel developing 255bhp at 1,800rpm (14,778cc)
Crew: 1 + 2
Speed: 53km/hr
Range: 800km
Fuel: 500 litres
Gradient: 15%
Angle Approach: 23°
Angle Departure: 45°
T/Radius: 10.05m
Fording: .5m

Development
The Berliet TBO 15 M3 is based on a commercial Berliet design, the first prototype was completed in 1959 and the first production vehicle in 1961. It pulls a Coder type GSP BMT 35/45 semi-trailer, this has an overall length of 12.29m, width of 3.13m and a loaded height of 1.152m. This trailer can carry tanks of the AMX-30 and M-47 type. A Bonnier winch with a capacity of 15,000kg x 2 is fitted to assist in loading disabled armoured vehicles, in addition to self recovery of the vehicle, two ropes, each 90m in length are carried. The gearbox has 5F and 1R gears and a two-speed transfer box. The rear axles are fitted with dual tyres, air brakes are fitted and the steering is hydraulically assisted. The complete tractor and trailer empty weighs some 46,000kg, or with an AMX-30 MBT on the trailer, about 78,000kg.

Variants
A later model of the TBO 15 M3 is called the TBO 310, the prototype was completed in 1973 with production vehicles following later in the year, production was completed in 1974. This has similar dimensions to the earlier vehicle but is powered by a Berliet MIS 645, 6-cylinder diesel developing 289hp at 2,100rpm, it also has a different gearbox. Weight of the tractor is 19,000kg and its maximum towed load is 90,000kg.

Development of the new Berliet TBO 15 A, 6 x 6 transporter was stopped in 1974. This was powered by a 360hp diesel and had a maximum weight with trailer and load of 90-95,000kg.

Employment
France.

Below: *The Berliet TBO 15 M3 (6 x 4) Tractor*

Above: *The Berliet TBO 15 M3 (6 × 4) Tractor and semi-trailer carrying a M-47 MBT*

P3 (4 x 4) Truck and P2M (4 x 4) Truck   East Germany (GDR)

Length: 3.71m (3.755m)
Width: 1.95m (1.685m)
Height: 1.95m (1.835m)
G/Clearance: .33m (.3m)
Track: 1.42m(f) 1.4m(r) (1.44m)
Wheelbase: 2.4m
Weight: 1,860kg (1,770kg)
Engine: OM 6/35L 6-cylinder in-line water-cooled petrol engine developing 75hp at 3,750rpm. (OM 6/35 6-cylinder petrol engine developing 65hp at 3,500 rpm).
Crew: 1 + 5 (1 + 5)
Speed: 95km/hr (95km/hr)
Range: 520km (600km)
Gradient: 33° (33°)
T/Radius: 6m
Fording: .6m (.55m)
Tyres: 7.50 × 16 (6.50 × 16)

Data in brackets relates to the P2M.

P3 Development/Variants
The P3 entered production in 1962 as the replacement for the earlier P2M vehicle. Its payload is 700kg and its towed load is 750kg. Its gearbox has 4F and 1R gears and a two-speed transfer case. If required a canopy can be erected. Later production models had a different bonnet. There was to have been an amphibious model of the P3 but this did not enter production.

P2M Development/Variants
The P2M was the standard field car of the East-German Army until the P3 entered service in 1962. Its payload is 400kg and its towed load is 750kg. The gearbox has 4F and 1R gears and a two speed transfer case. The right wheelbase is 2.215m and the left wheelbase is 2.285m, this is because it has

transversal torsion bars. The vehicle is provided with a canopy and a fold-down windshield. The P2M was an unreliable vehicle in service as its cooling system

often overheated. There was also an amphibious model of the P2M called the P2S, this was built in small numbers and was similar to the World War II German Schwimmwagen. Basic data of the P2S is length 5.1m, width 1.83 and height 1.86m.

The East German border patrols use a 4 × 2 Trabant P601/A vehicle called the Grenztrabant which is based on the standard Trabant 601 car.

Employment
East German Army.

Above: *A P3 (4 × 4) vehicle of the East German Army*

Robur LO 1800A (4 x 4) 1.8-Ton Truck   East Germany (GDR)

Length: 5.38m
Width: 2.365m
Height: 2.735m (canvas top)
G/Clearance: .265m
Track: 1.636m(f) 1.664(r)
Wheelbase: 3.025m
Weight: 5,000kg (loaded)
3,200kg (empty)
Engine: Model LO 4, 4-cylinder in-line, air-cooled petrol engine developing 70hp at 2,800rpm
Crew: 1 + 2
Speed: 80km/hr
Range: 590km
Gradient: 25°
Fording: .8m
Tyres: 10.00 × 20

Development
The Robur LO 1800A was developed to replace the earlier Robur Garant 30K (4 × 4) truck. It is similar to the civilian Robur (4 × 2) LO 2500 truck, but has numerous modifications to the engine, transmission, suspension and body, it also has single tyres. Its payload is 1,800kg cross-country and 2,500kg on roads, its towed load is 2,100kg and is often used to tow artillery, for example the 57mm Soviet anti-tank gun. The gearbox has 5F and 1R gears and a two-speed transfer case.

Variants
Variants in service include ambulance, van (workshop, radio, command) and water purification vehicles. There was to have been a diesel model designated LD 1800A but it appears that this did not enter production.

Employment
East Germany, Hungary, Poland.

Robur Garant 30K — Production of this 4 × 4 vehicle was completed in 1960/61 but some still remain in service with border units and workers Militia. Basic data is as follows: length 5.49m, width 1.97m, height 2.56m (with canvas cover), speed 80km/hr, range 450km. It is powered by a Model 30K 4-cylinder in-line petrol engine developing 60hp at 2,800rpm. Its weight (empty) is 2,700kg and its payload is 1,000kg, towed load being 1,200kg. Some models had single rear wheels and others double, its chassis is used for the SK-1 armoured car.

Below: *A 4 × 4 Robur LO 1800A truck of the East German Army towing a 57mm auxiliary propelled anti-tank gun*

W 50 LA/A (4 x 4) 3-Ton Truck   East Germany (GDR)

Length: 6.53m
Width: 2.5m
Height: 3.2m (canvas top)
2.6m (cab)
G/Clearance: .3m
Track: 1.7m(f) 1.78m(r)
Wheelbase: 3.2m
Weight: 9,800kg (loaded)
5,080kg (empty)
Engine: Model 4 VD 14.5/12 SRW, 4-cylinder in-line, water-cooled diesel developing 125hp at 2,200rpm
Crew: 1 + 1
Speed: 83km/hr
Range: 720km

Fuel: 100 litres
Gradient: 28°
Fording: .8m
Tyres: 16.00 × 20

Development
The W 50 LA/A is a 4 × 4 military model of the civilian 4 × 2, W 50 L series of trucks which entered production in 1965 as a replacement for the earlier S 4000-1 (4 × 2) series. Whilst under development it was known as the S 4500 or the W45, the early models have a 100hp engine. It can carry 3,000kg of cargo cross-country, 4,700kg of cargo on dirt roads or 5,300kg of cargo on the highway. Its normal towed load is 8,000kg.

The gearbox has 5F and 2R gears, a central tyre pressure regulation system is fitted and a winch with a capacity of 4,500kg is mounted under the chassis and this can be used front or rear.

Variants
The 4 × 2 civilian trucks are all designated W 50 L whereas the 4 × 4 trucks are designated W 50 LA. The letters after the L or LA are for the type of vehicle: LA/A is the military truck, L/K is a dump truck (rear or three way types), L/L is a crane truck (HIAB type), L/W is a van for various roles and there is also a tractor truck.

Employment
East German Army.

Other trucks of East German manufacture which may be found in service include the 4 × 2 Barkas (.8t), 4 × 2 Barkas B1000, 4 × 2 Robur Garant, 4 × 2 Robur LD/LO 2500 series, 4 × 2 H3A series, 4 × 2 S4000-1 series, 4 × 2 H6 (6,500kg capacity).

Above: *The W 50 LA/A (4 × 4) 3-Ton Cargo Truck, note the observation hatch in the roof of the cab*

G5 Series (6 x 6) 3 ½-Ton Truck

Length: 7.3m
Width: 2.5m
Height: 3m (canvas top)
2.6m (cab)
G/Clearance: .255m
Track: 1.8m(f) 1.75m(r)
Wheelbase: 3.8m + 1.25m
Weight: 11,500kg (loaded)
8,000kg (empty)
Engine: EM6 6-cylinder in-line water-cooled diesel developing 120hp at 2,000rpm. Late G5s had 150hp engines.
Crew: 1 + 1
Speed: 60km/hr
Range: 585km
Fuel: 150 litres
Gradient: 23°
T/Radius: 9.5m
Fording: 1.05m
Tyres: 8.25 × 20

Development
The G5 series are no longer in production in East Germany and they are being replaced by the Soviet Ural-375D, or the 4 × 4 W 50 LA truck of East German manufacture. The G5 can carry 5,000kg of cargo on roads or 3,500kg of cargo cross-country. Its towed load is 8,000kg on roads or 4,600kg cross-country and it is often used to tow artillery. The first production G5s had an open cab with a folding windshield, later models had a fully enclosed cab with a roof observation hatch. The G5/2 is powered by a 150hp engine. The G5/3 is a much improved model with a more powerful 8-cylinder engine, new body and single tyres with a central tyre pressure regulation system. The G5 has a gearbox with 5F and 2R gears and a two-speed transfer case.

East Germany (GDR)

Variants
There are many variants of the G5 in service and these include a dump truck (standard and three way), van truck (repair and radio), two types of crane truck, fire fighting truck and a 4,000 litre fuel tanker. There are three decontamination trucks, these being designated GEW-1, GEW-2 and GEW-3. The GEW-1 is a liquid decontamination vehicle (4,500 litres) and can also be used as a fire truck. The GEW-2 is a dry decontamination vehicle (3,000kg) and can also be used in winter to put sand on icy roads. The GEW-3 is similar to the GEW-1 except that it has a separate engine for the pump, it can be used as a fire fighting vehicle or a mobile smoke generator. Tank capacity is 3,100 litres. The SK-2 armoured water cannon is based on the G5 chassis, the engine of the G5 is used in the H6 (4 × 2) truck.

Employment
East German Army.

Above right: *G5 (3 × 3) tankers taking on fuel from rail tankers*

Kraka 640 (4 x 2) Carrier

Germany (FGR)

Length: 2.78m
Width: 1.51m
Height: 1.28m
.755m (platform)
G/Clearance: .25m
Track: 1.138m (f) 1.13m(r)
Wheelbase: 2.058m
Weight: 1,610kg (loaded)
735kg (empty)
Load Area: 1.4m × 1.4m
Engine: BMW Model 427, two-cylinder petrol
engine developing 26hp at 4,500rpm. (697cc)
Crew: 1
Speed: 55km/hr
Fuel: 24.5 litres
Gradient: 55%
T/Radius 4.25m
Fording: .5m
Tyres: 22 × 12

Development

The Kraka (Kraftkarren) was designed by Nicholas
Straussler, the first models were built by Zweirad
Union who were later taken over by Faun, who now
manufacture the vehicle. Kraka is an abbreviation
from *Kraft* (power) and *Karren* (cart). It is available in
five different models with two different engine/gear-
box combinations—these are the 640, 641, 642, 643
and 644, the German Army uses the fully equipped
Model 640. The Kraka (LKW 0.75T) is a very small
vehicle that can be transported by aircraft or
helicopter and is used mainly by airborne forces. A
typical example is the CH-53 helicopter which can
carry a total of five folded Kraka's inside.

The engine is mounted at the rear and the gearbox
has 4F and 1R gears. The chassis is of all-welded
construction and is of the box type, the steering is of
the rack and pinion type and hydraulic brakes are
fitted. The rear end of the vehicle can be swung
through 180° for stowage purposes and in this case
the overall length is only 1.85m, the steering wheel
can also be folded down to reduce the overall height
to 1m.

Variants

The Kraka can be used for a variety of roles
including: load carrier, this can carry a maximum of
800kg of stores or ammunition, radio vehicle, cable
layer, fire fighting vehicle, mobile generator, water
purification vehicle, aircraft towing vehicle and so
on. It is capable of towing a two wheeled trailer. The
Kraka can mount a variety of weapons systems
including: 106mm M-40 recoilless rifle, fitted with
HOT, TOW, Milan or Cobra (five maximum)
ATGWs, carrying 120mm mortar and ammunition,
they can also mount 7.62mm or 12.7mm machine
guns and 20mm cannon. An armoured version of the
Kraka has been built for trials purposes.

Employment

German and Spanish Armies. It is reported that this
vehicle is also being built in Italy for the Italian Army.

Kraka with the Milan ATGW system installed

Auto-Union LKW (4 x 4) 0.25-Ton Vehicle   Germany (FGR)

Length: 3.445m
Width: 1.81m
Height: 1.75m (overall)
1.33m (lowest)
G/Clearance: .24m
Track: 1.206m
Wheelbase: 2.0m
Weight: 1,450kg (loaded)
1,085kg (empty)
Engine: Auto-Union 3-cylinder petrol engine developing 44bhp at 4,250rpm. (980cc)
Crew: 1 + 3
Speed: 95km/hr
Range: 350km (road)
Fuel: 45 litres
Gradient: 60%
Angle Approach: 43°
Angle Departure: 41°
T/Radius: 6.25m
Fording: .5m
Tyres: 6.00 × 16

Development
In 1954/55 three German manufacturers built prototypes of a 4 × 4 ¼-ton vehicle for the German Army. After trials a production contract was awarded to Auto-Union for their vehicle which is normally referred to as the Munga. The Munga was in production between 1954 and 1968 and the data

above relates to the late production model Munga 4. Earlier vehicles were powered by a 38bhp or 40bhp engine.

There are three basic models of the vehicle, these are the Munga 4 (four-seater), 6 (six-seater) and 8 (eight-seater). The Munga 4 and 8 can tow a 500kg trailer and the Munga 6 a 750kg trailer.

The chassis consists of an anti-distortion box-section frame with double side members. The steering is of the rack and pinion type. The suspension consists of traverse springs and double-action telescopic shock absorbers. The gearbox has 4F and 1R gears and a two speed transfer box. A waterproof folding hood is fitted and the doors can be removed if required.

The Munga 6 could be fitted with a PTO and all models could have a hitch rail and a trailer coupling.

Variants
The Munga 6 has the following data: length 3.595m, width 1.83m, height 1.973m, loaded weight, 1,315kg and range of approximately 400km.

The Munga is also used in some numbers by the German Army as an anti-tank vehicle fitted with the Cobra ATGW, these being mounted on the back of the vehicle, facing the rear.

Employment
France (in Germany), Germany, Great Britain (BAOR and Berlin), Indonesia and the Netherlands.

The Auto-Union LKW (4 × 4) ¼-Ton Vehicle with hood in stowed position.

VW 181 (4 x 2) 0.4-Ton Vehicle

Germany (FGR)

Length: 3.78m
Width: 1.64m
Height: 1.62m (PVC top)
G/Clearance: .205m
Track: 1.354m (front)
1.446m (rear)
Wheelbase: 2.4m
Weight: 1,340kg (loaded)
900kg (empty)
Engine: 4-cylinder, horizontally-opposed petrol engine developing 44bhp at 4,000rpm (1493cc). Later models have 1,584cc engines developing 53 bhp at 4,200rpm
Crew: 1 + 3
Speed: 113km/hr
Range: 230km
Fuel: 40 litres
Gradient: 48%
Angle Approach: 36°
Angle Departure: 31°
T/Radius: 5.48m
Fording: .396m

Developing/Variants

The Volkswagen 181 (German Army designation is Pkw 0.4t) uses many components of the standard VW 1500 vehicle including the same chassis, engine, front seats and steering column. An all-steel body is fitted and this is provided with four doors which can be quickly removed, as can the side windows, the windscreen and PVC top can be folded down, if required. The chassis is of all-welded construction and independent suspension with telescopic shock absorbers is fitted. The rear seats fold down to give an additional load carrying area, and the space-behind the rear seats has C-profile rails for securing equipment.

The gearbox has 4F and 1R gears, a dual braking system is fitted. Fittings on the vehicle include the following: rifle and machine gun mountings, towing hook, starting handle, headlamp blackout covers, wheel chock, towing eye and a map light. If required an additional dynamo can be installed when the vehicle is fitted with a radio.

Employment

2,000 issued to German Army in 1969/70. Denmark and the Netherlands have some of these vehicles. Also available on the civilian market. Under development by MBB is a 4 × 4 ½-ton amphibious vehicle for the German Army, first prototypes of which were completed in 1970.

Above: A VW 181 (4 × 2) vehicle of the German Army

UNIMOG Series

Germany (FGR)

Development/Variants

The famous UNIMOG (Universal Motor Gerät) series were developed shortly after the end of World War II and are built by Mercedes-Benz. Since then many models have been built for numerous civil and military applications.

Model 406: This has a wheelbase of 2.38m, other data being length 4.05m, width 2m, height 2.25m, track 1.536m. It can carry a maximum of 2,000kg of cargo, gross vehicle weight is 5,000kg.

Model 411: This was the earliest model to enter production and it has a very short wheelbase (only 1.72m) and is powered by a 4-cylinder diesel engine which develops 34bhp. Other data is length 3.46m, width 1.63m and a height of 2.035m payload is 1,100kg. A number of Air Forces (e.g. the RAF in Germany) use this model for towing aircraft.

Model 416: This is powered by a MB-OM 352 6-cylinder diesel which develops 110hp. Its gearbox has 6F and 2R gears. The rear cargo body has drop

	Model 416	**Model 421**
Length:	5.1m	4.55m
Width:	2.14m	1.8m
Height:	2.67m (tarpaulin)	2.2m
	2.325m (cab)	1.75m (reduced)
G/Clearance:	.44m	.415m
Track:	1.616m	1.384m
Wheelbase:	2.9m	2.57m
Weight:	6,000kg (loaded)	4,000kg (loaded)
	3,600kg (empty)	2,500kg (empty)
Crew:	1 + 1	1 + 1
Speed:	85km/hr	80km/hr
Range:	600km	500km
Fuel:	90 litres	90 litres
Gradient:	70%	70%
Angle Approach:	45°	42°
Angle Departure:	46°	55°
Fording:	1m	.8m
Tyres:	12.5 × 20	10.5 × 18
Load Area:	3m × 2m	2.4m × 1.55m

sides and a tailgate and is provided with bows and a canvas cover, the cab has a soft roof which can be quickly removed if required. It can carry a maximum of 2,400kg of cargo and its towed load is 2,500kg on both road and cross-country. The chassis of the 416 is also used as the basis for the Rheinstahl UR-416 Armoured Personnel Carrier which is in service in many countries.

Model 421: This is powered by a MB-OM 616 4-cylinder diesel that develops 66hp at 3,500rpm, a gearbox with 6F and 2R gears is provided. Its rear cargo body has drop sides and a tailgate and is also provided with bows and a tarpaulin cover. It can carry a maximum of 1,500kg of cargo on roads and its towed allowance is 1,500kg on roads and 1,000kg across country.

Model S-404: This is similar to the Model 416 but is powered by a MB/M 130 6-cylinder petrol engine which develops 118hp at 4,800rpm. The gearbox has 6F and 2R gears. It has the same wheelbase as the

416 but has a track of 1.63m as it has 10.5 × 20 tyres. The Unimog Model 'S' is similar to the S-404 and has the same transmission.

There are many optional extras for members of the Unimog family and these include front mounted winches, generators, enlarged cabs, hard-top cabs, pumps, PTOs and a wide variety of body styles. Variants used by the German Army include cargo trucks, ambulances, command vehicles, radio and fire control vehicles.

Employment
Used by many countries including Austria, Finland, France, Germany, Great Britain, Greece, India, Netherlands, Switzerland, Turkey, United States.

Below: *The Mercedes-Benz Unimog S (4 × 4) Truck*

The Unimog (4 × 4) Model 421 Truck

Unimog S being used as a radio vehicle by the German Frontier Service

The Unimog (4 × 4) Model S-404 Truck with front mounted winch

Ford G398SAM (4 x 4) 3-Ton Cargo Truck   Germany (FGR)

Length: 7.25m
Width: 2.445m
Height: 2.94m
2.135m (w/o cab)
G/Clearance: .32m
Track: 1.7m
Wheelbase: 4.013m
Weight: 7,840kg (loaded)
4,400kg (empty)
Engine: Ford Model G29T, V-8 petrol engine developing 92bhp at 3,500rpm. (3.924 litres)
Crew: 1 + 2
Speed: 80km/hr
Range: 300km
Fuel: 110 litres
Gradient: 60%
T/Radius: 10m
Fording: 1.1m
Tyres: 11.00 × 20
Load Area: 4.25 × 2.25m

Development
The Ford G398 SAM was developed from a commercial vehicle and was manufactured by Ford of Germany from 1957 to 1961. It can carry 3,000kg of cargo across country or 5,000kg of cargo on roads. A front mounted winch is fitted to some vehicles. The rear cargo body has drop sides and a tailgate, bows and a tarpaulin cover can be fitted. The cab has a soft roof which could be quickly removed as could the tops of the doors; the windscreen can be folded down flat. Some models were built with a hard cab. The gearbox has 4F and 1R gears and a two-speed transfer case is fitted. This vehicle is similiar in appearance to the 4 × 4 MAN 3-ton cargo truck.

Variants
These include ambulance, air defence radar vehicle (with AN/TPS-1D radar scanner mounted on the roof) and workshop vehicle.

Employment
Germany, Israel, Turkey.

Below: *A Ford G398SAM 3-Ton (4 × 4) Cargo Truck with hood, door tops, bows and tarpaulin cover removed*

Bottom: *A Ford G398SAM-Ton (4 × 4) Cargo Truck with windscreen, hood and tarpaulin in position*

MAN 630 Series of (4 x 4) 5-Ton Cargo Trucks   Germany (FGR)

Length: 7.9m
Width: 2.5m
Height: 2.845m (o/a)
2.2m (reduced)
G/Clearance: .35m
Track: 1.922m(f) 1.763(r)
Wheelbase: 4.6m
Weight: 13,000kg (loaded)
7,515kg (empty)
Load Area: 5m × 2.35m
Engine: MAN Model D 1246 MV3A/W, 6-cylinder
multi-fuel engine developing 130hp at 2,000rpm
Crew: 1 + 1
Speed: 66km/hr
Range: 440km
Fuel: 110 litres
T/Radius: 9.75m
Fording: .85m
Tyres: 11.00 × 20

Note: *The above data relates to the MAN 630 L2A.*

Development
This is one of the standard 5-Ton, 4 × 4 trucks of the
German Army. A latter model is the MAN 630 L2AE.
this has single rear wheels whereas the earlier L2A
has dual rear wheels.

The rear cargo body is provided with drop sides,
tailgate, bows and a tarpaulin cover. Most models
have a soft cab and some are fitted with a front
mounted winch. The gearbox has 6F and 1R gears
and a two-speed transfer box. Earlier models

included the MAN 415 series of 4-ton 4 × 4 trucks.
These are powered by a 6-cylinder multi-fuel engine
developing 100hp, and have single rear tyres and a
wheelbase of 4.2m. The MAN 415 has also been built
in India with a number of modifications including
dual rear tyres, the Indians call the vehicle the
Shaktiman.

Variants
Ambulance, basic data is length 7.73m, width 2.5m,
height 2.98m, weight 8,050kg.
    Decontamination vehicle designated TER-Kfz.
    Drone vehicle carrying the Canadian AN/USD-
501 reconaissance drone.
    Field kitchen.
    Radar vehicle with the American AN/TPS-1E
radar system installed in the rear.
    Tanker.
    Semi-trailer tractor with a wheelbase of 4.1m.

Employment
Belgium, Germany and India.

Above: *MAN 630 L2AE 5-Ton (4 × 4) Truck of the
German Army*

Mercedes-Benz LG 315/46 (4 x 4) 5-Ton Truck   Germany (FGR)

Length: 8.14m
Width: 2.5m
Height: 3.1m (overall)
2.68 (reduced)
G/Clearance: .408m
Track: 2.005m
Wheelbase: 4.6m
Weight: 12,850kg (loaded)
7,600kg (empty)
Load Area: 5m × 2.35m
Engine: Daimler Benz Model OM 315 V, 6-cylinder multi-fuel engine developing 145hp at 2,100rpm.
Crew: 1 + 1
Speed: 70km/hr
Range: 510km
Fuel: 140 litres
T/Radius: 10.7m
Fording: .85m
Tyres: 14.00 × 20

Development

This was developed in the early 1950s from a commercial model 4 × 4 vehicle. It has an all-steel body which is provided with drop sides, tailgate, bows and a tarpaulin cover. Most models have a cab with a soft top, although some have a hard top. The gearbox has 6F and 1R gears and a two-speed transfer case.

Variants

Observation vehicle with a hydraulically operated observation tower. Tanker: This has two tanks each holding 2,100 litres. Basic data is length 8.12m, width 2.5m, height 3.2m and weight 7,330kg.

Wrecker: This has a small crane mounted in the rear cargo area. Basic data is length 9.3m, width 2.5m, height 3m.

Employment

German Army.

Below: *A Mercedes-Benz LG 315/46 5-Ton (4 × 4) Truck*

Bottom: *The German Federal Border Police (BGS) uses a number of these Mercedes-Benz 3-Ton (4 × 4) Trucks, similar vehicles are used by a number of other countries.*

Magirus-Deutz (6 x 6) 7-Ton Truck

Germany (FGR)

Length: 8m
Width: 2.5m
Height: 2.95m
G/Clearance: .315m
Track: 1.927m(f) 1.915m (r)
Wheelbase: 4.16m + 1.28m
Weight: 15,250kg (loaded)
7,450kg (empty)
Load Area: 5m × 2.35m
Engine: Deutz Model F8 L 714A, 8-cylinder multi-fuel engine developing 178hp at 2,300rpm
Crew: 1 + 2
Speed: 73.6km/hr
Range: 500km
Fuel: 150 litres
T/Radius: 10.5m
Fording: .85m
Tyres: 11.00 × 20

Development

This was developed from a standard commercial vehicle and was introduced into the German Army in the early 1960s. Its German Army designation is LKW 7-ton gl Winde (Jupiter). The rear cargo body is of all steel construction and is provided with drop sides, tailgate, bows and a tarpaulin cover. Many models are fitted with a winch mounted behind the front bumper. Late models have a more powerful engine and slightly different cabs. The gearbox has 6F and 1R gears and a two-speed transfer case.

There was also a 4 × 4 Magirus-Deutz, 5-ton truck which entered service in the 1950s, and some of these may well remain in service.

Variants

There are many variants of this 6 × 6 truck in service, they include:

Aircraft refueller.

Decontamination truck with a full range of equipment. This is called the E-Kfz (*Dekontaminierungsgerat*).

Fire-fighting truck.

Light Artillery Rocket System. This is a standard 6X6 chassis with 36 launching tubes for 110mm rockets. Basic data of this model is as follows: weight fully loaded 15,000kg, length 7.85m, width 2.5m, height 2.9m. A total of 209 of these are in service with the German Army.

Tipper truck. This is a standard 6 × 6 chassis with a three way tipper mounted on the rear. Basic data is weight 8,650kg (empty), length 8m, width 2.5m, height 2.55m.

Tractor. 4 × 4 tractor for towing semi-trailers. Wheelbase is 4.41m, other data is length 7.16m, width 2.5m and height 2.6m, weight 7,200kg.

Wrecker. This has a crane with a telescopic jib, traverse throughout 360°, crane has a capacity of 4,000kg. Other data is length 9.4m, width 2.5m, height 3.15m and weight 14,500kg.

Employment

German Army and Air Force. Magirus-Deutz (6 × 6) trucks of various types are also used by Belgium, Denmark, India and Turkey.

Below: Magirus-Deutz 7-Ton (6 × 6) Truck of the German Army fitted with a front mounted winch.

Above: *Magirus-Deutz 7-Ton (6 × 6) Dump Truck with front mounted winch.*

Faun L 908/54 VA (6 x 6) 10-Ton Cargo Truck   Germany (FGR)

Length: 9.75m
Width: 2.5m
Height: 3.35m
G/Clearance: .37m
Track: 2.046m(f) 1.944m(r)
Wheelbase: 4.7m + 1.4m
Weight: 21,500km (loaded)
11,500kg (empty)
Load Area: 6.7m × 2.35m
Engine: Deutz Model BF 12 L 714A, 8-cylinder air-cooled multi-fuel engine developing 178hp at 2,300rpm
Crew: 1 + 2
Speed: 72km/hr
Range: 520km
Fuel: 200 litres
Gradient: 40%
T/Radius: 12m
Fording: 1m
Tyres: 14.00 × 20

Development
This can carry 10,000kg of cargo on both roads or cross-country. It is fitted with a Model AK6-55 gearbox which has 6F and 1R gear and a two-speed transfer box. The cab is of the forward control type and its roof can be removed if required. The rear body is provided with drop sides and a tailgate. Some models have a THEA crane fitted which can lift 1,000kg of cargo. A winch with a capacity of 10,000kg is standard.

Employment
German Army, some reports have stated that the Turkish Army has some of these vehicles.

Below: *The Faun L 908/54 VA (6 × 6) Cargo Truck using its TEHA hydraulic crane, note the stabilisers in position.*

Faun LK 1212/485 11 Crane Truck

Germany (FGR)

This is a highly mobile 6 × 6 crane and is powered by a Deutz air-cooled multi-fuel engine Model F12 L 714A which develops 265hp at 2,300rpm. The gearbox (Model AK6-75) has 6F and 1R gears and a two-speed transfer case. The crane can be traversed through 360° and can lift a maximum of 13,000kg, stabilisers are povided. A winch with a capacity of 10,000kg is fitted. Early models had a different crane. Basic data is as follows: length 9.14m, width 2.5m, height 3m, weight 17,000kg, speed 60km/hr, range 600km and wheelbase 4m + 1.7m.

Employment
German Army.

Above: Faun Crane Truck Model LK 1212/485 11 in travelling order.

Faun L912/45A (6 x 6) 10-Ton Truck

Germany (FGR)

Length: 7.65m
Width: 2.5m
Height: 3,44m
G/Clearance: .37m
Track: 2.055m(f) 1.81m(r)
Wheelbase: 3.77m + 1.46m
Weight: 27,000kg (loaded)
12,000kg (empty)
Load Area: 3.55m × 2.35m
Engine: Deutz 12-cylinder air-cooled multi-fuel engine type F 12 L 714A developing 265hp at 2,300rpm
Crew: 1 + 2
Speed: 76km/hr
Range: 660km
Fuel: 300 litres
Gradient: 40%

T/Radius: 11m
Fording: .9m
Tyres: 12.00 × 24

Development
This has been designed to carry 10,000kg of cargo across country or 15,000kg of cargo on roads. Its German Army designation is LWK 12-Ton *Gleitkipper*. The rear cargo body is provided with a tailgate, bows and a tarpaulin cover. A winch with a capacity of 8,000kg is standard equipment. Its gearbox has (Model AK 6-75-3) 6F and 1R gears and a two-speed transfer box.

Variants
Faun L 912/SA: This has the same chassis and engine as the above and is used to tow semi-trailers.

Basic data is length 7.61m, width 2.5m, height 2.82m and weight of 12,500kg.

Faun L 912/5050A: This has a longer wheelbase than the L 912/45A but has the same engine and gear box. Essential data is length 9.1m, width 2.5m, height 2.9m and gross vehicle weight of 25,200kg, wheelbase is 4.3m and 1.5m. The rear loading platform can be tilted to the rear and extended to the ground so that vehicles (such as bulldozers) can be quickly loaded.

Faun L 908/ATW (Tanker): This is powered by a Deutz F 8 L 714A multi-fuel engine developing 178hp at 2,300rpm, a AK 6-55 gearbox is fitted, this has 6F and 1R gears and a two-speed transfer case. Two models have been built, the airfield model carries 12,000 litres of fuel and the road model 15,000 litres of fuel.

Employment
German Armed Forces.

Below: *The Faun L 912/45A (6 × 6) Cargo Truck/Prime Mover*

Bottom: *The Faun L 908/ATW Fuel Tanker.*

New Range of German Tactical Trucks

	4-TON (4 × 4)	7-TON (6 × 6)	10-TON (8 × 8)
Length:	7.4m	8.43m	9.93m
Width:	2.49m	2.49m	2.49m
Height (o/a):	3.75m	3.75m	3.75m
Height (cab):	2.81m	2.81m	2.81m
G/Clearance:	.405m	.405m	.405m
Wheelbase:	4.3m	3.8m + 1.4m	1.9m + 3.7m + 1.4m
Track:	2.066m	2.066m	2.066m
Weight (loaded):	12,000kg	17,000kg	22,000kg
Weight (empty):	8,000kg	10,000kg	12,000kg
Crew:	1 + 2	1 + 2	1 + 2
Speed:	90km/hr	90km/hr	90km/hr
Range:	800km	800km	800km
Angle Approach:	45°	45°	45°
Angle Departure:	46°	42°	57°
Engine (Cyl/HP):	7/265	10/330	10/330

In the late 1950s and early 1960s the Federal Technical Office for Armament and Military Purchases drew up requirements for a new range of tactical trucks for the German Army. Basically this range consists of 4, 7 and 10-ton vehicles, some of which were to be amphibious. Also included were 4 × 4 and 6 × 6 armoured amphibious load carriers and 8 × 8 reconnaissance vehicles.

In 1964 various German automotive companies were approached to build the prototypes of this new range of tactical vehicles. In 1965 a Joint Project Office was set up and the following companies undertook development work: Büssing, Krupp, Rheinstahl/Henschel, Klöckner-Humboldt-Deutz and MAN. In addition Daimler Benz also developed some vehicles. After various prototypes were built, it was decided in 1970 that the Joint Project Office would concentrate on the unarmoured tactical trucks whilst Daimler Benz carried on with the armoured vehicles.

Wherever possible commercial components have been used such as axles and engines, and all of the trucks have similar wheels and cabs. Trials with the prototypes have been conducted in various parts of the world including Canada, Norway, Germany and Italy. In addition to carrying cargo some of the trucks will be adopted for carrying fuel or ammunition.

Below: *On the left is the 6 × 6 7-Ton Tactical Cargo Truck and on the right is the 4 × 4 4-Ton Tactical Cargo Truck.*

By the end of 1974 none of the vehicles was in service although Rheinstahl had been awarded a contract for the construction of 408 of the 8 × 8 reconaissance vehicle known as the *Spähpanzer 2*. It is expected that the 4 × 4 armoured load carrier will be dropped from the range and the 6 × 6 model, which is called the *Transportpanzer 1* (TPz 1), will be adopted.

Variants

(4 × 4) 4-Ton Tactical Cargo Truck (Lkw 4-Ton, Pritsche): This is designed to carry 4,000kg of cargo on both roads and cross-country. An amphibious model, which is propelled in the water by two propellers may also enter production. There is also a normal transport model with a longer wheelbase (5.15m) and this can carry 6,600kg of cargo on roads. **(6 × 6) 7-Ton Tactical Cargo Truck (Lkw 7-Ton, Pritsche):** This is designed to carry 7,000kg of cargo on both roads and cross-country. An amphibious model has also been developed but this, as far as is known, will not enter production. In addition there is a standard transport truck that can carry 10,000kg of cargo on roads and this has a wheelbase of 4.7m + 1.4m.

(8 × 8) 10-Ton Tactical Cargo Truck: This has been designed to carry 10,000kg of cargo on both roads and cross-country. All of these trucks have rear cargo bodies with dropsides, tailgate, bows and a tarpaulin cover.

Employment

It is expected that these vehicles will enter production in 1976 and total requirements of the German Army are said to be at least 60,000 trucks.

Above: The 6 × 6 7-Ton Tactical Cargo Truck undergoing trials.

Faun GT 8/15 (4 x 4) Artillery Tractor   Germany (FGR)

Length: 7.4m
Width: 2.8m
Height: 3.22m (overall)
2.5m (reduced)
G/Clearance: .44m
Track: 1.99m(f) 1.995m(r)
Wheelbase: 3.4m
Weight: 20,000kg (loaded)
15,250kg (empty)
Engine: Deutz Model F 8 L 714A, 8-cylinder multi-fuel engine developing 178hp at 2,300rpm
Crew: 1 + 7
Speed: 67.5km/hr
Range: 520km
Fuel: 185 litres
Gradient: 50%
Angle Approach: 35°
Angle Departure: 60°
T/Radius: 9m

Fording: 1.4m
Tyres: 16.00 × 24

Development

This 4 × 4 vehicle, which is called the *Geräteträger* in the German Army, has been designed to carry a standard American M-101 105mm Howitzer in the rear of the vehicle. To enable this weapon to be removed quickly it is fitted with a hydraulic tailgate which places the gun in its exact firing position. At the front is a hydraulically operated dozer blade which is used to clear obstacles or prepare fire positions. A winch with a capacity of 10,000kg is also fitted. The gearbox (Model AK 6-55) has 6F and 1R gears and a two-speed transfer case. An early model of this vehicle was the GT 6/15, this had a 6-cylinder engine. Some GT 8/15s have a crane mounted on the rear and these are known as GK 8/15s.

Variants

FAUN Z 12/31 A [*Zugmashine*]: Although in some respects similiar to the above vehicle, this has a different engine (Deutz F 12 L 614, developing 250hp at 2,300rpm) and gearbox. It is used to tow trailers up to a maximum stated weight of approximately 80,000kg. Basic data of the Z 12/31A is length 6.79m, width 2.5m, height 2.8m, wheelbase 3.1m, maximum road speed 65km/hr, range 580km, and fuel 290 litres. It weighs 14,400kg which includes 3,150kg of ballast. A winch is mounted at the front of the vehicle. So far only two of these vehicles have been built.

Employment

German Army.

Below: A Faun GT 8/15 (4 × 4) Artillery Tractor carrying a M-101 (modified) Howitzer.

Faun Z 912/21-203 (6 x 6) Artillery Tractor   Germany (FGR)

Length: 8.4m
Width: 2.5m
Height: 3.45m
G/Clearance: .44m
Track: 1.99m(f) 1.995m(r)
Wheelbase: 1.78m + 3.11m
Weight: 26,400kg (loaded)
16,400kg (empty)
Load Area: 5m × 2.35m
Engine: Deutz Model F 12 L 714A, 12-cylinder air-cooled multi-fuel engine developing 265hp at 2,300rpm.
Crew: 1 + 13
Speed: 60km/hr
Range: 600km
Fuel: 300 litres
Gradient: 50%
T/Radius: 11.4m
Fording: 1.4m

Tyres: 15.00 × 25

Development

This 6 × 6 vehicle was designed by Faun-Werke (Nuremberg) to tow medium artillery (e.g. 155mm) and carry its complete crew plus ammunition and stores.

The gearbox has 6F and 1R gears (AK 6-55) and a two-speed transfer case, steering is on the front two axles. A winch with a capacity of 10,000kg is provided. The cab is of the forward control type, the rear body has drop sides and a tailgate, bows and a tarpaulin cover are provided.

Variants

Faun L 912/21 MUN: This is similar to the Z 912/21-203 but is used to carry a maximum of 10,000kg of stores or ammunition. To assist in unloading the ammunition it is fitted with a hydraulic

crane that can lift a maximum of 1,000kg at 4m. Gross weight of this vehicle, fully loaded, is 27,200kg.

Faun Z 912/21 A 1 (Geräteträger): This has the same engine, gearbox as the above vehicles but has a wheelbase of 1.78m + 2.61m. It has a hydraulic dozer blade at the front and a hydraulic lift at the rear to off-load cargo, a winch with a capacity of 10,000kg is fitted. Empty weight is 16,800kg and loaded weight is 22,000kg.

Faun LK 12/21-400: This has the same engine and chassis as the Z 912/21-203. On the rear of the chassis is a crane with a capacity of 11,000kg. A dozer blade is fitted at the front of the vehicle and

jacks to stabilise it when the crane is in use are also fitted. Has not yet entered service; trials only.

Employment
German Army.

Above left: *Faun Z 912/21-203 (6 × 6)* Artillery Tractor

Faun LK 1212/45 VSA (6 x 6) Tractor

Germany (FGR)

Length: 7.838m
Width: 2.9m
Height: 3.04m
G/Clearance: .39m
Track: 2.133m + 2.071m
Wheelbase: 3.785m + 1.5m
Weight: 18,100kg
Engine: Deutz Model BF 12 L 714 12-cylinder air-cooled diesel developing 340hp at 2,300rpm
Crew: 8
Speed: 57km/hr
Range: 720km
Fuel: 400 litres
T/Radius: 11.5m
Fording: .9m
Tyres: 14.00 × 24

following basic data: length 14.75m, width 2.5m and empty weight of 14,200kg. This can carry both the Leopard and M-48s which are the MBTs used by the German Army.

It has a Model AK 6-75-3 gearbox with 6F and 1R gears and a two-speed transfer case, a dual winch with a capacity of 20,000kg each is fitted as standard equipment. A latter Faun tank transporter is the L 1212/50 VS, this has not however, entered service.

Employment
The Faun LK 1212/45 VSA is in service with the German Army.

Development/Variants
This tractor, which entered service in the early 1960s is known as the *Sattelzugmaschine* 25 T (6 × 6) and is the standard tank transport tractor of the German Army. It is used with a semi-trailer which has the

Above right: *The Faun LK 1212/45 VSA towing a semi-trailer carrying a M-47 tank.*

Faun L 912/VSA (6 x 6) Tractor

Germany (FGR)

Length: 7.74m
Width: 2.9m
Height: 2.306m
G/Clearance: .38m
Track: 2.12 + 2.007m
Wheelbase: 3.75m + 1.5m
Weight: 17,000kg
Engine: Deutz Model BF 12 L 614, 12-cylinder air-cooled diesel developing 300hp at 2,300rpm
Crew: 8
Speed: 57km/hr

Range: 800km
Fuel: 400 litres
T/Radius: 11.5m
Fording: .9m
Tyres: 14.00 × 24

Development/Variants/Employment
This was the forerunner of the Faun L 1212/45 VSA and entered service in the late 1950s. It is still used by the German Army.

Faun SLT 50-2 (8 x 8) Tractor

Germany (FGR)

Length: 21.378m
Width: 3.07m
Height: 3.235m
Wheelbase: 1.5m + 2.7m + 1.5m
Weight: 87,600kg (loaded)
23,030kg (empty)
Engine: MTU MB 837 EA 500 8-cylinder diesel developing 730hp
Speed: 65km/hr
Range: 600km
Gradient: 50%
Tyres: 18.00 × 22.5

Development/Variants
By the end of 1974 Faun had built a total of seven of these tractors, these being pre-production models and are based on the American/German HET-70 (Heavy Equipment Transporter), which was designed to carry the now defunct MBT-70. The trailer, which has eight wheels, all of which can be steered, has been designed and built by the GST (Gesellschaft Für System-Technik), this being a subsidiary of Krupp. The German Army has a requirement for around 120 of these units. As of

December 1974, no production contracts had been awarded for this vehicle, although it is anticipated that orders will be placed in the near future.

Employment
Pre-production for the German Army.

The Faun SLT 50-2 (8 × 8) Tractor Unit.

The Faun SLT 50-2 (8 × 8) Tractor Unit and its LH 70-420 Trailer

The American HET-70 with a M-60 MBT on its semi-trailer.

Land Rover (4 x 4) ½-Tonne Truck

Great Britain

Length: 3.67m
Width: 1.52m
Height: 1.95m (hood up)
1.47m (w/o windscreen)
G/Clearance: .21m
Track: 1.31m (f and r)
Wheelbase: 2.23m
Weight: 2,160kg (loaded)
1,460kg (empty)
Load Area: 1.14m × 1.40m
Engine: Rover 2.25 litre four-cylinder petrol engine developing 81bhp at 4,500rpm
Crew: 1 + 2
Speed: 95km/hr
Range: 560km
Fuel: 91 litres
Gradient: 39% (high) 115% (low)
Angle Approach: 49°
Angle Departure: 36°
T/Radius: 6.4m (maximum)
Fording: .5m
Tyres: 6.50 × 16

Development
This has been developed by the Rover Company and MVEE to meet the airportable requirement for the British armed forces. Its full designation is Truck, General Service (Rover ½-Tonne, 4 × 4). This vehicle is replacing the standard 88" (2.23m) Land Rover and is capable of being airlifted by the Wessex and Puma helicopters. The first prototypes were built in 1965, with production commencing in 1968. The prototype vehicles differed in a number of ways, the most obvious being that they had their headlamps in front of the radiator, on production models the headlamps are on the front of the wings.

The engine, transmission, axles, suspension and steering are all similar to the standard Land Rover, the new components are the chassis, body and wheels. To save weight, the hood, body sides, windscreen, bumpers, doors and spare wheel can quickly be removed.

The vehicle has a maximum payload of 500kg and an installed power-to-weight ratio of 35.2bhp/Ton, a trailer, or light weapons, can be towed up to a maximum weight of 1,130kg. The normal seating arrangement is three men in the front and two men either side at the rear, when being used as a radio vehicle only two men (including the driver) can be seated in the front, the space between the seats being used for the 2 × 12 volt batteries. The gearbox has 4F and 1R gears and a two-speed transfer box. The front and rear suspension consists of semi-elliptical springs with double acting hydraulic shock absorbers. Both LHD and RHD models are available as are 12 and 24-volt electrical systems, the latter being for radio installations.

Variants
At the present time only the basic model is in service although trials have been carried out enabling the vehicle to be used as an emergency ambulance and for carrying a 120mm Wombat recoilless anti-tank rifle. The basic model, without doubt, can be adopted for a wide variety of roles.

Employment
Belgium, Brunei, Dutch Marines, Great Britain (Army, Royal Marines and Royal Air Force), Guyana, Hong Kong, Jamaica, Libya.

Below: *Early model of the Land Rover (4 × 4) ½-tonne Truck with doors, sides, hood and windscreen removed.*

Current production model of the Land Rover (4 × 4) ½-Tonne Truck.

Land Rover (4 x 4) ¼ and ¾-Ton Trucks Great Britain

	SWB	LWB
Length:	3.8m	4.56m
Width:	1.676m	1.676m
Height:	1.96m (with hood)	2.03m (with hood)
G/Clearance:	.203m	.228m
Wheelbase:	2.23m	2.768m
Track:	1.31m	1.33m
Weight Loaded:	2,020kg	2,760kg
Weight Empty:	1,530kg	1,680kg
Load Area:	1.206m × 1.448m	1.85m × 1.44m
Crew:	1 + 2	1 + 2
Speed:	105km/hr	96km/hr
Range:	560km	450/500km
Fuel:	91 litres	91 litres
Gradient:	39% (high) 115% (low)	25% (high) 58% (low)
Angle Approach:	46°	47°
Angle Departure:	34°	29°
T/Radius:	5.79m	7.5m (maximum)
Fording:	.5m	.5m
Tyres:	6.00 × 16, 6.50 × 16, 7.50 × 16 or 8.20 × 15	7.50 × 16, 8.20 × 15, or 9.00 × 15
Engine:	Rover 4-cylinder petrol, 77bhp at 4,250rpm	Rover 4-cylinder petrol, 81bhp at 4,500rpm

Note: *The above data relates to late production models, earlier vehicles may vary slightly in detail.*

Development

Without doubt the Land Rover is one of the most famous of all British post-war vehicles. Development of the Land Rover started in 1947 when a number of prototypes were built. It was first shown to the public at the Amsterdam Motor Show in April, 1948, the vehicle entered production at Solihull in July, 1948. The first models had a wheelbase of 80" (2.032m) and were powered by a 1.6 litre petrol engine. The 86" (2.184m) model followed in 1954 as did the 107" (2.717m). In 1956 the 88" (2.235m) and 109" (2.768m) models appeared, also in 1956 the Land Rover was officially adopted by the British Army, although by that time it had been in service for a number of years, these Land Rovers were known as the Series 11. In 1961 came the Series 11A and by 1966 half a million Land Rovers had been built, the majority of which went for export. From 1968 the head-lamps were moved from the grille to the wings to comply with new legal requirements in a number of countries.

The chassis of the Land Rover is of welded steel

construction, the body being of light alloy construction. The suspension consists of underslung semi-elliptical springs and double acting hydraulic shock absorbers. The gearbox has 4F and 1R gears and a two-speed transfer box, provision is made for a PTO which can be adapted for a wide variety of roles, including the fitting of a winch.

Variants
SWB Land Rover (Truck, General Service, ¼-Ton (4 × 4): This is no longer in production for the British Army as it is being replaced by the new airportable ½-Tonne Land Rover (refer to separate

Top: *LWB Land Rover with ambulance body.*

Above: *LWB Land Rover in service with the Australian Army. Of note are the modified wings and the guard on the front of the vehicle.*

entry for full details). It can carry 408kg of cargo on both road and cross-country and can also tow a trailer.

LWB Land Rover (Truck, General Service, ¾-Ton (4×4): This is still in production for the British Army and can carry 908kg of cargo on roads or 816kg of cargo across country. The LWB chassis is used for the successful Shorland Armoured Patrol Vehicle and the new Shorts SB.301 Armoured Personnel Carrier. Both the ¼ and ¾-ton model have been built as FFR (fitted for radio). Scottorn Trailers Limited have developed a powered trailer for use with the LWB Land Rover, thus making it an effective 6×6 combination. The standard Land Rover can be adapted for use with this trailer as well, with the aid of a kit.

There are many variants of the Land Rover in service including various types of ambulance, Special Air Service, crash rescue, repair vehicle, recovery vehicle and so on. The LWB models are also used for towing the following: 105mm Italian Pack Howitzer, Rapier Surface to Air Missile System, Cymbeline Motor Locating Radar System and various trailers, all of these have reinforced axles. The Land Rover can also be fitted with a variety of armament including the 120mm Wombat Recoilless Anti-Tank Rifle or the American M-40 106mm Recoilless Rifle, various machine guns, cannon or anti-tank guided weapons.

In addition there are also many local modifications all over the world as the Land Rover is built under licence, or assmbled locally, in many countries.

Employment
Land Rovers are in service with some 140 overseas armed forces.

Note: *There is also a 110" (2.794m) forward control Land Rover which is used by a number of armies including Spain.*

Old production model of the LWB Land Rover (Truck, General Service, ¾-Ton (4×4)).

New production model of the LWB Land Rover (Truck, General Service, ¾-Ton (4×4))

The SWB Land Rover (Truck, General Service, ¼-Ton, (4 × 4), this is now being replaced by the new ½-Tonne Land Rover.

The SWB Land Rover mounting a 7.62mm LMG. Note the additional water cans at the front and the radio aerials on the wings.

Spanish built LWB Land Rover in service with the Spanish Army.

Land Rover (4 x 4) 1-Tonne Truck

Great Britain

Length: 4.127m
Width: 1.842m
Height: 2.283m (hood)
2.138m (top of windscreen)
G/Clearance: .254m (axles)
Track: 1.524m(f) 1.549m(r)
Wheelbase: 2.565m
Weight: 3,143kg (loaded)
1,924kg (empty)
Load Area: 2.491m × 1.72m
Engine: Rover V-8 petrol engine developing 156bhp
at 5,000rpm (3,528cc)
Crew: 1 + 1
Speed: 120km/hr
Range: 560km
Fuel: 109 litres
Gradient: 60%
Angle Approach: 50°
Angle Departure: 51°
T/Radius: 5.63m
Fording: .8m
Tyres: 9.00 × 15

Development

The 1-Tonne Land Rover has been designed by Rover and the MVEE to meet a British Army requirement for a 1-Tonne vehicle with added capacity of towing a 1½-ton powered-axle trailer. This vehicle is now in volume production at the Rover factory at Solihull, Birmingham. The Royal Artillery will use this vehicle to tow the new British 105mm Light Gun which is now entering service.

It is powered by the successful light-weight Rover 3.5 litre petrol engine which is similar to the standard civilian engine but with a reduced compression ratio of 8.5 to 1 to enable it to operate on low octane fuels, power to weight ratio (laden) is 40.7bhp/Ton.

Its gearbox has 4F and 1R gears with high and low transfer box, this provides a total of 8F and 2R speeds. Permanent 4 × 4 drive eliminates the necessity for the 4 × 2 control lever. A third differential between the front and rear axles obviates

transmission wind-up associated with 4 × 4 transmissions.

The chassis is of all-steel construction with the body panels of aluminium. The suspension consists of semi-elliptical springs and hydraulic shock absorbers. A PTO is provided for a winch and a powered axle trailer as previously mentioned. This trailer, which is manufactured by Scottorn Trailers Limited of Chartridge, Buckinghamshire can carry a maximum of 1,000kg of cargo. British Army vehicles are RHD although LHD models are available, both 12-Volt and 24-Volt electrical systems are available.

The complete hood, body sides, windscreen, bumpers and spare wheel can be removed from the vehicle and in this form weighs only 1,580kg and can be airlifted by Wessex and Puma helicopters. If required the Land Rover can carry 8 fully equipped men in the rear in lieu of 1,000kg of cargo.

Variants

There are no variants in service at the present time although this vehicle could be adopted for a very wide range of roles including repair, recovery, ambulance and so on. Trials have been carried out with a 1-Tonne Land Rover fitted with a special infantry mounting called Beeswing, this has six Swingfire ATGWs, the vehicle can also mount and fire various types of recoilless rifle including the Wombat.

Employment

In service with the British Army.

Right: *The Land Rover (4 × 4) 1-Tonne Truck.*

Below right: *The Land Rover (4 × 4) 1-Tonne Truck towing a Scottorn 1-Tonne Powered Trailer.*

Below: *The Land Rover (4 × 4) 1-Tonne Truck towing the new British 105mm Light Gun.*

Bedford MK (4 x 4) 4-Ton Cargo Truck Great Britain

Length: 6.579,
Width: 2.489m
Height: 3.404m (overall)
2,501m (cab)
G/Clearance: .343m
Track: 2.05m(f) 2.03m(r)
Wheelbase: 3.962m
Weight: 9,450kg (loaded)
5,910kg (empty)
Load Area: 4.28m × 2.01m
Engine: Bedford 6-cylinder multi-fuel engine developing 107bhp at 2,800rpm
Crew: 1 + 1
Speed: 73km/hr
Range: 560km
Fuel: 150 litres
Gradient: 45%
Angle Approach: 41°
Angle Departure: 38°
T/Radius: 8.94m
Fording: .762m
Tyres: 12.00 × 20

Development

In the early 1960s various companies including Austin, Bedford and Commer, built a number of prototypes for a 4-ton truck to replace the Bedford RL series. Bedford were the winners of this competition with the truck based on the civilian TK range. The cab is of all-steel construction and is of the forward control type, some models are provided with an observation hatch in the roof of the cab. The cargo body is also of all-steel construction and this is built by Marshall of Cambridge (Engineering) Limited. It features drop sides and a tailboard which can be quickly removed to provide a platform for pallet loads or containers. If required, bows and a tarpaulin cover can be fitted.

The suspension consists of semi-elliptical springs front and rear, together with telescopic, hydraulic double acting dampers. The transfer box provides 4 × 4 drive in both high and low ranges, with 4 × 2 drive in high only. The braking system consists of dual air/hydraulic drum type on all wheels. It can tow a trailer with a maximum weight of 5,284kg.

Variants

The basic models are the FV 13801/FV 13802, or when fitted with a winch with a capacity of 3,500kg and 76m of rope, it becomes the FV 13803/FV 13804. Vauxhall also offer, for export LHD, petrol or diesel engines in places of the multi-fuel engine, and twin instead of single rear wheels. A dump truck model has been developed and this is already in production. A number of special vehicles have been developed for use by the Royal Air Force with their Harrier VTOL aircraft, these include bomb carrying vehicles, demountable bulk fuel dispensing unit (4,320 litre capacity) and a 4,500 litre capacity tactical refueller.

Employment

Eire, Great Britain, Kenya, Netherlands.

Right and below: The Bedford MK 4-Ton (4 × 4) Cargo Truck.

Below right: The Bedford MK 4-Ton (4 × 4) Cargo Truck fitted with a mine-proof cab by Reynolds Boughton Limited.

Bedford (4 x 4) 4-Ton Cargo Truck Great Britain

Length: 6.36m
Width: 2.39m
Height: 3.11m (overall)
2.602m (cab)
Track: 1.854m (f and r)
Wheelbase: 3.962m
Weight: 8,800kg (loaded)
4,500kg (empty)
Load Area: 4.267m × 2.178m
Engine: Bedford 6-cylinder OHV petrol engine developing 130bhp at 3,200rpm
Crew: 1 + 1
Speed: 75km/hr
Range: 400km
Fuel: 118 litres
Gradient: 33%
Angle Approach: 36°
Angle Departure: 30°
T/Radius: 9.13m
Tyres: 11.00 × 20

Note: *Data relates to the FV 13112*

Development
This range of vehicles (also known as the RL or RS, L = LWB and S = SWB) is basically an adaption of the commercial 7-ton (4 × 2) chassis to military requirements. They were developed by Vauxhall Motors Limited in the early 1950s and were in production from 1952 until 1969. According to Vauxhall 73,135 of these were built for both civilian and military use. Originally they were rated at 3,000kg, but more recently they have been re-rated at 4,000kg, their replacement is the Vauxhall MK series of 4 × 4 trucks. The vehicle has a gearbox with 4F and 1R gears and a two-speed transfer case, the cab is of the forward control type and is of all-steel construction, an observation hatch is provided in the roof of the cab. The rear body is of all-steel construction and is provided with bows and a tarpaulin cover, if required the sides and tailboard can be removed or dropped. The bodies were made by a number of companies, the largest manufacturer being Marshall of Cambridge (Engineering) Limited. Many models are fitted with a winch with a capacity of 5,000kg.

Variants
There are many variants of the RL/RS truck, the first production model being the FV 13101 cargo truck. Other models have included the following: FV 13104 charging vehicle, FV 13106 3,636 litre tanker, FV 13109 cargo truck, FV 13110 signals van, FV 13111 3,000kg tipper (SWB), FV 13112 cargo truck (dropside), FV 13113 MT repair vehicle, FV 13115 3-ton light recovery vehicle, FV 13120 1,728 litre tanker (also armoured model), FV 13136 for container bodies, FV 13142 cargo dropside (air-portable), FV 13143 3-ton cargo (LHD), FV 13149 2,728 litre tanker, FV 13165 dental surgery and FV 13197 water tanker (4 × 2). Other models include various fire trucks, roadway-laying vehicles, artillery towing trucks, a more recent model is fitted with the Midge reconnaissance drone.

Employment
Belgium, Eire, Great Britain, Malaysia, Netherlands, Pakistan, South Africa.

Below: *The basic Bedford RL (4 × 4) cargo truck with bows and tarpaulin cover in position.*

Top right: *The Bedford 3-Ton (4 × 4) Light Recovery Vehicle (FV 13115)*

Centre right: *Bedford RL fitted with the Canadian Midge (AN/USD-501) reconnaissance drone which is now in service with the British, German and United States Armies.*

Bedford RL fitted with a
system for laying Class 30
trackway, this has been
developed by Laird
(Anglesey) Limited.

AEC Militant Mk 3 (6 x 6) 10-Ton Cargo Truck   Great Britain

Length: 9.08m
Width: 2.49m
Height: 3.5m (inc. bows)
Track: 2m(f) 2.06m(r)
Wheelbase: 4.877m
Weight: 22,000kg (loaded)
11,850kg (empty)
Engine: AEC AV760 6-cylinder diesel developing 226bhp at 2,200rpm
Speed: 53km/hr
Range: 483km
Fuel: 218 litres
T/Radius: 11.4m
Tyres: 15.00 × 20
P/W Ratio: 10bhp/ton
Load Area: 6.25m × 2.34m

Development

The Militant MK 3 was designed by AEC (now a part of the British Leyland Motor Corporation) to a British Army specification for a 10-Ton General Service Cargo Truck. It is based on commercial components, its full Army designation is FV 11047 Truck Cargo with winch, AEC 10-Ton Mk 3, 6×6. The basic chassis is designed FV 11046. The vehicle is no longer in production.

The gearbox has 6F and 1R gears and a two-speed transfer box. The front suspension consists of semi-elliptical springs with double acting shock absorbers. The fully articulated rear bogie has inverted springs pivoted on a cross tube mounted in cast brackets. The steering is power-assisted and air brakes are fitted as standard.

The cab is of all-steel construction and is provided with an observation hatch in the roof. The rear cargo body, which was built by Marshalls of Cambridge Limited has drop sides and a drop down tailgate. If required these can be quickly removed, bows and a tarpaulin cover are provided. A winch with a capacity of 7,000kg and 76.3m of rope is provided.

Variants

There was an Armoured Command Vehicle on a SWB chassis, this was built by the ROF at Leeds in 1966 and was designated FV 11061, it did not, however, enter service. The FV 11044 is a 6×6 Medium Recovery Vehicle and is based on the SWB chassis. This has been designed to recover vehicles up to 10,000kg in weight. It is fitted with a hydraulic power operated jib crane (traverse 240°), a winch with a capacity of 15,000kg (bottom layer of the drum) and a hydraulically operated spade is mounted at the rear of the vehicle. Basic data of the FV 11044 is length 8.23m, width 2.5m, height 3.1m, maximum speed 78km/hr, range 483km, fuel 218 litres and weight 21,000kg.

Employment

British Army.

Below: *A AEC Militant, Mk. 3 (6 × 6) Cargo Truck undergoing trials.*

The FV 11002 (6 × 6) Artillery Tractor is used to tow the Bofors 40mm Light Anti-Aircraft guns of the Light A/A Regiments.

A Militant Mk. 1 (6 × 6) Cargo Truck with sides removed and a HIAB crane fitted so that it can handle pallets.

AEC Militant Mk 1 (6 x 6) 10-Ton Cargo Truck   Great Britain

Length: 9.14m
Width: 2.49m
Height: 3.6m
Track: 1.99m(f) 1.91m(r)
Wheelbase: 4.877m
Weight: 21,200kg (loaded)
11,100kg (empty)
Engine: AEC 6-cylinder diesel developing 150bhp at 1,800rpm
Speed: 40km/hr
Fuel: 218 litres
Range: 480km
Tyres: 14.00 × 20
P/W Ratio: 7.16hp/ton
Load Area: 5.486m × 2.324m

Development
This vehicle was developed by AEC (which is now a part of the British Leyland Motor Corporation) using standard commercial components, the 6 × 6 models were 0860s while the 6 × 4 models were 0859s. It was built in both 6 × 6 and 6 × 4 models and there were two different wheelbase models available. The full Army designation of the Militant Mk 1 was Truck, 10-Ton Cargo (dropside with winch), 6 × 6, AEC Mk 1.

The cab is provided with an observation hatch in the roof, the sides and tailgate drop down to assist in loading the vehicle, they can also be removed if required. The winch has a capacity of 7,000kg and this is provided with 76.2m of rope. The gearbox has 5F and 1R gears and a two speed transfer case. Recently some of these vehicles have had their sides and tailgates removed, and a HIAB crane has been mounted behind the cab, these vehicles have then been used for carrying pallets.

Variants
There are many variants of the Militant Mk 1 including the following:

FV 11001 6 × 4 Artillery Tractor (W/B 3.92m)
FV 11002 6 × 6 Artillery Tractor (LAA) (WB 3.92m)
FV 11003 6 × 6 Bridging Crane (W/B 4.493m)
FV 11005 6 × 4 Tipper (W/B 3.92m)
FV 11008 6 × 4 Cargo Truck (W/B 4.877m)
FV 11009 6 × 4 Tanker (W/B 4.877m)
FV 11010 6 × 6 Tractor Semi-Trailer (W/B 3.92m)
FV 11013 6 × 4 Crane (W/B 3.924m)
FV 11014 6 × 6 Excavator (W/B 3.924m)
FV 11041 6 × 6 Cargo Truck (W/B 3,924) Called Militant Mk 2, trials only

Employment
British Army.

Leyland (6 x 6) Artillery Tractor   Great Britain

Length: 8.185m
Width: 2.591m
Height: 3.073m
Track: 2.089m(f) 2.096(r)
Wheelbase: 4.42m
Weight Loaded: 18,640kg
Weight Empty: 14,310kg
Engine: Rolls-Royce B81 Mk. 5H 8-cylinder petrol engine developing 195bhp at 2,150rpm
Crew: 1 + 2
Speed: 56.3km/hr
Range: 563km
Fuel: 446 litres
T/Radius: 10.67m
Tyres: 15.00 × 20
P/W Ratio: 10.5bhp/ton

Development

The chassis of this vehicle was built by Leyland and the body by Park Royal Vehicles Limited. The full designation of this vehicle is FV 1103, Tractor, 10-Ton Medium Artillery (6 × 6 Leyland), and it is often referred to as the Martian. The primary role of the vehicle is to tow artillery, for example the 5.5″ Gun. The body has seating for 12 men, and in addition there is sufficient room for kit and small arms. The rear of the vehicle is provided with racks for up to 4,500kg of ammunition and stores. A hatch is provided in the roof of the vehicle for the mounting of a LMG. A winch with a capacity of 9,800kg is fitted and 107m of rope is provided. The gearbox has 4F and 1R gears and a three speed transfer box, the steering is power assisted.

Variants

FV 1110, Truck 10-Ton, 6 × 6, Cargo — this is a LWB model (W/B being 5.41m), basic data is length 9.068m, width 2.591m, height 3.607m, weight 23,610kg (laden), 13,440kg (unladen), range 560km and maximum road speed 42km/hr.

FV 1119, Recovery Vehicle, Wheeled-Heavy (Leyland 10-Ton, 6 × 6) — this uses the same chassis as FV 1103 and has been designed to recover vehicles up to 10-tons in weight. On the rear of the vehicle is a hydraulic power-operated crane, this slews through 240°, its jib can be extended from 3.048m to 5.486m and can lift a maximum of 15,000kg. A hydraulic winch is fitted incorporating two speed ranges (high and low). At the rear is an hydraulically operated spade, when this is in position, rear pulls of up to 40,000kg can be exerted. Basic data of the FV 1119 is as follows: length 8.89m, width 2.59m, height 3.1m, wheelbase 4.42m and weight 21,604kg.

FV 1121, Truck Cargo, Dropside (Leyland 10-Ton, 6 × 6) — the chassis and winch of this vehicle are identical to the FV 1103. The cargo body is provided with dropsides and a tailgate, these can be quickly removed if required. The rear cargo area, which can be covered by bows and a tarpaulin cover when required, is 4.88m long and 2.44m wide. Basic data is as follows: length 8.38m, width 2.59m, height 3.58m, wheelbase 4.42m, weight loaded 14,310kg (unladen), 24,600kg (laden), range 563km at a speed of 42km/hr.

FV 1122, Tractor, Wheeled, General Service for 8″ Howitzer (Leyland 10-Ton, 6 × 6). This was designed to tow the 8″ Howitzer and carry its crew of 11, plus stores and ammunition. Basic data is length 8.23m, width 2.59m, height 3.29m and unladen weight 14,310kg.

Employment

British Army.

Below: *The FV 1103, Tractor, 10-Ton, Medium Artillery (6 × 6 Leyland)*

Below right: *The FV 1110, Truck, 10-Ton (6 × 6 Cargo) this has a longer wheelbase.*

Right: *The FV 1119, Recovery Vehicle, Wheeled-Heavy (Leyland 10-Ton, (6 × 6))*

New Foden Military Vehicles Great Britain

	FH 70 (6 × 6) LIMBER	FH 70 (6 × 6) TRACTOR	CARGO (8 × 4)
Length:	8.92m	9.15m	10,278m
Width:	2.502m	2.502m	2.502m
Height:	3.607m	3.75m	3.137m
Wheelbase:	3.97m + 1.516m	3.97m + 1.516m	1.372 + 3.614m + 1.516m
Weight (loaded):	28,448kg	25,500kg	29,553kg
Speed:	109km/hr	109km/hr	76km/hr
Fuel:	409 litres	409 litres	227 litres
T/Radius:	12.45m	12.45m	12.25m
Tyres:	16.00 × 20	16.00 × 20	11.00 × 20

Fodens, of Sandbach, Cheshire, have been awarded a contract by the Ministry of Defence (Army), to develop a new range of vehicles for the British Army. There are basically two ranges—a 6 × 6 medium mobility range and a 8 × 4 and 6 × 4 low mobility range. Wherever possible, standard and well-tried commercial components have been used.

MEDIUM MOBILITY RANGE (6 × 6)

These are powered by a Rolls Royce Eagle 305 Mk. 111 6-cylinder (turbocharged) engine developing 305hp at 2,100rpm, a Foden gearbox with 9F and 1R gears is fitted. The auxiliary gearbox is a Kirkstall K.F.700 and has two speeds, high and low. It has been designed to give matched drive-line characteristics for operation with hydrostatic and mechanically driven powered axle trailers. The cab is of the forward control type and is of all-steel construction, it can be tilted forward to allow access to the engine and an observation hatch is provided in the roof of the cab. By late 1974 prototypes had been built and were being tested.

Marshall of Cambridge have designed the following bodies for the basic chassis:

6 × 6 FH 70 GUN TRACTOR

This will tow the 155mm FH 70. A removable heated cabin behind the cab provides accommodation for eight men, four pallets of ammunition are carried and a hydraulic crane is provided for unloading these, additional stores are carried at the rear of the vehicle.

6 × 6 FH 70 GUN LIMBER

This carries eight pallets of ammunition and is also provided with a hydraulic crane.

6 × 6 CARGO TRUCK

This can carry eight standard NATO pallets and is provided with a hydraulic crane, dropsides and removable rear bulkhead.

6 × 6 RECOVERY VEHICLE

This is under development.

LOW MOBILITY RANGE (8 × 4 and 6 × 4)

These have been designed to operate satisfactorily when laden to its GVW on both highway and unsurfaced tracks. With the use of differential locks the performance can be much improved. It is powered by a Rolls Royce Eagle 220 Mk. 111 6-cylinder engine developing 220hp at 2,100rpm. A Foden gearbox with 9 (or 8) F and 1R gears is fitted. It has the same S90 cab as the 6 × 6 vehicles.

By the late 1974 prototypes of these had been built and full production had started. Marshall of Cambridge have designed some of the bodies for these vehicles. The variants announced so far are tankers 6 × 4 (12,000 litre), 8 × 4 (22,500 litre), cargo 8 × 4 carrying 16,000kg or 20,000kg and a 8 × 4 tipper truck.

Below: *The Foden (8 × 4) Low Mobility Chassis.*

One of the Medium
Mobility range (6 × 4)
undergoing trials. Note
the Atlas hydraulic crane.

The Foden FH 70 (6 × 6)
Tractor. The pallets in the
centre of the rear body
carry ammunition for the
155mm FH 70 weapon.

The Foden (8 × 4) Low
Mobility Chassis, this has
the same cab as the 6 × 6
Tractor.

Scammell Contractor (6 x 6) Prime Mover Great Britain

This vehicle has been developed by Scammel Motors (a part of British Leyland) of Watford and although it has not been adopted by the British Army, significant numbers have been sold overseas, especially to the Middle East. The maximum gross combination weight, i.e. tractor, trailer and MBT is 101,604kg.

The Contractor is powered by a Cummins NTC Model 335 6-cylinder diesel developing 335hp at 2,100rpm, a Type VT-50 turbo-charger is fitted. The gearbox is a Fuller RT-915 complete with gearbox oil-cooler. This has a total 10F and 1R gears and three ranges, high, low and deep reduction. The steering is power-assisted and air brakes are provided. The rear suspension consists of two semi-elliptical springs, one each side, mounted in trunnions provided with oil bath lubrication. The front suspension also consists of semi-elliptical springs, these are, however, provided with shock absorbers.

Two 318 litre fuel tanks are provided under the cab. The silencer discharges vertically behind the cab. The cab is of all-steel construction and is insulated to waistline. The cab is provided with a single seat for the driver and the co-driver has a bench-type seat. Full cab air-conditioning equipment is provided by a Kysor air-conditioning plant mounted on the cab roof. Seating is provided behind the cab and over the winch for the tank crew.

The Scammel vertical winch comprises a fabricated steel frame carrying the drive assembly and the fabricated steel drum. Primary reduction is by fully enclosed worm and wheel. 107m of 22mm-diameter wire core rope is provided which has a breaking load of 30,988kg. Maximum pull on the first layer is 15,300kg.

The Contractor has been designed for use with the Crane Fruehauf Heavy Duty Trailer Model 60 which can carry all current MBTs, such as the Chieftain, AMX-30, M-60 or T-55. Basic data of the trailer is as follows: Overall length 11.29m, unladen weight 15,850kg, effective platform length 6.248m, overall width 3.658m, height of main deck (laden) 1.295m, ground clearance under frame (laden) .864m. Retractable gear is mounted to support the front end of the semi-trailer when disconnected from the tractor. A total of four loading ramps are provided. Two hydraulic jacks are also provided for use at the rear of the frame to prevent any danger of tipping and are used additionally to jack up the trailer for the removal of tyres. There is ample space for the stowage of lashing gear, petrol-cans, tools, jacks, chocks and so on. There is also a 52 litre water tank.

Below: *The Scammel Contractor (6 × 4) Prime Mover, carrying a Chieftain MBT on its trailer.*

Thornycroft Antar Mk 3 (6 x 6) Tractor

Great Britain

Length: 8.7m
Width: 3.2m
Height: 3.15m
Track: 2.25m(f) 2.29(r)
Wheelbase: 4.88m
Weight: 23,040kg (empty)
Engine: Rolls Royce C8SFL-843, 8-cylinder diesel engine developing 333bhp at 2,100rpm (16,200cc)
Speed: 32km/hr
Range: 700km
Fuel: 910 litres
T/Radius: 10.6m (vehicle only)
Tyres: 14.00 × 24
P/W Ratio: 3.16bhp/ton

Development/Variants

The first Antar was the Mk. 1 (FV 12001) and this was based on the civilian Mighty Antar designed and built by Transport Equipment (Thornycroft) Limited. Production was undertaken at Thornycroft's factory at Basingstoke, Hampshire. The Mk. 1 Antar was followed by the Mk. 2 Antar (FV 12002). The Mk. 2 is powered by a Meteorite 8-cylinder petrol engine developing 285bhp at 2,000rpm, it had a 4-speed gear box and a 3-speed transfer case. The FV 12003 was similiar to the FV 12002 but had a ballast body and was used to tow tank trailers rather than semi-trailers. The Antar Mk. 3 (FV 12004) was a development of the earlier Antars, the most significant improvements were the new cab, new transmission and a new supercharged engine. A winch with a capacity of 20,000kg is fitted for loading disabled vehicles, its gearbox has 6F and 1R gears and the transfer box has six speeds, steering is power-assisted. Production of all Antars has now been completed. The Mk. 3 Antar is used in conjunction with the 50 and 60 ton tank transporter trailers and used to transport Chieftain MBTs, the vehicles are operated by the Royal Corps of Transport.

The Antar is normally used in conjunction with the FV 3011 semi-trailer tank transporter, basic data of this is length 11.93m, width 3.353m, height 3.086m, inner track .876m, outer track 2.692m and unladen weight of 16,360kg. When a ballast body is fitted the Antar can tow the FV 3601 tank trailer, this trailer takes AFVs up to 50,000kg and its basic data is as follows: length with tow bar 10.2m, length w/o tow bar 9.07m, width 3.2m, height 2.21m and unladen weight of 18,660kg.

Employment

Great Britain, India, Netherlands, Pakistan, South Africa, Turkey.

Below: *Antar Mk. 3 and semi-trailer crossing a bridge constructed of amphibious bridging units.*

Scammell Constructor (6 x 6) Tractor (FV 12102)　　Great Britain

Length: 7.46m
Width: 2.85m
Height: 3.1m
Track: 2.11(f) 2.1m(r)
Wheelbase: 4.8m
Weight: 14,682kg
Engine: Rolls Royce, C6 NFL-140, 6-cylinder diesel developing 184bhp at 2,100rpm
Crew: 1 + 2
Speed: 40km/hr
Range: 805km
Fuel: 500 litres
T/Radius: 12.72m
Tyres: 14.00 × 20

Development

This was designed and built by Scammell Lorries Limited (who are now part of the British Leyland Motor Corporation) in the early 1950s. It was designed to tow 30-ton semi-trailers for Royal Engineers' Plant. The trailer used usually being the FV 3541, basic data of this being length 12.287m, width 2.743m, height 3.2m, unladen weight 15,890kg and laden weight 46,760kg. The ramps at the rear were hydraulically operated as were the jacks at the rear of the semi-trailer. The FV 12102 had a gearbox with 6F and 1R gears and a two speed transfer box, steering was power assisted.

Variants

The earlier FV 12101 was similar to the latter FV 12105 and was used to tow 20-ton full trailers, a winch with a capacity of 15,000kg was fitted as standard. Basic data was length 7.214m, width 2.642, height 3.048m, weight loaded 26,950kg and weight unladen of 14,290kg.

The FV 12105 (Tractor, Wheeled, General Service, Scammell 20-ton, 6 × 6) was also used to tow trailers of up to 30-tons, and was also fitted with a winch of 15,000kg capacity. Basic data was length 7.66m width 2.86m, height 3.28m, weight loaded 26,926kg and weight empty 17,022kg. There was also a 4 × 4 model called the Mountaineer, this was sold overseas. The vehicle has been further developed into the so called Super Constructor which has been exported.

Employment

Australia, Great Britain, Netherlands.

Below: *Scammel Constructor (6 × 6)* Tractor.

Alvis Stalwart (HMLC) (6 x 6) FV 622   Great Britain

Length: 6.356m
Width: 2.616m
Height: 2.64m (inc. cover)
2.312m (top of cab)
G/Clearance: .42m (laden)
Track: 2.04m
Wheelbase: 1.524m + 1.524m
Weight: 14,480kg (laden)
8,970kg (empty)
Load Area: 3.6m × 2.4m × .925m
Engine: Rolls Royce B-81 Mk. 8B, 8-cylinder, water-cooled petrol engine developing 220bhp at 3,750rpm (6,522cc)
Crew: 1 + 2
Speed: 63km/hr
Range: 515km
Fuel: 455 litres
Gradient: 60% (loaded)
Angle Approach: 44°
Angle Departure: 40°
T/Radius: 8.38m
Fording: Amphibious
Tyres: 14.00 × 20

Development
The original Stalwart (PV1) was built by Alvis Limited of Coventry in 1959 as a private venture. This vehicle was not amphibious, and was simply a load carrier and was based on components of the FV 652 Salamander fire tender. This was followed in 1961 by the PV2. The first production model was the Mk. 1 (FV 620), followed by the Mk. 2 (FV 622) in 1966, production of the Mk. 2 continued until 1972.

The Mk. 2 Stalwart HMLC (High Mobility Load Carrier) incorporated a number of features found necessary during trials with the Army. These included improving the visibility from the cab, this was achieved by making some of the windows deeper, improving the layout on the cab, reduced maintenance and improved reliability. The Stalwart uses many components of the FV 600 series of fighting vehicles (Saladin and Saracen). The Stalwart can carry 5,000kg of cargo on both roads or cross-country, if not carrying cargo the rear of the vehicle can carry 38 fully equipped troops. The sides of the rear cargo body fold down to assist in loading the vehicle. At the front of the vehicle is a winch with a capacity of 4,990kg for self recovery, many Stalwarts are fitted with a HIAB crane.

Below: *The Alvis Stalwart (6 × 6) High Mobility Load Carrier showing its cross country capabilities.*

It is fully amphibious being propelled in the water by two water-jets which give it a speed of 10.2km/hr (unloaded) or 9.6km/hr (loaded) before entering the water a trim board is erected at the front of the vehicle. The Stalwart has independent suspension on all six wheels and the steering is hydraulically assisted on the front four wheels, air brakes are fitted. The gearbox has 5F (2nd, 3rd, 4th and 5th are synchromesh), the transfer box contains a no-Spin differential which transfers the drive direct to each centre bevel box, and thence via transmission shafts to the front and rear bevel boxes.

Variants
Variants in service include the FV 623 artillery limber and the FV 624 REME fitters' vehicle. Trials have

been carried out with a Stalwart fitted with 2'' rockets to assist the vehicle leaving mud or steep river banks. Some Stalwarts have a large tank in the rear cargo compartment for the bulk transport of fuel.

Employment
Austria, Great Britain, Sweden (Coastal Artillery). France and Germany have had them for trials purposes.

Above: *Alvis Stalwart showing its amphibious capabilities.*

Csepel D-344 (4 x 4) 3-Ton Truck

Hungary

Length: 6.716m
Width: 2.56m
Height: 2.43m
G/Clearance: .27m
Track: 1.78m(f) 1.72m(r)
Wheelbase: 3.75m
Weight: 7,500kg (loaded)
4,500kg (empty)
Engine: D-414h, 4-cylinder, in-line, water-cooled diesel developing 100hp at 2,300rpm
Crew: 1 + 1
Speed: 82km/hr
Range: 530km
Fuel: 145 litres
Gradient: 18°
Tyres: 9.00 x 20

Development/Variants
The Csepel D-344 is a 4 x 4 model of the Csepel D-350 4 x 2 truck which in turn is based on an Austrian Steyr truck. It has a payload of 3,500kg on paved roads or 3,000kg across country, its towed load being 2,000kg. It is the only 4 x 4 truck in production in Hungary at the present time. Its gearbox has 5F and 1R gears and a two-speed transfer case, an unusual feature of the D-344 is that its rear wheels have dual tyres. It normally has a body of the dropside type which is often provided with bows and a tarpaulin cover. A dump truck model is designated D-445.

Employment
Hungary.

Other Hungarian trucks
The Csepel 130 is a 4 x 4 1¼-ton truck that is no longer in production, it was based on the American WW2 Doge ¾-ton weapons carrier. The vehicle is powered by a Model 130 4-cylinder, water-cooled petrol engine developing 85hp at 2,200rpm. This gives a maximum road speed of 80km/hr. Overall dimensions are—length 4.237m, width 2.103m, height 2.195m and ground clearance 269mm. Weight empty was 3,178kg. A van type model was built in addition to the basic cargo model. The Csepel K300 (6 x 6) 3-ton truck was based on the 4 x 2 Csepel D-350 but is not found in large numbers. The D-350 (later models were known as the D-352) is no longer in production. This 4 x 2 vehicle was built in various models including cargo carriers and dump trucks, and a fuel tanker. The Csepel D-450 (4 x 2) series are a development of the D-420, variants in service include the D-450 N tractor truck, and the D-450 B and D-455 B dump trucks. The D-450 series is reported to be being replaced by the Csepel D-457 (4 x 2) series. The Csepel D-700 series (4 x 2) is built in a wide variety of models including truck (road capacity of 7,000kg), tractor, tanker, dump truck and crane truck. The D-708 is the replacement for the D-700 series. Under development in 1968 was a new 6 x 6 truck known as the D-717 series, in 1971 came the D-566 (6 x 6) and the D-588 (8 x 8) trucks.

The Csepel D-344 (4 × 4) 3-Ton Truck.

Csepel K-800 Light Tracked Tractor

Hungary

Length: 5m
Width: 2.4m
Height: 2.2m
G/Clearance: .3m
Track: 2.1m
Weight: 8,200kg (loaded)
6,400kg (empty)
G/Pressure: .45kg/cm²
Engine: Model D-613, 6-cylinder water-cooled, in-line diesel developing 125hp at 2,200rpm
Crew: 2 + 14
Speed: 35km/hr
Range: 300km
Fuel: 280 litres
Gradient: 60%
Trench: 1.5m
Vertical Obstacle: .5m
Fording: .6m

Development
The Csepel K-800 is essentially a Hungarian copy of the old Soviet M-2 light tracked artillery tractor, this is no longer in service with any of the WPF. The Csepel K-800 can carry a maximum of 1,800kg of cargo and tow a maximum load of 800kg (i.e. artillery). The rear cargo area is provided with bows, a tarpaulin cover and a tailgate. In the Hungarian Army the Soviet AT-S medium tracked artillery tractor and 6 × 6 trucks have replaced many K-800s.

Variants
The K-800 has also been built in Yugoslavia, these models are powered by a FAMOS 6-cylinder water-cooled engine developing 120hp. The Yugoslav vehicle is designed GJ-800 and has the same cab as the Yugoslav FAP truck.

Employment
China, Hungary and Yugoslavia.

Below: *The Soviet M-2 light artillery tractor, the main differences between the Soviet and Hungarian vehicles is that the latter has a different bonnet and a slightly different cab.*

Fiat Campagnola (4 x 4) ½-Ton Series   Italy

Length: 3.596m
Width: 1.57m
Height: 1.8m (inc. hood)
1.4m (w/o hood)
G/Clearance: .203m
Track: 1.254m(f) 1.26(r)
Wheelbase: 2.25m
Weight: 1,920kg (loaded)
1,440kg (empty)
Load Area: 1m × .825m
Engine: 4-cylinder liquid-cooled, in-line petrol engine developing 56hp at 4,000rpm
Crew: 1 + 5
Speed: 110km/hr
Range: 450km
Fuel: 58 litres
Gradient: 89%
Angle Approach: 60°
Angle Departure: 35°
T/Radius: 5.4m
Fording: .6m
Tyres: 6.40m × 16

Development
The Fiat Campagnola was developed shortly after the end of the Second World War and the prototype was completed in 1950. The Italian Army adopted it in 1951 and called it the AR 51. Basic data of the AR-51 was length 3.64m, width 1.48m, height 1.87m, laden weight, 1,712kg, empty weight 1,176kg, it was powered by a 4-cylinder petrol engine developing 53hp, this gave it a top road speed of 100km/hr. The AR-51 remained in production until 1955 when the vehicle was redesigned and called the AR-55. The AR-55 had a 59hp engine and a loaded weight of 1,815kg. The last production model was the AR-59, and the data above relates to this model, the Fiat designation of the AR-59 is Model 1101B. It can carry 480kg of cargo, or a total of six men, two in the front and four in the rear.

A new Campagnola has recently been developed although it is not yet in service with the Italian Army.

This is powered by a four cylinder petrol engine developing 80hp at 4,600rpm, and it has a loaded weight of 2,300kg and an empty weight of 1,690kg. When being used to transport men it can carry six troops in addition to the driver. Its gearbox has 4F and 1R gears and a two-speed transfer case. Independent suspension is fitted, the front wheels are provided with a single shock absorber each and the rear wheels each have twin shock absorbers. A dual braking system is fitted as standard. The body is of all-steel construction and is provided with a tailgate. Three men (including the driver) can be seated at the front of the vehicle and another four at the rear, these being provided with seats that fold up to enable the vehicle to carry cargo. The windshield can be folded flat against the bonnet and the hood can be removed. The vehicle can carry 500kg of cargo on both road and cross-country and its maximum towed load is 500kg.

Variants
The basic AR-59 can be used as a cargo/personnel transport, radio truck or command vehicle. Modified AR-59s are fitted with 106mm recoilless rifles, twin SS11 ATGWs and a 24 round mutliple rocket launcher.

Employment
The AR-59 is in service with the Italian Army. It is also built in Yugoslavia where it is known as the *Zastava* and is used to tow 120mm mortars, recoilless rifles and anti-aircraft guns. Undergoing tests by Fiat is the Fiat 6640 4 × 4 amphibious vehicle, this can carry a maximum of 2,000kg of cargo and is propelled in the water by a propeller.

Below: *A Fiat AR 59 (4 × 4) vehicle of the Italian Army.*

Fiat 6601 (4 x 4) 4-Ton Cargo Truck   Italy

Length: 6.191m
Width: 2.368m
Height: 2.952m (canvas top)
2.857m
G/Clearance: .265m (axles)
Track: 1.88m(f)
Wheelbase: 3.27m
Weight: 9,366kg (loaded)
5,216kg (empty)
Load Area: 3.95m × 2.23m × .55m
Engine: 4-cylinder liquid-cooled diesel developing
89hp at 2,000rpm
Crew: 1 + 1
Speed: 58.5km/hr
Range: 450km
Fuel: 91 litres
Gradient: 40%
Angle Approach: 35°
Angle Departure: 25°
T/Radius: 7.32m
Fording: .609m
Tyres: 10.00 × 20

Development/Variants

The Fiat 6601 is designated Autocarro Medio CM.52
(4 × 4) by the Italian Army. It can carry 4,150kg of
cargo on roads or 3,150kg of cargo across country.
Its towed load is 6,490kg on roads or 3,000kg across
country. It is a forward control type vehicle with the
engine under the cab. The cab is of all-steel
construction and is fully enclosed, a ring hatch is
provided on the left side of the roof and a heater is
fitted. The cargo body is of steel construction and is
lined with wood. It has fixed front and side racks,
tiltable and removable tailgate with swing out steps.
Tiltable troop seats are incorporated in the side

racks. The tarpaulin is supported by six bows, when
the bows are not required they are stowed on the rear
of the cab.

The gearbox has 4R and 1R gears and a two-speed
transfer case. The suspension consists of front: leaf
springs and hydraulic shock absorbers; rear: leaf
springs. No power-assistance is provided for
steering purposes and air brakes are provided. An
earlier model was the Fiat CM.50, this was powered
by a petrol engine.

Employment

In service with the Italian Army, some have also been
exported to South America.

Other trucks used by the Italian Army include the
unusual Moto Guzzi Mulo Meccanico three wheeled
vehicle which is used by the Alpine Divisions,
various OM 1½ and 2-ton (4 × 4) vehicles and
various Lancia 4 × 4 vehicles.

Above: *The Fiat 6601 (4 × 4) 4-Ton Cargo Truck.*

Fiat 6602 CM (4 x 4) 5-Ton Truck

Italy

Length: 6.55m
Width: 2.46m
Height: 2.97m (canvas top)
2.133m (reduced)
G/Clearance: .244m
Track: 1.87m
Wheelbase: 3.57m
Weight: 12,570kg (loaded)
7,460kg (empty)
Load Area: 4.28m × 2.23m × .58m
Engine: 6-cylinder in-line liquid-cooled diesel developing 192hp at 2,500rpm
Crew: 1 + 1
Speed: 74km/hr
Range: 650km
Fuel: 230 litres
Gradient: 60%
Angle Approach: 45°
Angle Departure: 35°
T/Radius: 8.11m
Fording: .87m
Tyres: 11.00 × 20

Development/Variants

The Fiat 6602 CM is called the Autocarro Pesante CP.70 by the Italian Army and it uses many components of the Fiat 6607 6 × 6 vehicle.

It can tow 9,980kg of cargo on roads or 3,900kg across country. The Fiat 6602 can be used as a load carrier, personnel carrier or to tow artillery, and is air-transportable. A fuel tanker model has also been built. The cab is of steel construction with removable canvas top and side curtains, the windshield can be folded flat against the front of the vehicle. The cab is provided with a heater. The body is of all-steel construction with a removable tailgate with swing out steps, the floor of the body is lined with wood. A winch with a capacity of 9,072kg with an automatic safety brake is mounted at the rear of the vehicle, 60m of rope is provided.

The manual gearbox has 5F (2nd-5th are synchromesh) and 1R gears and a two-speed transfer case. The suspension consists of semi-elliptical springs front and rear with double-acting shock absorbers on the front wheels. The steering gear is power assisted and the brakes are of the drum type and are air-operated.

Employment

Used by the Italian Army.

Below: *The Fiat 6602 (4 × 4) 5-Ton Cargo Truck, note the bows in the stowed position.*

Fiat 6607 CM (6 x 6) 5-Ton Truck   Italy

Length: 7.82m
Width: 2.43m
Height: 2.7m (canvas top)
1.98m (reduced)
G/Clearance: .244m
Track: 1.87m
Wheelbase: 3.567m + 1.25m
Weight: 13,970kg (loaded)
8,829kg (empty)
Load Area: 5.54m × 2.26m × .58m
Engine: 6-cylinder in-line liquid-cooled diesel engine
developing 192hp at 2,500rpm
Crew: 1 + 1
Speed: 74km/hr
Range: 650km
Fuel: 230 litres
Gradient: 60%
Angle Approach: 45°
Angle Departure: 29°
T/Radius: 8.96m
Fording: .85m
Tyres: 11.00 × 20

Development/Variants
The Fiat 6607 was developed from the Fiat 6602 CM
(4 × 4) truck, its Italian Army designation is Autocarro Pesante CP 70. The Fiat 6607 is a 5-ton 6 × 6
truck and is airportable.

The cab is of the forward control type and is of
all-steel construction, the windshield can be folded
flat against the front of the vehicle if required, the
side windows and canvas top can be removed. The
driver sits on the RHS of the vehicle, the cab is
provided with a heater. The cargo body is of all-steel
construction with drop sides and a removable
tailgate, the floor is wood-lined. A winch with a
capacity of 9,072kg with an automatic safety brake is
mounted at the rear of the vehicle, 60m of rope is
provided.

The manual gearbox has 5F (2nd-5th are synchromesh) and 1R gears and a two-speed transfer
case. The suspension consists of: front: leaf-springs
and double-acting shock absorbers; rear: parallelogram torque arm with two, constant rate leaf-
springs. The steering is power assisted and the
brakes are air operated. The Fiat 6607 can tow
9,980kg of cargo on roads or 3,990kg of cargo across
country.

Employment
Italy.

Below: *A Fiat 6607 CM (6 × 6) 5-Ton Cargo Truck.*

Fiat 6605N (6 x 6) Artillery Tractor

Italy

Length: 7.33m
Width: 2.5m
Height: 2.921m (canvas top)
2.139m (reduced)
G/Clearance: .3m (axles)
Track: 2.07m
Wheelbase: 3.219m + 1.365m
Weight: 16,000kg (loaded)
11,793kg (empty)
Load Area: 3.42m × 2.38m × .6m
Engine: 6-cylinder in-line water-cooled diesel developing 213hp at 1,900rpm (13,798cc)
Crew: 1 + 11
Speed: 78.8km/hr
Range: 700km
Fuel: 364 litres
Gradient: 60%
Angle Approach: 45°
Angle Departure: 40°
T/Radius: 8m
Fording: 1.5m
Tyres: 14.00 × 20

Development/Variants

The Fiat 6605 N is designated Trattore Medio TM.69 by the Italian Army and its primary role is to tow artillery up to and including 155mm and 8'' weapons. An earlier model of the TM.69 was called the TM.65, this was powered by a 10,676cc engine.

The vehicle can carry twelve men with their equipment and a days supply of ammunition. Its maximum towed load is 14,969kg. The cab is of all-steel construction and is fitted with a heater, the side windows can be removed as can the canvas cover of the cab, the windscreen can be folded flat against the front of the vehicle. The rear body is also of all-metal construction with head, side boards and a tailgate, which can be removed if required. The floor has a plank lining. The cargo body has movable cross partitions providing three compartments — one for stores, one for projectiles and one for charges. The rear compartment is covered by canvas cover which is supported by four bows, when the cover is not required the bows are stowed under the central area of the cargo body floor and the cover in the stores compartment.

The transmission consists of a set of gears mounted on four shafts (input, primary, layshaft and reverse) giving eight speeds forward, four low and four high and two reverse (low and high). Air brakes are fitted and the steering is power-assisted.

The suspension consists of front: leaf-springs and hydraulic shock absorbers; rear: leaf-springs swinging on a rocker arm and slide-fixed to axles. Torque arms from axles to central support. A winch is mounted at the rear of the vehicle and this can be used through the front or rear, it has a maximum pull of 15,000kg and has 60m of rope.

In 1973 prototypes of a modified TM.69 were built with a hydraulic crane, this is for use with the FH.70, this is a 155mm gun at present under development by England, Germany and Italy. The Fiat 6605 DM has a recovery crane mounted on the rear.

Employment

In service with the Italian Army.

Below: *The Fiat 6605N (6 × 6) Artillery Tractor.*

Japanese Military Trucks

Vehicle	Manu	Type	Model	Length	Width	Height	Weight	Speed
¼-Ton Truck (4 × 4)	Mitsubishi	J54-A	1970	3.33m	1.595m	1.85m	1,655kg	92km/hr
¾-Ton Truck (4 × 4)	Nissan	Q4W73	1967	4.775m	2.025m	2.233m	4,025kg	97km/hr
¾-Ton Ambulance	Toyota	HQ15V	1967	5.165m	2.13m	2.815m	4,300kg	85km/hr
2½-Ton Truck (6 × 6)	Isuzu	TWD21	1967	6.765m	2.28m	2.995m	10,615kg	85km/hr
2½-Ton Truck (6 × 6)	Isuzu	TWD30	1969	8.69m	2.4m	2.995m	11,850kg	74km/hr
2½-Ton Dumper (6 × 6)	Isuzu	TWD21	1970	6.795m	2.29m	2.975m	10,485kg	65km/hr
2½-Ton Tanker (6 × 6)	Isuzu	TWD21	1967	6.70m	2.25m	2.65m	10,405kg	74km/hr
4-Ton Truck (6 × 6)	Hino	ZC48	1964	7.69m	2.44m	2.92m	16,200kg	78km/hr
4-Ton Wrecker (6 × 6)	Hino	C48C	1964	9.30m	2.45m	2.88m	14,020kg	78km/hr
6-Ton Truck (6 × 6)	Mitsubishi	W121P	1970	7.00m	2.48m	3.145m	18,110kg	83km/hr

The Japanese Defence Force (Army) uses a large variety of wheeled vehicles of local manufacture. Below is a resume of some of these vehicles.

J54-A (4 × 4) ¼-TON TRUCK
This is built under licence from Kaiser Jeep by Mitsubishi. It is powered by a four-cylinder petrol engine developing 75hp at 3,800rpm, its gear box has 3F and 1R gears and a two-speed transfer box. It can carry 250kg of cargo and a crew of two, or four men. It has 6.00 × 16 tyres and its wheelbase is 2.03m. It has been built with 12V and 24V electrical systems right and left-hand drive and with petrol or diesel engines. Various models are in service including ambulances, anti-tank missile vehicle with two KAM-3D (Type 64 ATM-1) ATGW mounted in the vehicles rear, recoilless rifle vehicle with a Type 60 (i.e. M-40) 106mm recoilless rifle in the rear and radio versions. Nissan have also built 4 × 4 trucks and the Toyota 4 × 4 Land Cruiser is used by a number of armed forces, for example India, some of their vehicles have three SS 11 ATGWs mounted on the rear of the vehicle.

Q4W73 (4 × 4) ¾-TON TRUCK
This is powered by a petrol engine developing 98hp at 4,000rpm. It can carry 750/1,000kg of cargo plus a crew of two, or a total of 11 men. The cab has a soft roof and the windscreen folds down flat when required. This vehicle has also been built under licence in India for the Indian Army.

HQ15V (4 × 4) ¾-TON AMBULANCE
This is powered by an engine developing 95hp at 3,600rpm, its gearbox has 4F and 1R gears. It has a crew of two and can carry five stretcher patients, or two crew and nine sitting patients. There is also a ¾-ton 4 × 4 cargo truck based on the same chassis, basic data of this vehicle, which is designated 2FQ15L, is length 5.08m, width 2.02m, height 2.32m, wheelbase 3m, tyres 7.50 × 20

TWD21 (6 × 6) 2½-TON TRUCK SERIES
Developed from 1952/53 and entered production in 1957. The basic vehicle is powered by a 6-cylinder in-line diesel developing 130hp at 2,600rpm. It can carry 2,500kg of cargo across country or 5,000kg on roads, or 20 fully equipped troops. There are numerous differences between production runs, for example dual and single rear tyres and hard and soft cabs. The TWD21 are the more recent models.

Variants in service include air compressor, dump truck, shop/van, tanker and a wrecker. A latter model is the TWD30 which is longer and can carry a maximum of 26 troops when being used in this role. Some of these vehicles have a winch mounted at the front. There is also a 4 × 4, 2½-ton Isuzu truck based on the 6 × 6 model, this also has a front mounted winch. Toyota has also built a range of 6 × 6 trucks and these are used by Japanese Self Defence Force (Army). Models include an air compressor and cargo truck.

ZC48 (6 × 6) 4-TON TRUCK SERIES
A whole series of these 6 × 6 Hino trucks have been developed including the ZC35, ZC36, ZC37, ZC46 and ZC47. The ZC48 is powered by a 6-cylinder diesel developing 160hp at 2,400rpm and can carry 4,000kg of cargo across country or 8,000kg on roads. There are many variants in service including the following: cargo, dump, rocket launcher carrying two Type 30 surface-to-surface rockets, rocket resupply vehicle carrying six Type 30 rockets, tractor, snow plough, water sprinkler, and a wrecker. Some models have a winch mounted behind the cab. Other Hino trucks in service include a 4½-ton 4 × 4 truck based on commercial components and a 5-ton 4 × 4 tractor truck.

W121P (6 × 6) 6-TON TRUCK
This is powered by an engine developing 250hp at 2,200rpm and it can carry a maximum of 8,000kg of cargo or 14 fully equipped troops, a winch is mounted behind the cab. Variants include a tractor truck for towing pontoon boats. Early Mitsubishi trucks still in service include the Fuso series, these include cargo, tractor and wrecker models.

Employment
All of the above are used by the Japanese Defence Force (Army). In addition many of the 4 × 4 and 6 × 6 (2½-ton) trucks are used by the Phillipines, South Korea, Vietnam and the United States (Far East only).

Mitsubishi ¼-ton (4 × 4) truck, fully enclosed.

Mitsubishi ¼-ton (4 × 4) truck with two KAM-3D anti-tank missiles on rear.

Below: *Nissan Q4W73 ¾-Ton (4 × 4) Cargo Truck.*

Toyota HQ15V ¾-Ton Ambulance.

Isuzu 2½-Ton (6 × 6) Cargo Truck

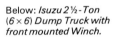

Below: *Isuzu 2½-Ton (6 × 6) Dump Truck with front mounted Winch.*

Above: *Isuzu 2½-Ton
(6 × 6) TWD21 Tanker
with hard-topped cab.*

Left: *Isuzu 2½-Ton (6 × 6)
Long Wheel Based Cargo
Truck with front mounted
winch.*

Top: *Hino (6 × 6) Wrecker Model C48C.*

Centre: *Hino 4-Ton (6 × 6) Cargo Truck Model ZC48.*

Right: *Mitsubishi 6-Ton (6 × 6) Cargo Truck Model W121P. Note winch behind cab.*

The DAF 66 YA (4 × 2) being used as a radio vehicle.

The DAF 66 YA (4 × 2) with hood and windscreen down.

DAF 66 YA (4 x 2) 0.4-Ton Utility Vehicle   Netherlands

Length: 3.75m
Width: 1.5m
Height: 1.58m (overall)
1.11m (w/o windscreen)
G/Clearance: .2m
Track: 1.31m(f) 1.24(r)
Wheelbase: 2.255m
Weight: 1,295km (loaded)
870kg (empty)
Engine: BB 100E, liquid-cooled, 4-cylinder in-line petrol engine developing 47hp at 2,700rpm
Crew: 1 + 3
Speed: 115km/hr
Range: 500km
Fuel: 50 litres
Gradient: 20%
Angle Approach: 27°
Angle Departure: 30°
Fording: .2m
Tyres: 14.50 × 14

Development
The prototype of the DAF 66 YA was built in 1970 and it was previously known as the 55 YA. The vehicle entered production in 1973 and production is expected to continue until 1977.
The body is of all-welded construction and a total of four seats are provided, two at the front and two at the rear. The rear seats can be folded foward to increase the load carrying area. Its maximum load is 425kg. Collapsible bows and a cover are provided, the windscreen can be folded flat against the bonnet. The vehicle has rear wheel drive through a stepless automatic transmission (forward, neutral and reverse). The differential can be fitted with a locking device if required. The front suspension consists of independent longitudinal torsion bars with an anti-roll bar and telescopic double-acting hydraulic shock absorbers. The rear suspension consists of single friction-free semi-elliptic leaf-springs and telescopic double-acting hydraulic shock-absorbers. Hydraulic brakes are fitted; front brakes have discs and the rear, drums. Standard equipment includes map-reading light, inspection lamp socket, hazard warning lights, hand throttle, and cable connectors for radio operations.

Variants
The basic vehicle can be adopted for a number of roles including military police vehicle, radio vehicle and an ambulance. In the latter role it can carry two stretcher patients, attendant and the driver.

Employment
In service with the Netherlands Army.

DAF YA 126 (4 x 4) 1-Ton Truck (Weapons Carrier)   Netherlands

Length: 4.55m
Width: 2.1m
Height: 2.22m (overall)
1.828m (lowest)
G/Clearance: .4m
Track: 1.72m
Wheelbase: 2.83m
Weight: 4,230kg (loaded)
3,230kg (empty)
Load Area: 2.006m × 1.905m × 1.295m
Engine: Hercules, JXC, 6-cylinder in-line petrol
engine developing 102bhp at 3,200rpm
Crew: 1 + 1
Speed: 84km/hr
Range: 330km
Fuel: 110 litres
Gradient: 65%
Angle Approach: 45°
Angle Departure: 45°
T/Radius: 7.01m
Fording: .76m
Tyres: 9.00 × 16

Development
The prototypes of the YA 126 were built around 1950 and the vehicle was in production from 1952 until 1960. The DAF YA 126 is designed for the transportation of men and cargo in the battlefield area. The rear body is provided with a tailgate, bows and a tarpaulin cover, when not carrying cargo the body can carry eight fully equipped men. If required,

the windscreen can be folded flat and the side-screens and canvas cab roof can be removed.

The gearbox has 4F and 1R gears and a two-speed transfer case is fitted. If required, a rear mounted winch with a capacity of 2,500kg can be fitted. It can tow a trailer with a maximum weight (with cargo) of 3,000kg.

Both the front and rear wheels are suspended on two longitudinal trailing arms which are connected at the front with traversely mounted tubular beams containing the torsion bars. Between the upper trailing arms and the chassis, auxiliary rubber springs are mounted. The front and rear wheels are fitted with hydraulic telescopic shock absorbers.

On each side of the vehicle is a spare wheel, this is mounted on a fixed axle, these wheels are free to rotate, acting as supporting wheels when traversing rough terrain, in addition they help to protect the transmission.

Variants
Models in service include an ambulance, workshop, and a radio/command vehicle. The DAF ¼-ton truck, YA 054, was only developed to prototype stage.

Employment
Only in service with the Netherlands Army.

Below: *The DAF YA 126 (4 × 2) 1-Ton Cargo Truck.*

DAF YA 314 (4 x 4) 3-Ton Truck

Netherlands

Length: 6.09m
Width: 2.42m
Height: 2.79m (canvas top)
2.108m (w/o windscreen)
G/Clearance: .36m
Track: 1.905m
Wheelbase: 3.6m
Weight: 7,500kg (loaded)
4,500kg (kerb)
Load Area: 4.2m × 2.15m × 1.6m
Engine: Hercules JXC, 6-cylinder, in-line, water-cooled petrol engine developing 102bhp at 3,200rpm
Crew: 1 + 1
Speed: 76km/hr
Range: 630km
Fuel: 210 litres
Gradient: 40%
Angle Approach: 40°
Angle Departure: 35°
T/Radius: 9m
Fording: .76m
Tyres: 11.00 × 20

Development
The prototype of the YA 314 was built around 1952 and the vehicle was in production from 1955 to 1966. It uses the same engine and gearbox as the DAF YA 126 vehicle. The YA 314 can carry 3,000kg of cargo on both roads and cross-country, it can also tow a trailer with a maximum weight of 3,000kg. The cab top and tops of the doors can be quickly removed to reduce the overall height of the vehicle and the windscreen can be folded flat against the radiator guard. The rear body is of all-steel construction and is provided with a tailgate, bows and a tarpaulin.

The gearbox has 4F and 1R gears and a two-speed transfer case. The vehicle is fitted with air/hydraulic brakes. If required a winch with a capacity of 4,000kg can be fitted at the front.

The extended wheel arches of the rigid cargo body constitute the seats when personnel are carried in the rear, a flat loading platform may be formed by means of wooden panels adapting the vehicle for the carrying of wider loads.

Variants
Variants of the YA 314 include the following: air compressor, bomb carrier, fuel carrier, office/command vehicle, radar vehicle, three-way tipper and a workshop. Late production models are designated YA 324. The YA 314 is also manufactured in Spain where it is known as the Pegaso 3045D, this has a different engine and numerous other modifications. Refer to the page on the Pegaso 3045D for further details.

Employment
Netherlands.

Below: *The DAF YA 314 (4 × 4) 3-Ton Cargo Truck.*

DAF YA 328, (6 x 6) 3-Ton Truck

Netherlands

Length: 6.19m
Width: 2.4m
Height: 2.65m (canvas top)
1.905m (w/o cab)
G/Clearance: .42m
Track: 2.08m
Wheelbase: 3.40m
Weight: 9,000kg (loaded)
6,100kg (curb)
Load Area: 4.2m × 2.15m × 1.6m
Engine: Hercules JXLD, 6-cylinder, in-line, water-cooled petrol engine developing 131bhp at 3,200rpm
Crew: 1 + 1
Speed: 80km/hr
Range: 315km
Fuel: 210 litres
Gradient: 50%
Angle Approach: 40°
Angle Departure: 40°
T/Radius: 8m
Fording: .76m
Tyres: 9.00 × 20

Development
The DAF YA 328 was preceded by the YA 318 which was built around 1950 and produced in very small numbers. The improved YA 328 was in production from 1957 to 1959. It has been designed as a general cargo carrier and can also be used to tow artillery (e.g. the American M-101 105mm howitzer), or trailers up to a maximum weight of 4,000kg. It is provided with an all-steel body with removable roof, side screens and windscreen. The rear body is provided with a tailgate, bows and a tarpaulin. The gearbox has 5F and 1R gears and a two-speed transfer case is provided. Brakes are of the air/hydraulic type. A winch can be fitted if required, this runs through the rear of the vehicle and is operated from the cab. The winch has a capacity of 4,500kg and is provided with 50m of cable.

The front wheels have independent suspension, each wheel being supported by two trailing arms and sprung by two cross-mounted torsion bars. The rear wheels are mounted on horizontal beams. These beams are mounted on a cross axle connected to the frame by means of leaf springs. Hydraulic shock absorbers of the double acting telescopic type are fitted front and rear.

Variants
YA 328 fire truck, YC 328 crash tender, YF 328 oil refueling truck. There were also some tractor-trucks based on the YA 328.

Employment
Netherlands Army; it is no longer used to tow artillery some models have been fitted with a 12.7mm anti-aircraft machine gun on a ring mount over the cab.

Below: *A DAF YA 328 3-Ton (6 × 6) Truck showing its paces through rough country.*

DAF YA 616 (6 x 6) 6-Ton Truck

Netherlands

Length: 7.27m
Width: 2.45m
Height: 3.32m (with tarpaulin)
2.49m (w/o windscreen)
G/Clearance: .36m
Track: 1.95m(f) 1.86(r)
Wheelbase: 4.16m
21,000kg (road loaded)
17,000kg (c/c loaded)
10,850kg (curb)
Load Area: 4.19m × 2.159m × 1.71m
Engine: Continental Model R 6602, 6-cylinder water-cooled petrol engine developing 232hp at 2,800rpm
Crew: 1 + 1
Speed: 80km/hr
Range: 400km
Fuel: 400 litres
Gradient: 59%
Angle Approach: 45°
Angle Departure: 40°
T/Radius: 11m
Fording: .75m
Tyres: 14.00 × 20

Development

The first prototype DAF YA 616 was built around 1956 and the vehicle was in production from 1957 until 1968 and can carry 6,000kg of cargo across country or 10,000kg of cargo on roads, it can tow a trailer to a maximum weight of 14,500kg, or various types of artillery, for example the American 155mm M-2.

The cab is of all-steel construction and the roof and sides can be removed if required, the front windscreen can be folded down. The rear body is of all-steel construction and is provided with a tailgate, bows and a tarpaulin cover. A winch with a capacity of 9,000kg is mounted behind the cab, this can be used through the front or rear of the vehicle.

The gearbox has 5F and 1R gears and a two-speed transfer case, hydraulic steering is provided and the brakes are of the air/hydraulic type. The tandem rear axle is suspended by leaf-springs placed lengthwise and pivoting around a central shaft. Double-acting hydraulic shock absorbers are mounted on both axles.

Variants

The YA 616 VL is similar but has a front mounted winch and removable side boards. Variants of the basic vehicle are as follows: YB 616 Wrecker, YF 616, 7,000 litre tanker, YK 616 three-way tipper and the YT 616 tractor, this has been designed to tow semi-trailers up to 20,000kg.

Employment

Netherlands Army and Air Force.

Below: *A DAF YA 616 (6 × 6) 6-Ton Truck undergoing trials in the Pyrénées Mountains.*

Above right: *A DAF YA 616 VL (6 × 6) 6-Ton Truck, note the drop sides and tailgate.*

New Generation of DAF Military Trucks

Netherlands

	YA 2442	YA 4440
Length:	5.48m	7.05m
Width:	2.44m	2.44m
Height:	3.325m	3.429m
G/Clearance:	.34m	.30m
Wheelbase:	3.2m	4.05m
Track:	1.91m	1.91m
Crew:	1 + 1	1 + 1
Speed:	92km/hr	87km/hr
Range:	600km	800km
Gradient:	50%	50%
Angle Approach:	43°	41°
Angle Departure:	46°	30°
Fording:	.9m	.9m
Tyres:	11.00 × 20	12.00 × 20

In November, 1974, DAF of Eindhoven, announced provisional details of two new 4 × 4 high mobility military trucks. Both vehicles have standard cabs, axles and numerous other components and are based on current commercial types and therefore spare parts are available from commercial sources. The cab is of the forward control type and tilts forward to allow access to the power unit, the roof of the cab incorporates a manhole and a mount for a light machine gun. The rear cargo body has removable bows, tarpaulin, sideboards and tailgate, this facilitates the loading of pallets and containers. The steering is power assisted and the brakes are air-hydraulic, dual-circuit; electrical system is 24 volts.

The YA 2442 is a 4 × 4 truck and can carry 2,500kg of cargo on both roads and cross country, in addition it can tow a trailer with a payload of 2,000kg. The vehicle is powered by a DAF Model DF 615, 6-cylinder direct injection diesel which develops 126hp. Its transmission has 5F and 1R gears and a two-speed transfer case.

The YA 4440 can carry 4,500kg of cargo on both roads and cross country and also tow a trailer with a load of 4,000kg. It has the same engine as the YA 2442 but for this vehicle it is turbocharged and develops 153hp, the transmission is the same as the YA 2442.

Optional extras for the YA 2442 include a rear mounted winch. Optional extras for the YA 4440 includes a hydraulic crane with a capacity of 7,000kg, rear mounted winch with a capacity of 5,000kg and stabilisers on either side. DAF are also developing a heavier cargo truck. At the present time the YA 2442 and YA 4440 are engaged in extensive trials.

The DAF YA 4440 4-Ton Cargo Truck.

The DAF YA 2442 2-Ton Cargo Truck with the cab tilted forward to allow access to the engine.

Below: *The DAF YA 4440 4-Ton Cargo Truck with stabilisers in position and hydraulic crane ready for use.*

Truck, Tractor, Coe, YT 1500L (4 x 2) 5-Ton   Netherlands

Length: 5.05m
Width: 2.3m
Height: 2.46m (cab)
1.96m (w/o windscreen)
G/Clearance: .36m
Track: 1.752m
Wheelbase: 3.11m
Weight: 3,700kg (vehicle only)
Tyres: 9.00 × 20
Engine: Hercules JXLD, 6-cylinder in-line water-cooled petrol engine developing 131bhp at 3,200rpm
Crew: 1 + 1
Speed: 80km/hr
Range: 500km
Fuel: 210 litres
Gradient: 24%
Angle Approach: 35°
Angle Departure: 50°
T/Radius: 7.6m
Fording: .76m

Development
The vehicle was manufactured from 1955 using components of civilian trucks and the YA 314 (4 × 4) vehicle. It is designed to tow semi-trailers with a maximum weight of 10,000kg. The gearbox has 5F and 1R gears and the rear axle has two speeds, high and low. The front and rear axles are suspended by semi-elliptical leaf-springs of the sliding end type. Rubber bushings in the front and rear spring mountings eliminate noise and squeak. Double acting hydraulic shock absorbers are fitted to both axles. Brakes are of the air hydraulic type. The cab is provided with a canvas cover which can be removed if required, the windscreen can be folded down if required.

Variants
None in service. The YT 514 (4 × 4) tractor is similar in appearance to the YT 1500L but has a more powerful 6-cylinder diesel engine.

Employment
Netherlands Army.

Trailers — DAF have built a very large range of trailers and semi-trailers including the following:
YAA 602 van type semi-trailer, load 6,000kg
YF 101 aircraft refueller (10,000 litre)
YF 102 aircraft refueller (9,500 litre)
YF 121 aircraft refueller (12,000 litre)
YEW 400, two wheel water tank trailer
YTT 10050 tank trailer (see page on DAF FFT-3500 for further details)
YTT 10060 tank trailer
YTT 1004 cargo trailer, maximum load 10,000kg (semi-trailer), used with YT 1500L
YQM 2200-960 aircraft transporter (semi-trailer)
YVW 1214 4 wheel flatbed trailer
M 390-17 and M 390-17C, 2 ton, 2 wheel chassis trailers
Treadway Bridge, KL20, 2 wheel, type YEE 2000 SB
The YVW 1414B is a pontoon boat trailer (production from 1967) and is towed by a YA 616 (6 × 6) truck with a winch for launching purposes.

Below: *The DAF YT 1500L (4 × 2) Tractor towing a DAF YTT 1004 cargo trailer.*

DAF Tractor Truck FTT 3500

Netherlands

Length: 7.97m
Width: 3.1m
Height: 3.15m
G/Clearance: .45m
Track: 2.54(f) 2.3m(r)
Wheelbase: 4.5m
Weight: 19.000kg
Engine: Detroit Diesel (GMC), 12-cylinder, developing 475hp at 2,100rpm
Crew: 1 + 1
Speed: 64km/hr
Fuel: 800 litres
Gradient: 15%
Angle Approach: 30°
Angle Departure: 55°
Tyres: 14.00 × 24

Development/Variants
The prototype of the FTT 3500 was completed in 1972 and it is expected that a production order will be awarded in the near future, the FTT 3500 has been developed from standard commercial components. The cab is the same as that fitted to the commercial 2600 series, in addition to the two seats fitted (driver and assistant), a further two seats can be fitted if required. The cab can be tilted forward so that the engine can be inspected. If required a hydraulic retarder can be fitted. A double drum hydraulic winch is mounted behind the cab, each winch has a capacity of 20 tons in the first layer of rope. An

Allison CLBT 5960 automatic gearbox with 6F and 1R gears is fitted. Two circuit air brake systems are provided, one serving the front axle and the other the rear axle. An additional hand brake control lever is mounted on the steering column for braking the semi-trailer. Hydraulic steering is fitted as standard.

The FTT 3500 has been designed to be used in conjunction with the DAF YTS 10050 tank trailer. The basic data of this trailer is as follows: overall length 11.72m, overall width 3.4m, height to top of ramps (travelling order) 1.81m, wheelbase 1.5m, weight unladen 15,000kg, maximum load 55,000kg, tyres 11.00 × 20. Overall length of the Tractor FTT 3500 and the YTS 10050 trailer in travelling order is 17.1m. The trailer is already in service with Belgium, Denmark, Netherlands and Sweden. The Swedish Army uses the Scania-Vabis LT76A truck for towing the tank transporter.

Employment
The FTT 3500 is not yet in service.

Below: *The DAF Tractor Truck FTT 3500 with a DAF YTS 10050 tank semi-trailer.*

Bottom: *The DAF Tractor Truck FTT 3500 with a DAF YTS 10050 tank semi-trailer carrying a Leopard MBT.*

The Star 66 (6 × 6)
2½-Ton Truck towing a
122mm Field Howitzer.

Star 66 (6 x 6) 2 ½ -Ton Truck

Poland

Length: 6.594m
Width: 2.4m
Height: 2.485m (cab)
2.875m (canvas top)
G/Clearance: .28m
Track: 1.804m
Wheelbase: 2.858m + 1.2m
Weight: 5,700kg (empty)
Engine: S-47, 6-cylinder in-line water-cooled petrol
engine developing 105hp at 3,000rpm
Crew: 1 + 1
Speed: 73.4km/hr
Range: 940km
Trench: .6m
V/Obstacle: .5m
Gradient: 28°
Fording: .8m
Tyres: 11.00 × 20

Development
The Star 66 first appeared in 1958 as the A66 and is
the only all-wheel drive truck manufactured in
Poland. Its payload is 2,500kg on a dirt road or
4,000kg on a paved highway. Towed load is 3,500kg
on a dirt road or 4,400kg on the highway. The
gearbox has 5F and 1R gears and a two-speed
transfer case, a winch with a capacity of 5,900kg is

fitted. It has a metal cab with a canvas top, the body
is metal with removable bows and a canvas cover.

Variants
Later models of the basic truck are the Star 660 M1
(from 1965), Star 660 M2 (from 1968, has water-
proofed ignition), both the M1 and M2 have larger
12.00 × 18 tyres. The Star 660D has the S530A1
diesel engine developing 180hp at 2,800rpm.

Variants in service include tank trucks, ZSH-6
crane truck, KS-251 shovel truck, van trucks, SMT-1
truck launched treadway bridge, decontamination
truck, signals and command vehicles, workshop
truck T574 on Star 660 M2 (has a jib crane at the front
when travelling this is stowed on the side), and two
pontoon vehicles carrying either the old TPP or the
more recent PMP pontoon.

Employment
Polish and Vietnamese Armed Forces, also available commercially. Under development is the
Star 266 (6 × 6) vehicle, this can carry 3,500kg of
cargo and is powered by a 150hp 6-cylinder diesel
engine, this gives the Star 266 a top road speed of
90km/hr. There are a large number of different Star
4 × 2 trucks as well as the more recent Star 244 (4 × 4)
truck.

Medium Tracked Artillery Tractor Mazur 350

Poland

Length: 5.81m
Width: 2.89m
Height: 2.695m (o/a)
2.6m (cab)
G/Clearance: .475m
Weight: 17,100kg (loaded)
13,600kg (empty)
G/Pressure: .65kg/cm²
Engine: Model D-350, V-12 water-cooled diesel
engine developing 300hp
Crew: 2 + 7
Speed: 53km/hr
Range: 390km
Gradient: 50%
Trench: 1.45m

V/Obstacle: .6m
Fording: 1m

Development
The prototypes of this vehicle were known as the
Mazur 300 (or ACS), the production vehicles were
the Mazur 350 which had a more powerful engine.
The vehicle entered service in the early 1960s,
production has now been completed and Poland is
manufacturing the Soviet ATS-59 in place of the
Mazur 350. The Mazur 350 has a payload of 5,000kg
on roads or 3,500kg across country. Its towed load is
15,000kg on roads or 10,000kg across country. It is
often used to tow artillery up to 152mm in calibre. It is
recognisable by its large cab with four doors and the

stake type cargo area which can be covered by a tarpaulin supported by bows. There is an observation hatch in the cab roof. The suspension consists of five road wheels, four return rollers, idler at the rear and the drive sprocket at the front. As far as it is known there are no variants in service.

Employment
Warsaw Pact Forces including Czechoslovakia and Poland.

A Mazur 350 Medium Tracked Artillery Tractor towing a Soviet 152mm M-1937 Gun/Howitzer.

SR-132M (4 x 4) 2-Ton Truck

Romania

Length: 5.78m
Width: 2.263m
Height: 2.1m
G/Clearance: .27m
Trench: 1.75m
Wheelbase: 3.4m
Weight: 3,750kg (empty)
Engine: SR-211 8-cylinder water-cooled petrol engine developing 140hp at 3,600rpm
Crew: 1 + 1
Speed: 95km/hr
Range: 800km (est)
V/Obstacle: .46m
Gradient: 32°
Fording: .7m
Tyres: 9.75 × 18

Development
The SR-132M is a 4 × 4 model of the Carpati truck and can be distinguished from the SR-131 Carpati and the SR-113 Bucegi as it has single rear tyres.

It is used as a cargo-carrier, troop-carrier and light prime-mover. Its normal payload is 2,000kg on dirt roads and 3,000kg on the highway, towed load is 2,000kg. The gearbox has 4F and 1R gears and a two-speed transfer case.

Variants
The SR-114M is similar in appearance but has dual rear wheels, this is a 4 × 4 3½-ton truck and is powered by an 8-cylinder engine developing 140hp, maximum road speed is 90km/hr. Commercial models of both the SR-132RM and SR-114M are available.

Employment
Romanian Armed Forces.

Other Romanian vehicles include the 4 × 2 (3½-ton) SR-101 series which are similar to the Soviet ZIL-150, 4 × 2 (5-ton) SR-113 Bucegi series including cargo SR-116 dump truck and SR-115 tractor. The 4 × 2 (3-ton) SR-131 Carpati has the same engine (SR-211, 140hp) as the SR-113 series. There is also a 4 × 4 vehicle built in Rumania called the UMM M-461, this is very similar to the Soviet UAZ-69 but has a different engine and gearbox.

UAZ-469B (4 x 4) Truck

Soviet Union

Length: 4.025m
Width: 1.785m
Height: 2.05m (o/a)
G/Clearance: .22m
Track: 1.442m
Wheelbase: 2.38m
Weight: 2,300kg (loaded)
1,600kg (empty)
Engine: UMZ-451M, 4-cylinder in-line water-cooled petrol engine developing 75hp
Crew: 1 + 6
Speed: 100km/hr
Range: 750km
Fuel: 78 litres
Gradient: 60%
Angle Approach: 52°
Angle Departure: 42°

T/Radius: 6.5m
Tyres: 8.40 × 15
Fording: .7m

Development
The UAZ-469B is the replacement for the UAZ-69 vehicle. The first prototypes were known as the UAZ-460B, and these appeared in 1960. Although these were extensively tested they were not placed in production. The final model, known as the UAZ-469B, entered production late in 1972 with first deliveries to the Soviet Army taking place early in 1973.

The UAZ-469B uses many components of the UAZ-452 (4 × 4) truck. The vehicle can carry two men and 600kg of cargo or a total of seven men. Its maximum towed load on both road and cross-country is 850kg. The UAZ-469 has four doors, the tops of which can be removed if required, the windscreen and hood can also be folded down. The gearbox has 4F and 1R gears and a two-speed transfer case.

In 1973 the UAZ-469 was unveiled, this is reported to be powered by a slightly more powerful engine which gives it a top road speed of 120km/hr and new axles which increase its ground clearance from .22m to .3m.

*The UAZ-469B with hood
and windscreen down.*

Variants
There is an ambulance model called the UAZ-469BG in service, recently a van model has been introduced. This vehicle will also be available commercially in due course.

Employment
In service with the East German and Soviet Armies.

GAZ-69 (4 x 4) Series

Soviet Union

Length: 3.85m
Width: 1.75m
Height: 1.92m
G/Clearance: .21m
Track: 1.44m
Wheelbase: 2.3m
Weight: 1,960kg (loaded)
1,535kg (empty)
Tyres: 6.50 × 20
Engine: GAZ-69 4-cylinder, side-valve, in-line petrol engine developing 52hp at 3,600rpm
Crew: 1 + 4
Speed: 90km/hr
Range: 430km
Fuel: 60 litres
Gradient: 60%
Angle Approach: 45°
Angle Departure: 35°
T/Radius: 6m
Fording: .7m

The above data relates to the GAZ-69A

Development
The first model was known as the GAZ-69 and was manufactured from 1952 to 1956 at the Gor'kiy Plant. In 1956 production was transferred to the Ulyanovsk Plant, after which it was known as the UAZ-69. More recent production models are the UAZ-69M and the UAZ-69AM, these have the M-21 petrol engine developing 70hp at 4,000rpm.

The GAZ-69 is a light cargo carrier with two seats at the front and a bench seat either side of the body, the GAZ-69A is a passenger type vehicle and has a larger fuel tank. Both models can tow 800kg of cargo. The gearbox has 3F and 1R gears and a two-speed transfer box, suspension consists of semi-elliptical springs front and rear with hydraulic shock absorbers front and rear.

Variants
There is a tractor truck called the UAZ-456 and the UAZ-450 series of vehicles use some components of the UAZ-69. The GAZ-46 MAV (4 × 4) amphibious truck was based on the UAZ-69 and is very similar in design to the World War II amphibious American jeep. It has a weight of 1,750kg, length 4.93m, width 1.86m, height 1.778m and it is powered by a 4-cylinder M-20 petrol engine developing 55hp. Road speed is 95km/hr and water speed is 8km/hr, road range is about 400km. It can carry five men or 360kg of cargo.

Four Snapper anti-tank missiles are mounted on the rear of one model of the UAZ-69. Whilst travelling these missiles are vertical and are covered by a canvas cover. The missiles can be fired from within the cab or away from the vehicle with the aid of a remote control cable. There is also a mine detector vehicle and an anti-tank vehicle fitted with the 82mm B-10 recoilless gun. The GAZ-69 is often used as a command or radio vehicle, and is also widely used by civilian interests.

Employment

In service with most members of the Warsaw Pact as well as those countries that have received Soviet aid in one form or another, these include Cuba, Egypt, Finland, India, Iran, Israel (captured) and Syria. It is also built in Romania where it is known as the M-461.

In the 1960s the Soviets built a 4×4 ¼-ton vehicle called ZaZ-969, although this was tested it did not enter production. A development of this vehicle called the LuMZ-969 did, however, enter production in 1972. This light 4×4 vehicle weighs only 820kg and is powered by a MeMZ-966 4-cylinder engine that develops 27hp, this gives the vehicle a top speed of 75km/hr. Basic data is length 3.2m, width 1.6m, height 1.77m and a wheelbase of 1.8m. This would appear to be a useful vehicle for the Soviet Airborne units or other units where light vehicles are essential.

The GAZ-69 (4×4) vehicle with its hood and windscreen down.

The UAZ-69 with four Snapper ATGW at the rear.

Below: The UAZ-69 (4×4) amphibious vehicle in travelling order.

UAZ-452D (4 x 4) Light Truck

Length: 4.46m
Width: 2.044m
Height: 2.07m
G/Clearance: .22m
Track: 1.442m
Wheelbase: 2.3m
Weight: 2,500kg (loaded)
1,700kg (empty)
Load Area: 2.6m × 1.87m
Engine: Model ZMZ-451E, 4-cylinder petrol engine developing 72hp
Crew: 1 + 2
Speed: 95km/hr
Range: 400km
Fuel: 56 litres
Gradient: 60%
Angle Approach: 33°
Angle Departure: 30°
T/Radius: 6.8m
Fording: .3m
Tyres: 8.40 × 15

Development

The UAZ-452D has been in production at the Ul'yanovsk Autombile Plant since 1966. The cab is of the forward control type and is of all-steel construction, the rear cargo body consists of a wooden platform with dropsides and a tailgate. The vehicle can carry a maximum of 800kg of cargo on both roads and cross-country and can also tow a maximum of 800kg. Its gearbox has 4F and 1R gears and a two-speed transfer case. Other models are the UAZ-452A (Ambulance), UAZ-452V (bus) and the UAZ-452P tractor truck.

Variants

The first vehicles built were the UAZ-450 (van), UAZ-450D (truck), UAZ-450A (ambulance) and the UAZ-450V (bus), these were produced from 1958 to 1966 as were all 4 × 4s, they were powered by a M-20 4-cylinder petrol engine which developed 65hp, their transmission had 3F and 1R gears and a two-speed transfer case. Basic data was—length 4.35m, width 2.04m, height 2.05m, track 1.436m and fuel 55 litres. From 1961 4 × 2 models were built as well—UAZ-451 (van), UAZ-451D (cargo) and UAZ-451DM. In 1966 the improved 4 × 2 UAZ-451M entered production. The UAZ-455 is similar to the UAZ-452.

Employment

Warsaw Pact Forces.

GAZ-51 (4 x 2) and GAZ-63 (4 x 4) Trucks

	GAZ-51A	GAZ-63
Length:	5.725m	5.525m
Width:	2.28m	2.2m
Height (Cab):	2.13m	2.245m
G/Clearance:	.245m	.27m
Wheelbase:	3.3m	3.3m
Track:	1.589m(f) 1.65m(r)	1.588m(f) 1.6m(r)
Weight (loaded):	5,350kg	5,430kg
Weight (empty):	2,710kg	3,280kg
Load Area:	3.07m × 2.07m × .61m	2.94m × 1.99m × .89m
Crew:	1 + 1	1 + 1
Speed:	70km/hr	65km/hr
Range:	450km	780km
Fuel:	90 litres	90 or 105 litres
Gradient:	15°	28°
Angle Approach:	40°	48°
Angle Departure:	32°	32°
T/Radius:	7.6m	8.7m
Tyres:	7.50 × 20	10.00 × 18
Fording:	.6m	.8m

GAZ-51 Development

The GAZ-51 entered production in 1946 at the Gor'kiy Plant where it was produced until 1955 after which time the GAZ-51A was placed in production. The GAZ-51A can carry, 2,000kg of cargo across country or 2,500kg on roads. It has a metal cab and a wooden platform with hinged sideboards and tailgate. The gearbox has 4F and 1R gears and there is no transfer case. It is powered by a GAZ-51, 6-cylinder in-line petrol engine developing 70hp at 2,800rpm, and has dual rear wheels.

GAZ-51 Variants

There are many variants of the GAZ-51 vehicle and these include the GAZ-51P tractor truck, GAZ-93 dump truck, GAZ-51U (export), GAZ-51V (export), GAZ-51Yu (export, tropical), GAZ-51Zh (gas cylinder), GAZ-51R (freight/passenger), GAZ-51S (two fuel tanks), GAZ-51N (two fuel tanks, seats along either side), PAZ-653 and AS-3 ambulances, DDA-53 disinfestation vehicle, MZ-51M motor oil supply truck (920 litres), and various water and fuel trucks etc. The GAZ-51 was built in Poland for some time under the designation Lublin-51.

GAZ-63 Development

The GAZ-63 is basically a 4 × 4 model of the GAZ-51, it was in production from 1948 until 1968. It can carry 2,000kg of cargo both on roads or cross-country and tow a load of 1,500kg. The gearbox has 4F and 1R gears and a two speed transfer case and single rear wheels. The GAZ-63 chassis was used for the BTR-40 APC, and its replacement is the GAZ-66. The GAZ-63 has been built in China.

GAZ-63 Variants

Variants of the GAZ-63 include the GAZ-63A with a winch, DD-53A disinfestation vehicle, GAZ-63 with 140mm (17 round) BM-14-17 multiple rocket system, GAZ-63 with winch, GAZ-63AE with shielded electrical system, GAZ-63D truck/tractor, GAZ-63AYu export, GAZ-63P truck/tractor, GAZ-63U and GAZ-63AU export models, and many others.

Employment

The GAZ-51 may still be found in some second line units, the GAZ-63 is still in large scale use although it is being replaced by the GAZ-66.

Above: *The GAZ-63 (4 × 4) Cargo Truck.*

Below: *The GAZ-51 (4 × 2) Cargo Truck.*

GAZ-66 (4 x 4) 2-Ton Truck   Soviet Union

Length: 5.655m
Width: 2.342m
Height: 2.44m (cab)
2.52m (canvas top)
G/Clearance: .315m
Track: 1.8m(f) 1.75m(r)
Wheelbase: 3.3m

Weight: 5,770kg (loaded)
3,440kg (empty)
Load Area: 3.33m × 2.05m × .89m
Engine: ZN6-66, V-8, water-cooled petrol engine developing 115hp at 3,200rpm
Crew: 1 + 1
Speed: 95km/hr

Range: 875km
Fuel: 2 × 105 litres
Gradient: 30%
Angle Approach: 41°
Angle Departure: 32°
T/Radius: 9.5m
Fording: .8m
Tyres: 12.00 × 18

Development

The GAZ-66 entered production late in 1963 at the Gor'kiy plant and is the replacement for the earlier GAZ-63, an earlier model of the GAZ-66 was powered by an 85hp engine. It has a forward control type cab that can be swung forwards to provide access to the engine, the body consists of a metal platform with a hinged tailgate, provision has been made for the fitting of a canopy with five arch supports. The engine used is the same as that used in the GAZ-53, the gearbox has 4F and 1R gears with a two-speed transfer case. Suspension consists of semi-elliptical springs with telescopic shock absorbers front and rear. It can carry 2,000kg of cargo on roads or cross-country and can also tow a trailer of 2,000kg, it can also be used to tow artillery or mortars.

Variants

There are many civilian and military versions of the GAZ-66 in service including the following: GAZ-66-01 with tyre pressure adjustment system, GAZ-66-02 with tyre pressure adjustment system and winch with a capacity of 3,500kg (also known as GAZ-66A), GAZ-66-03 with shielded electrical system (also known as the GAZ-66E), GAZ-66-04 is similar to the GAZ-66-03 but has a tyre pressure adjustment system, the GAZ-66-05 is the GAZ-66-04 but with the shielded electrical system (it is also called the GAZ-66-EA). GAZ-66s are also built with soft top cabs. Other models include the GAZ-66P tractor truck, GAZ-66 vans, MZ-66 motor oil supply truck (820 litres), ATs PT-1.7 (1,700 litres) tank truck and the DDA-66 decontamination truck. The GAZ-66B (it has also been called the GAZ-62) is a special lightweight model for the use of the airborne forces and features removable canvas cab top, removable doors and windows and telescopic steering column. Reference has also been made to a 6 × 6 model called the GAZ-34, this can carry 3,500kg of cargo.

Employment

In service with members of the Warsaw Pact. All models built since 1968 have the tyre pressure regulation system fitted.

A GAZ-66 (4 × 4) 2-Ton Truck.

ZIL-157K (6 x 6) 2 ½-Ton Truck

Soviet Union

Length: 6.922m
Width: 2.315m
Height: 2.915m (canvas top)
2.36m (cab)
G/Clearance: .31m
Track: 1.755m(f) 1.75m(r)
Wheelbase: 3.665m + 1.12m
Weight: 8,450kg (loaded)
5,800kg (empty)

Load Area: 3.57m × 2.09m × .355m
Engine: ZIL-157K 6-cylinder, in-line, water-cooled petrol engine developing 109hp at 2,800rpm
Crew: 1 + 2
Speed: 65km/hr
Range: 510km
Fuel: 215 litres
Gradient: 28%
Angle Approach: 35°

Angle Departure: 28°
T/Radius: 11.2m
Fording: .85m
Tyres: 12.00 × 18

Development

The ZIL-157 was in production at the Imeni Kirhachev Plant from 1958, the ZIL-157K being introduced in 1961. The ZIL-157 was the replacement for the earlier ZIL-131. The cab is of all-steel construction and the body consists of a wooden platform with a hinged tailgate, folding benches are incorporated in the sides of the vehicle. The tyre pressures can be regulated whilst the vehicle is travelling and a crane is mounted behind the cab. The gearbox has 5F and 1R gears and a two-speed transfer case. The front suspension consists of semi-elliptical springs and hydraulic shock absorbers, the rear suspension consists of longitudinal springs. A winch is normally mounted at the front of the vehicle. It can carry 4,500kg of cargo on roads or 2,500kg of cargo across country, its maximum towed load is 3,600kg.

In addition to its role of carrying cargo it is also used to tow artillery, for example the 122mm Howitzer D-30.

Variants

There are many variants of the ZIL-157K and they include: ZIL-157KG truck with shielded ignition system, ZIL-157KV truck tractor, ZIL-157KE which is a KIL-157K for operations in temperate climates (export), ZIL-157KYu which is an export model for operating in tropical climates, ZIL-157GT which is the ZIL-157KG with a shielded electrical system for operations in tropical climates, ZIL-157KYe chassis for special truck beds and bodies, ARS-12U decontamination truck, ZIL-157KYe chassis with high output generator, VMZ-ZIL-157K water/motor oil tank truck, ATsM-4-157K tank truck (4,040 litres of water or fuel), ATZ-2-157K fuel service truck, crane truck, command/radio vehicle, carrying TPP pontoons, carrying span of KMM bridge, ZIL-157KYeG which is a ZIL-157KG chassis with shielded electrical system, ZIL-157YeT which is a ZIL-157KYe chassis (tropical climate export model), ZIL-157YeGT which is a ZIL-157KYeG chassis (tropical climate export model), ZIL-157KYeGT which is a ZIL-157KYeG chassis for use in tropical climates and is for export, ZIL-157YeT is a ZIL-157KYe tropical climate export model (chassis has features of the ZIL-157KYu. The ZIL-157 chassis is also used to mount the following rocket launchers: 140mm (16 round) BM-14-16, 200mm (4 round) BMD-20 and 240mm (12 round) BM-24. Later production models of the ZIL-157K are the ZIL-157W.

Employment

Widely used in Warsaw Forces, exported overseas including Egypt, Finland and Syria. It is now being replaced by the ZIL-131. Romania has some ZIL-151s and ZIL-157s fitted with the 130mm (32 round) M-51 Rocket Launcher on the rear. Romania is the only country to use this combination as this system is normally mounted on the Czech Praga V3S chassis.

Above: *The ZIL-157V (6 × 6) Tractor Truck.*

ZIL-151 (6 x 6) 2½-Ton Truck

Length: 6.93m
Width: 2.32m
Height: 2.74m (canvas cover)
2.32m (cab)
G/Clearance: .265m
Track: 1.59m(f) 1.72m(r)
Wheelbase: 3.665m + 1.22m
Weight: 7,830kg (loaded)
5,580kg (empty)
Engine: ZIL-121, 6-cylinder in-line water-cooled petrol engine developing 92hp at 2,600rpm
Crew: 1 + 2
Speed: 60km/hr
Range: 600km
Gradient: 28%
Angle Approach: 36°
Angle Departure: 30°
T/Radius: 10m
Fording: .8m
Tyres: 8.25 × 20

Development

The ZIL-151 was the standard 2½-ton truck of the Soviet Army for many years. The prototype ZIS-151 was built in 1946 and it was in production from 1947 until 1958, later it was known as the ZIL-151. It can carry 2,500kg of cargo across country or 4,500kg on roads, its towed load was 3,600kg and it was extensively used to tow artillery up to 152mm calibre. Its gearbox has 5F and 1R gears and a two-speed transfer case, a tyre pressure regulation system is installed and many vehicles were fitted with a winch. Late production ZIL-151s had the radiator and cab of the ZIL-157 as the ZIL-157 replaced the ZIL-151 in production from October, 1958. Early models of the BTR-152 APC used the ZIL-151 truck chassis.

Variants

Variants include the BM-14-16 (16-round) 140mm rocket launcher, 200mm rocket launcher (4-round) BMD-20, 240mm rocket launcher (12-round) BM-24, ZIL-121D and ZIL-151D tractor trucks, ARS-12D decontamination truck, ATs 4-151 4,000 litre tanker, ATZ 3-151 3,500 litre fuel service truck, van truck VMZ-ZIL-151 that can carry fuel and water, TPP Pontoon truck, the Romanian Army has some ZIL-151s with the 130mm (32-round) M-51 Rocket Launcher mounted on the rear, and 3t crane truck. The ZIL-151D tractor truck was also used to tow SAMs.

Employment

No longer in large scale used with Soviet Forces but still in use in other members of the WPF and numerous foreign countries that have received Soviet aid. The ZIS-150 was a 3½-ton (4 × 2) cargo truck, this is no longer in service with WPF.

Below: *The ZIL-151 (6 × 6) 2½-Ton Truck.*

ZIL-131 (6 x 6) 3½-Ton Truck

Soviet Union

Length: 7.04m
Width: 2.5m
Height: 2.48m (cab)
2.975m (canvas top)
G/Clearance: .33m
Track: 1.82m (f and r)
Wheelbase: 3.35m + 1.25m
Weight: 10,425kg (loaded)
6,700kg (empty)
Load Area: 3.6m × 2.322m × .346m
Engine: ZIL-131, OHV, 8-cylinder petrol engine developing 150hp at 3,200rpm
Crew: 1 + 2
Speed: 80km/hr
Range: 850km
Fuel: 2 × 170 litres
Gradient: 30%
Angle Approach: 36°
Angle Departure: 30°
T/Radius: 10.2m
Fording: 1.4m
Tyres: 12.00 × 20

Development
The ZIL-131 has been in production at the Moscow (imeni Kikhachev) Plant since December, 1966, and is the replacement for the ZIL-157. It has been developed from the ZIL-130 (4 × 2) and is also related to the ZIL-133 (6 × 4). The cab is of metal construction and the body consists of a wooden platform with metal fittings and a hinged tailgate. The inside of the body is provided with baggage grating and hinged benches, a canopy and bows can be fitted. Its maximum capacity is 5,000kg of cargo on hard roads or 3,500kg of cargo on dirt roads, it can tow 5,000kg of cargo. A winch with capacity of 4,500kg is fitted, and the tyre pressures can be adjusted from the inside of the cab. The gearbox has 5F and 1R gears with a two-speed transfer case. The front suspension consists of longitudinal semi-elliptical springs with double-acting shock absorbers the rear suspension consists of an equaliser arm (on sliding bearings) and semi-elliptical springs.

Variants
ZIL-131D dump truck, ZIL-131V for towing semi-trailer, ZIL-131A with standard ignition system instead of shielded sealed ignition system, ZIL-137 tractor truck with powered trailer, this makes it a 10 × 10 vehicle with a considerable increase in cross-country capability. The ATZ-3 4-131 is a 3,400 litre fuel truck. Variants of the ZIL-133 (6 × 4) include the ZIL-133B dump truck, ZIL-133D construction dump truck, ZIL-133G LWB truck and ZIL-133V tractor truck.

Employment
Warsaw Pact Forces.

The ZIL-131 (6 × 6)
3½-Ton Cargo Truck.

The ZIL-133V (6 × 4)
Tractor Truck.

MAZ-502 (4 x 4) 4-Ton Truck

Length: 7.15m
Width: 2.7m
Height: 3.025m (stakes)
2.725m (cab)
G/Clearance: .29m
Track: 2.03m
Wheelbase: 4.52m
Weight: 11,925kg (loaded)
7,700kg (empty)
Load Area: 3.5m × 2.03m × 1.018m
Engine: YaAZ-M204V 4-cylinder, in-line, water-cooled diesel developing 135hp at 2,000rpm
Crew: 1 + 2
Speed: 65km/hr
Range: 590km
Fuel: 450 litres
Gradient: 20%
Angle Approach: 52°
Angle Departure: 30°
T/Radius: 12.5m
Fording: 8m
Tyres: 15.00 × 20

Above: *The MAZ-502A (4 × 4) 4-Ton Cargo truck with front mounted winch.*

Development
The MAZ-502 was manufactured at the Minsk Plant from 1957 until 1966. The MAZ-502 is based on the MAZ-501 4 × 4 timber hauling truck which in turn was based on the MAZ-200V tractor truck. The MAZ-502 has a payload of 4,000kg across country or 5,000kg on roads, its towed load is 4,000kg.

The vehicle has an all-metal cab and body. The body is provided with a hinged tailgate and grilled sideboards, hinged benches, removable canopy supports and a canopy. The gearbox has 5F and 1R gears and a two-speed transfer case. The front suspension consists of longitudinal, semi-elliptical springs with double acting hydraulic shock absorbers, the rear suspension consists of longitudinal, semi-elliptical springs with helper springs.

Variants
The MAZ-502A has a winch, the MAZ-502V is a truck/tractor and is often used to tow missiles, there are also various radio and repair van type models.

Employment
Warsaw Pact Forces. The MAZ-502 is being replaced by the MAZ-505 series of 4 × 4 trucks.

GAZ-53A (4 x 2) 4-Ton Cargo Truck

Length: 6.395m
Width: 2.38m
Height: 2.22m (cab)
G/Clearance: .265m
Track: 1.63m(f) 1.69m(r)
Wheelbase: 3.7m
Weight: 7,250kg (loaded)
3,250kg (empty)
Load Area: 3.75m × 2.17m
Engine: ZMZ-53, V-8, OHV petrol engine developing 115hp at 3,200rpm

Crew: 1 + 1
Speed: 80km/hr
Range: 375km
Fuel: 90 litres
Gradient: 30%
Angle Approach: 41°
Angle Departure: 25°
T/Radius: 8m
Fording: .6m
Tyres: 8.25 × 20

Development
Whilst under development this vehicle was referred to as the GAZ-52. The GAZ-53A can carry 4,000kg of cargo and tow a trailer with a maximum weight of 4,000kg. It has twin rear wheels and its gearbox has 4F and 1R gears. The front and rear suspension consists of longitudinal semi-elliptical springs, the front springs have two-way hydraulic shock absorbers. If required an auxiliary fuel tank with a total capacity of 150 litres can be fitted on the LHS of the chassis.

Variants
There are many variants of the GAZ-53, these include the following:
GAZ-53-03: Has 2,500kg cargo capacity and is powered by an engine that develops 75hp at 2,800rpm
GAZ-53A-02: Dump truck chassis
GAZ-53A-016: Cargo truck with two fuel tanks with a total capacity of 195 litres, weight w/o load is 3,325kg
GAZ-53B: 4 × 2 three way dump truck
ATZ-3.8-53A: 3,800 litre fuel servicing truck
ATs-2.6-53F: Tank truck
ATs-2.9-53F: Tank truck
ATs-4.2-53A: Tank truck
ATsPT-2.8: Tank truck

Employment
Warsaw Pact Forces. (Is also built in Bulgaria).

Above: *The GAZ-53A (4 × 2) 4-Ton Cargo Truck.*

ZIL-164 (4 x 2) 4-Ton Truck

Length: 6.7m
Width: 2.47m
Height: 2.18m
G/Clearance: .265m
Track: 1.7m(f) 1.74m(r)
Wheelbase: 4m
Weight: 8,250kg (loaded)
4,100kg (empty)
Load Area: 3.54m × 2.25m × .584m

Soviet Union

Engine: ZIL-164, 6-cylinder in-line water-cooled petrol engine developing 100hp at 2,800rpm
Crew: 1 + 2
Speed: 75km/hr
Range: 550km
Fuel: 150 litres
Gradient: 15%

Below: *The ZIL-164N (4 × 2) Tractor Truck.*

Angle Approach: 40°
Angle Departure: 24°
T/Radius: 8m
Tyres: 9.00 × 20

Development
The ZIL-164 was in production from 1957 until 1961 at the imeni Kikhachev (Moscow Plant, from 1961 to 1965 the ZIL-164A was produced. The ZIL-164 is very similar to the earlier ZIL-150 (in production from 1946-1957). Many components of the ZIL-164, such as the engine, are used in the ZIL-157 (6 × 6) truck. Its normal payload is 4,000kg on the road, 3,500kg on dirt roads or 4,500kg with special tyres, its towed load is 6,400kg on roads. The gearbox has 5F and 1R gears, there is no transfer case.

Variants
The ZIL-164 differs from the ZIL-164A in the construction of the transmission and its lower powered engine. There are many variants of the ZIL-164 including the ZIL-164N tractor truck, crane truck, ZIL-164D and ZIL-164AD with shielded electrical system, ZIL-164R and ZIL-164AR with air brake connection for towing trailer, ZIL-166 operating on compressed gas or petrol, ZIL-166A truck operating on liquefied gas or petrol, ZIL-164E and ZIL-164S export models, ZIL-164G and ZIL-164AG dump trucks, ZIL-164Yu tropical export model, ZIL-164N and ZIL-164AN for towing semi-trailers. The ZIL-16AR has a more powerful engine, and is fitted with a winch. The ZIL-MMZ-585 L is a construction dump truck and the ZIL-MMZ-585 M is an agricultural dump truck.

Employment
Still in use with most members of the Warsaw Pact although it has been replaced in many units by the ZIL-130. The ZIL-164 is also built in China where it is known as the Jay-Fong CA10Z.

Ural-375D (6 x 6) 4½-Ton Truck

Soviet Union

Length: 7.35m
Width: 2.69m
Height: 2.68m (cab)
2.98m (canvas top)
G/Clearance: .4m
Track: 2m
Wheelbase: 3.5m + 1.4m
Weight: 13,300kg (loaded)
8,400kg (empty)
Load Area: 3.9m × 2.43m × .872m
Engine: ZIL-375, OHV, 8-cylinder petrol engine developing 180hp at 3,200rpm
Crew: 1 + 2
Speed: 75km/hr
Range: 750km
Fuel: 360 litres
Gradient: 30%
Angle Approach: 44°
Angle Departure: 40°
T/Radius: 10.5m

Fording: 1.5m
Tyres: 14.00 × 20

Development
The Ural-375D has been in production at the Ural Plant since 1961. The cab and body are of metal construction and the body is provided with hinged bench seats along its sides and a detachable canopy and bows. A winch with a capacity of 7,000kg is fitted and the tyre pressures can be adjusted as required. The gearbox has 5F and 1R gears and a two speed transfer case, hydraulic assisted steering is provided. The front suspension consists of semi-elliptical springs (interchangeable with the MAZ-500) and shock absorbers, the rear suspension consists of a centraliser arm on two longitudinal semi-elliptical springs. It can tow 5,000kg of cargo cross-couintry or 10,000kg on roads, it is used to tow artillery up to and including the 152mm M-1955 (M-20) Field Howitzer.

The URAL-375D (6 × 6) Truck carrying pontoon bridge sections.

Variants

The Ural-375 has a soft cab, the Ural 375A has its frame extended 335mm to take the K375 van body, the Ural-375S has a shorter frame (135mm) and is used to tow semi trailers, for example, a trailer carrying the Griffon SAM. The Ural-375D is also widely used to mount the 122mm Multiple Rocket Launcher BM-21 (40 rounds), and for towing the pontoon boat BMK-150, this model has a winch for recovering the boat, and for carrying the RF-68 pontoon bridge sections. The tanker models of the Ural-375D include the ATMZ-4.5-375 fuel lubricant truck carrying 4,500 litres of fuel, TZ-5 fuel truck carrying 5,000 litres of fuel (5 hoses are provided for refueling other vehicles) and the ATs-5-375 5,000 litre tank truck. The 6 × 4 Ural 377 series have a longer cargo body, variants of this model include the Ural-377M with tyre pressure regulations system, Ural-377S tractor for towing semi-trailers and the Ural-377V dump truck.

Employment

Used by most members of the Warsaw Pact Forces.

The ZIL-130 5-Ton (4 × 2) Dump Truck.

ZIL-130 (4 x 2) 5-Ton Truck   Soviet Union

Length: 6.675m
Width: 2.5m
Height: 2.35m (cab)
G/Clearance: .27m
Track: 1.8m(f) 1.79(r)
Wheelbase: 3.8m
Weight: 9,300kg (loaded)
4,300kg (empty)
Load Area: 3.75m × 2.325m
Engine: ZIL-130, 8-cylinder, OHV petrol engine developing 170hp at 3,600rpm
Crew: 1 + 2
Speed: 90km
Range: 600km
Fuel: 170 litres
Gradient: 30%
Angle Approach: 38°
Angle Departure: 27°
T/Radius: 8m
Fording: .7m
Tyres: 9.00 × 20

Development

The ZIL-130 was manufactured from 1962 at the imeni Likhachev truck plant, models built before 1965 were rated to carry 4,000kg of cargo. It can carry 5,000kg of cargo on the highway or 4,000kg of cargo on dirt roads, its maximum towed load is 8,000kg.

Its rear cargo body has dropsides and a tailgate. The ZIL-130 has a gearbox with 5F and 1R gears. The front and rear suspension consists of longitudinal semi-elliptical springs front and rear and two-way hydraulic shock absorbers are mounted on the front only.

Variants

There are many variants of the ZIL-130, these include the following:
ZIL-130V1: Truck/tractor, wheelbase 3.3m
ZIL-130G: LWB Cargo truck from 1964
ZIL-130D1: Chassis for ZIL-MMZ-555 dump truck, w/b 3.3m
ZIL-130D2: Dump truck chassis
ZIL-130E: Temperate climate export model of basic ZIL-130
ZIL-130V1E: Temperate climate export model of ZIL-130V1 truck/tractor
ZIL-130GE: Temperate climate export model of ZIL-130G
ZIL-130D1E: Temperate climate export model of ZIL-MMZ-555
ZIL-130Ye: ZIL-130 with shielded electrical system

ZIL-130YeE: Temperate climate export model of ZIL-130Ye

ZIL-130YeT: Tropical climate export model of ZIL-130Ye

ZIL-130T: Tropical climate export model of ZIL-130

ZIL-130V1T: Tropical climate export model of ZIL-130V1

ZIL-130GT: Tropical climate export model of ZIL-130G

ZIL-130D1T: Tropical climate export model of ZIL-130D1

ZIL-136I: ZIL-130 export model with Perkins diesel

ZIL-136IG: ZIL-130G export model with Perkins diesel

ZIL-136IDI: Dump truck chassis with Perkins diesel

ATs-4.2-130: Tank truck, 4,200 litre capacity

ATZ-3.8-130: Fuel truck with a capacity of 3,800 litres

PAZS-3152: Mobile fueling unit

The 4×2 KAZ-608 (Kolkhida) vehicle uses the engine, transmission and axles of the ZIL-130.

Employment
Warsaw Pact Forces.

MAZ-200 Series (4 x 2) 5-7-Ton Trucks   Soviet Union

Length: 7.62m
Width: 2.65m
Height: 2.43m
G/Clearance: .29m
Track: 1.95m(f)
1.92m(r)
Wheelbase: 4.52m
Weight: 11.400kg (loaded)
6,400kg (empty)
Load Area: 4.5m × 2.48m × .6m
Engine: YaAZ-M204A, 4-cylinder, in-line, water-cooled diesel developing 120hp at 1,200rpm. Early vehicles had 110hp engine.
Crew: 1 + 2
Speed: 65km/hr
Range: 590km
Fuel: 225 litres
Gradient: 20%
Angle Approach: 43°
Angle Departure: 26°
T/Radius: 10.1m
Fording: .8m
Tyres: 12.00 × 20

Development
The MAZ-200 series of trucks were manufactured at the Minsk Plant from 1947 until 1966 and for a time were known as the YaAZ-200 series. Payload is 5,000kg across country, 7,000kg on roads and a towed load of 9,500kg. The gearbox has 5F and 1R gears. The front suspension consists of longitudinal, semi-elliptical springs with double acting hydraulic shock absorbers, the rear suspension is similar but has helper springs in place of the shock absorbers. The cab has a wooden frame with a metal sheet covering, the rear body consists of a platform bed with three hinged sideboards. A later model was designated MAZ-200G, this was in production from 1951 until 1957. This has a body with higher sides with removable extensions, folding seats were provided so that it could carry men, a canopy could be erected over the rear body if required. Late production models of the MAZ-200 and MAZ-200V were built with the same engine (the YaMZ-236 6-cylinder diesel developing 180hp at 2,100rpm) as the MAZ-500 series of trucks and were called the MAZ-200P and MAZ-200M respectively.

Below: *The MAZ-200 (4 × 2) Cargo Truck.*

Variants

M-205 dump truck, MAZ-501 (4 × 4) timber truck, MAZ-200V and MAZ-200M tractor trucks, crane and tanker models were also built. Other 4 × 4 models included the MAZ-502 and MAZ-502A cargo trucks, MAZ-501V and 502V tractor trucks, and the TZ-200 fuel servicing truck.

Since 1965 the MAZ-200 series has been replaced by the MAZ-500 series of 4 × 2 trucks, these have a maximum payload of 7,500kg and various models have been built including cargo, tractor, dump truck, crane and so on.

Employment

Warsaw Pact Forces.

Above: The MAZ-200V (4 × 2) Tractor Truck.

KrAZ-214 (6 x 6) 7-Ton Truck   Soviet Union

Length: 8.53m
Width: 2.7m
Height: 2.8m (cab)
3.17m (canvas top)
G/Clearance: .36m
Track: 2.03m (f and r)
Weight: 19,325kg (loaded)
12,100kg (empty)
Load Area: 4.565m × 2.5m × .935m
Engine: YaAZ M206B, 6-cylinder in-line diesel, OHV, developing 205hp at 2,000rpm
Crew: 1 + 2
Speed: 55km/hr
Range: 850km
Fuel: 2 × 225 litres
Gradient: 30%
Angle Approach: 48°
Angle Departure: 32°
T/Radius: 13m
Fording: 1m
Tyres: 15.00 × 20

Development

The KrAZ-214 was originally produced between 1956 and 1959 as the YaAZ-214 at the Yaroslavl plant. In late 1959 production was transferred to the Kremenchug plant when it became known as the KrAZ-214. The first models were known as the KrAZ-214A and had a 12V electrical system, the latter KrAZ-214B has a 24V electrical system. It has a gearbox with 5F and 1R gears and a two-speed transfer case, the front wheels are provided with hydraulic shock absorbers and the rear bogie has longitudinal semi-elliptical springs. A canvas cover with bows is provided and there is a winch with a capacity of 8,000kg at the front of the vehicle. The KrAZ-214 is used to tow trailers (up to 50,000kg on roads) and artillery.

Variants

The KrAZ-214 is related to the KrAZ-219 and YaAZ-210 trucks, both of which have dual rear tyres, variants of the KrAZ-219 include the KrAZ-219A with 12V electrical system, KraZ-219B with 24V electrical system, KrAZ-221B for towing semi-trailers, KrAZ-222B dump truck, all of these are 6 × 4 vehicles and recent models have a V-8 diesel engine.

There are numerous variants of the KrAZ-214 in service including the BM-25 multiple rocket system with six 250mm rockets, there is also a model with the E-305V crane/shovel and another model carries the TMM scissors bridging system. The KrAZ-214 will probably be replaced by the KrAZ-255B which is undergoing trials. This has a YaMZ-238 engine developing 240hp at 2,100rpm as used in the KrAZ-250 series of vehicles, it has a payload of 7,500kg and has large tyres with a central tyre regulation system.

Employment

In service with members of the Warsaw Pact Forces as well as countries in the Middle East.

Below: *A KrAZ-214 (6 × 6) Truck with a PMP pontoon bridge section on the rear.*

Bottom: *KrAZ-214 (6 × 6) Trucks crossing a PMP bridge.*

KrAZ-255B (6 x 6) 7 ½ -Ton Truck
Soviet Union

Length: 8.645m
Width: 2.75m
Height: 3.17m (canvas cover)
2.94m (cab)
G/Clearance: .36m
Track: 2.16m
Wheelbase: 4.6m + 1.4m
Weight: 19,675kg (loaded)
11,950kg (empty)
Load Area: 4.565m × 2.5m × .924m
Engine: YaMZ-238, 8-cylinder, OHV, water-cooled
diesel developing 240hp at 2,100rpm
Crew: 1 + 2
Speed: 71km/hr
Range: 750km
Fuel: 330 litres
Gradient: 30%
Angle Approach: 47°
Angle Departure: 32°
T/Radius: 13m
Fording: 1m
Tyres: 13.00 × 53

Development
The KrAZ-255B has been in production at the Kremenchug Plant since 1967. Its normal payload across country is 7,500kg, it can tow 10,000kg of cargo across country or 30,000kg on roads. The cab is of metal construction with a wooden frame. The rear body is of metal construction and is provided with a tailgate, bows and a cover. A winch with a capacity of 12,000kg is fitted.

The gearbox has 5F and 1R gears and a two-speed transfer case. The front suspension consists of longitudinal semi-elliptical springs and hydraulic shock absorbers, the rear suspension consists of longitudinal semi-elliptical springs, a rear suspension locking mechanism is installed. A central tyre pressure regulation system is installed and the steering is power-assisted.

Variants
The KrAZ-225V is a truck tractor.

Employment
Warsaw Pact Forces.

Below: *The KrAZ-255B (6 × 6) 7 ½ - Ton Cargo Truck.*

126

MAZ-500 (4 x 2) 7 ½-Ton Truck

Soviet Union

Length: 7.33m
Width: 2.65m
Height: 2.64m
G/Clearance: .295m
Track: 1.95m(f) 1.9m(r)
Wheelbase: 3.85m
Weight: 14,000kg (loaded)
6,500kg (empty)
Load Area: 4.86m × 2.352m
Engine: YaMZ-236, 6-cylinder water-cooled diesel developing 180hp at 2,100rpm
Crew: 1 + 2
Speed: 75km/hr
Range: 900km
Fuel: 200 litres
Gradient: 25%
Angle Approach: 30°
Angle Departure: 28°
T/Radius: 9m
Tyres: 12.00 × 20

Development

This has been in production at the Minsk Autombile Plant since 1965 and is the replacement for the earlier MAZ-200 series of trucks. The MAZ-500 can carry 7,500kg of cargo on roads and tow a maximum load of 12,000kg. The cab is of the forward control type and is of all-steel construction and swings forward to allow access to the engine and transmission. The rear cargo body has dropsides and a tailgate. The gearbox has 5F and 1R gears. The front suspension consists of semi-elliptical springs with telescopic hydraulic shock absorbers and the rear suspension consists of semi-elliptical springs with helper springs.

Variants

There are many variants of the MAZ-500, these are:
MAZ-500G LWB cargo truck, also crane mounted model.
MAZ-503B (4 × 2) standard dump truck, from 1965 wheelbase 3.2m.
MAZ-504 (4 × 2) tractor truck, wheelbase 3.2m. Also MAZ-504B dump truck.
MAZ-505 (4 × 4) cargo truck, same engine as the MAZ-500.
MAZ-508V (4 × 4) tractor truck.
MAZ-509 (4 × 4) timber truck.
MAZ-510 (4 × 2) rear dump truck.
MAZ-511 (4 × 2) side dump truck.
MAZ-512 (4 × 2) arctic truck.
MAZ-513 (4 × 2) tropical truck.
MAZ-514 (6 × 4) cargo truck.
MAZ-515 (6 × 4) tractor truck.
MAZ-516 (6 × 2) cargo truck has been in production since 1968. Basic data is length 8.52m, width 2.5m, height 2.65m, weight 8,800kg, cargo capacity 14,000kg, it has the same engine as the MAZ-500.

Employment

Warsaw Pact Forces.

Above: *The MAZ-500 (4 × 2) 7 ½-Ton Cargo Truck.*

ZIL-135 (8 x 8) 10-Ton Truck

Soviet Union

Length: 9.27m
Width: 2.8m
Height: 2.53m
G/Clearance: .58m
Track: 2.3m
Wheelbase: 2.415m + 1.5m + 2.415m
Weight: 22,000kg (loaded)
12,000kg (empty)
Engines: 2 × ZIL-375, 8-cylinder, water-cooled petrol engines developing 180hp at 3,200rpm (6.96 litre)
Speed: 65km/hr
Range: 600km (estimated)
Gradient: 60%
Trench: 2.63m
V/Obstacle: .685m
Fording: .58m
Tyres: 16.00 × 20

Development
The ZIL-135 is a fairly new vehicle and is also known as the BAZ-135 or ZIL-135L4. It can carry 10,000kg of cargo on both roads or cross-country and can tow a trailer with a total weight of 18,000kg on both roads or cross-country. It has an all-steel cab and a body of the stake type with a tailgate. If required, bows and tarpaulin can be fitted and many ZIL-135s have a hydraulic crane fitted between the cab and the body.

One of the unusual features of the ZIL-135 is that it has two engines, one engine drives the four wheels on one side and the other engine drives the other side it can keep going should one engine fail. The front and rear wheels are steerable whilst the middle four are fixed.

Variants
The ZIL-135 is used as a launching vehicle for the FROG-7 surface-to-surface missile and the Shaddock surface-to-surface missile. There is also a FROG-7 missile resupply vehicle that carries three FROG-7 missiles. A more recent model is the 6 × 6 ZIL-E167 which weighs, 7,000kg and has a central tyre pressure regulation system fitted. This has been designed for use in very rough country and will be available in a number of roles including tanker, cargo truck and tractor truck.

Employment
Warsaw Pact Forces.

Below: *The ZIL-135 (8 × 8) vehicle being used as a transporter/launcher for the FROG-7 surface-to-surface missile.*

YaAZ-210 (6 x 4) 10-Ton Cargo Truck

Length: 9.66m
Width: 2.65m
Height: 2.575m
G/Clearance: .29m
Track: 1.95m(f) 1.92m(r)
Wheelbase: 5.05m + 1.4m
Weight: 21,300kg (loaded)
11,300kg (empty)
Engine: YaAZ-M206A, 6-cylinder in-line water-cooled diesel engine developing 180hp at 2,000rpm
Crew: 1 + 2
Speed: 55km/hr
Range: 820km
Gradient: 40%
Fording: 1m
Tyres: 12.00 × 20

Development
The YaAZ-210 was in production from 1951 to 1958 and was replaced by the KrAZ-219, this uses the same engine as the YaAZ-210. The KrAZ-214 (6 × 6) vehicle is based on the YaAZ-210 series.

The YaAZ-210 can carry 10,000kg of cargo on dirt roads or 12,000kg of cargo on the highway, its maximum towed load is 15,000kg. The rear cargo body is provided with dropsides and a tailgate. Some models have been fitted with a winch and these are known as the YaAZ-210A.

Variants
YaAZ-210 standard dump truck.
YaAZ-210D (6 × 4) tractor truck (for semi-trailers).
YaAZ-210G (6 × 4) prime mover (with ballast).
YaAZ-218 (6 × 4) side dump truck, there is some doubt as to when this model went into production.

Employment
Warsaw Pact Forces.

Below: *The YaAZ-210G (6 × 4) Prime Mover.*

KrAZ-219 (6 x 4) 12-Ton Truck

Length: 9.66m
Width: 2.65m
Height: 3.15m (canvas top)
2.62m (cab)
G/Clearance: .29m
Track: 1.95m(f) 1.92m(r)
Wheelbase: 5.05m + 1.4m
Weight: 23,530kg (loaded)
11,300kg (empty)
Load Area: 5.77m × 2.48m × .825m
Engine: YaAZ-M2061 6-cylinder in-line, water-cooled diesel developing 180hp at 2,000rpm
Crew: 1 + 2
Speed: 55km/hr
Range: 800km
Fuel: 450 litres
Gradient: 20%
Angle Approach: 42°
Angle Departure: 18°
T/Radius: 12.5m
Fording: .8m
Tyres: 12.00 × 20

Development
This replaced the earlier YaAZ-210 series and was manufactured between 1958/59 at the Yaroslavl Plant during which time it was known as the YaAZ-219. Since 1959 it has been built at Kremenchug. The vehicle can carry 10,000kg of cargo on dirt roads or 12,000kg of cargo on the highway. Towed load in the highway is 15,000kg.

The gearbox has 5F and 1R gears, and a two-speed transfer box. The KrAZ-219 is related to the KrAZ-214 (6 × 6) truck.

Variants
The first production models had a 12V electrical system, the KrAZ-219B has a 24V electrical system. The KrAZ-221B is the KrAZ-219B with a semi-automatic fifth-wheel attachment device in place of truck bed, for hauling semi-trailers, the KrAZ-222B is a dump truck with tipping dump body, there is also a model with the K-104 crane. More recent models have a V-8 diesel engine and these are designated KrAZ-254 dump truck (three way), KrAZ-256 hopper dump truck, KrAZ-257 cargo truck and KrAZ-258 tractor truck. These are interim vehicles pending the large scale introduction of the KrAZ-250 series of 6 × 4 vehicles. These have 250hp diesels and the range includes the KrAZ-250 cargo truck, KrAZ-251 hopper type dump truck and the KrAZ-252 tractor truck (cab over engine type).

Employment
Warsaw Pact Forces.

The KrAZ-219 (6 × 4) 12-Ton Truck.

The KrAZ-250 (6 × 4) Truck.

MAZ-535 and MAZ-537 (8 x 8) Vehicles　Soviet Union

	MAZ-535A	MAZ-537A
Length:	8.78m	9.13m
Width:	2.805m	2.885m
Height:	2.915m (cab)	2.88m
G/Clearance:	.475m	.5m
Wheelbase (o/w):	5.75m	6.05m
Track:	2.15m	2.2m
Weight (loaded):	25,975kg	37,500kg
Weight (empty):	18,975kg	22,500kg
Load Area:	4.5m × 2.595m × .35m	4.562m × 2.53m × .5m
Crew:	1+3	1+3
Speed:	75km/hr	60km/hr
Range:	650km	650km
Fuel:	700 litres	840 litres
Gradient:	30°	23°
Angle Approach:	38°	38°
Angle Departure:	60°	52°
T/Radius:	13.5m	15.5m
Fording:	1.3m	1m
Tyres:	18.00 × 24	18.00 × 24

The MAZ-537 (8 × 8) Tractor.

Development/Variants

The MAZ-535 series of 8 × 8 vehicles are the most powerful trucks in use in the Soviet Union and are used in civilian roles as well as many military roles. They have been in service since the early 1960s.

MAZ-535: The primary role of the MAZ-535 is to carry cargo across rough country to a maximum load of 7,000kg, it can also tow a trailer with a maximum weight of 15,000kg. It is powered by a four-cycle, OHV, 12-cylinder diesel model D12A-375 developing 375hp at 1,650rpm. The gearbox has 3F and 1R gears and a two-speed transfer case. The front four wheels are steered and the steering is hydraulic-assisted. The front suspension consists of individual torsion bars with hydraulic shock absorbers on the front axle. The MAZ-535V is a truck tractor for towing semi-trailers.

MAZ-537: The first model was the MAZ-537 which could tow a 65-ton (gross weight) semi-trailer. The MAZ-537A can carry a load of 15,000kg or tow a trailer with a maximum weight of 75,000kg. It is powered by D12A-525 OHV, 12-cylinder diesel developing 525hp at 2,100rpm and has a similar transmission as the MAZ-535. Both the MAZ-535 and MAZ-537 have a tyre pressure regulation system installed.

Variants of the vehicle include the MAZ-537G truck/tractor for hauling 68-ton gross weight semi-trailers, MAZ-537D truck/tractor with AC generator unit for hauling 65-ton semi-trailer, MAZ-537Ye truck tractor with AC generator unit for hauling 65-ton gross weight 'active drive' semi-trailer and the MAZ-537K tractor for crane equipment.

The MAZ-537 truck/tractor has a fifth wheel and tows the ChMZAP-5247G or B two-axle heavy load semi-trailer with a load capacity of 50,000kg. Trailer weight is 18,000kg, length 15.23m, width 3.38m and has rear loading ramps.

The basic MAZ-537 can tow the ChMZAP-5208 Heavy Load Trailer, this has a capacity of 40,000kg and has three axles and a tow-bar, rear loading ramps are provided. Length (w/o tow-bar) is 7.48m and width 3.2m. Or it can tow the ChMZAP-5212 Heavy Load Trailer which has 4 axles and a capacity of 60,000kg. Length (w/o tow bar) is 8.85m and width is 3.3m.

The MAZ-543 is similar to the MAZ-535 but has a split cab, the normal model has a stake type body and is used for the transportation of cargo. The MAZ-543 is also used as a transporter/erector/launch vehicle for the SCUD-B surface-to-surface missile, and the Scaleboard (SS-12) surface-to-surface tactical missile, there is also a fire-fighting model.

The MAZ-537 truck/tractor is also used as a towing vehicle for the following missiles: Sasin (SS-8) ICMB, Sawfly (SS-N-6) naval Poseidon type missile, Scarp (SS-9) ICBM, Scrag (SS-10) ICBM, Skean (SS-5) IRBM and the Galosh (anti-missile-missile). There is also a 8 × 8 truck called the NAMI-058 (Octopus).

Employment
Soviet Armed Forces.

Above: *The MAZ-537 (8 × 8) Tractor towing a ChMZAP-524G semi-trailer with a T-55 MBT.*

Left: *The MAZ-543 (8 × 8) Cargo Truck.*

Light Tracked Artillery Tractor AT-L

Soviet Union

Length: 5.313m
Width: 2.214m
Height: 2.18m
G/Clearance: .3m
Weight: 8,300kg (loaded)
6,300kg (empty)
G/Pressure: .61kg/cm²
Engine: Model YaAZ-M204VKr, 4-cylinder in-line water cooled diesel developing 135hp at 2,000rpm
Crew: 1 + 2
Speed: 42km/hr
Fuel: 300 litres
Gradient: 60%
Trench: 1.524m
V/Obstacle: .6m
Fording: 1m

Development

The AT-L replaced the earlier M-2 light artillery tractor. The first models of the AT-L, which appeared in 1953, had a suspension consisting of six small road wheels, three return rollers, idler at the rear and drive-sprocket at the front. The later model, which appeared in 1956, and has become known as the AT-L (modified) has five large road wheels, no return rollers, drive-sprocket at the front and idler at the rear, this model is the more common of the two.

The truck-type cab has seats for the driver and two passengers and is provided with an observation hatch in the roof. The rear cargo body can carry 2,000kg of cargo or eight men and is provided with a tailgate, bows and a tarpaulin cover. Its maximum towed load is 6,000kg. The AT-L was originally used to tow heavy mortars (160mm and 240mm), anti-aircraft guns, anti-tank guns and field artillery. In recent years however, 6 × 6 high mobility trucks have taken over this role.

Variants

There are models fitted with radar (including battlefield surveillance), a geological survey vehicle and van-type models (e.g. command). The AT-L can also be fitted with the OLT dozer attachment at the front of the vehicle and retain its load carrying capability.

Employment

Warsaw Pact Forces.

Below: *The latter model of the AT-L had no return rollers and five road wheels.*

Medium Tracked Artillery Tractor ATS-59

Soviet Union

Length: 6.28m
Width: 2.78m
Height: 2.5m (o/a)
2.3m (cab)
G/Clearance: .425m
Weight Loaded: 16,000kg (loaded)
13,000kg (empty)

G/Pressure: .52kg/cm²
Engine: Model A-650, V-12 water-cooled diesel developing 300hp at 1,700rpm
Crew: 1 + 1
Speed: 40km/hr
Range: 350km
Gradient: 60%

*The Medium Tracked
Artillery Tractor ATS-59*

Trench: 2.5m
V/Obstacle: 1.1m
Fording: 1.5m

Development

The ATS-59 first appeared in 1959 and is the replacement for the earlier AT-S tracked artillery tractor. The ATS-59 has a payload of 3,000kg and can tow a maximum load of 14,000kg. When used to tow artillery, the gun crew and the ammunition are carried in the rear cargo area. If not carrying cargo a total of 14 men can be seated in the rear. The suspension is similar to the AT-L and consists of five road wheels, drive sprocket at the front and idler at the rear, there are no track return rollers. The truck-type cab is provided with an observation hatch in the roof.

Variants

There are some ATS-59s in service with a hydraulically operated dozer blade mounted on the front of the vehicle. Some are also used to tow SAM missiles (e.g. the SAM-2) on semi-trailers, in this model the rear cargo area has been removed. The ATS-59 has also been built in Poland.

Employment

Warsaw Pact Forces including East Germany, Poland, Soviet Union; United Arab Republic.

Note: *A new Soviet tracked artillery tractor was seen for the first time on November 7th, 1972, at the annual military parade in Moscow. This new vehicle has similar suspension to the ATS-59 but has a much larger forward control type cab which could seat the complete gun crew.*

Medium Tracked Artillery Tractor AT-S   Soviet Union

Length: 5.87m
Width: 2.57m
Height: 2.85m (o/a)
2.535m (cab)
G/Clearance: .4m
Weight: 15,000kg (loaded)
12,000kg (empty)
G/Pressure: .58kg/cm²
Engine: Model V-54-T, V-12, water-cooled diesel engine developing 250hp at 1,500rpm
Crew: 1 + 6
Speed: 35km/hr
Range: 380km

Fuel: 420 litres
Gradient: 50%
Trench: 1.45m
V/Obstacle: .6m
Fording: 1m

Development

Although this vehicle entered service over 20 years ago it is still in service in quantity. The AT-S can carry 3,000kg of cargo and tow a maximum load of 16,000kg, it is often used as a prime mover for artillery including the 130mm M-1946 Field Gun and 152mm Howitzers. The AT-S is recognisable by its

large cab which is fully enclosed and has seats for a total of seven men, including the driver, the rear cargo body is provided with a tailgate, bows and a tarpaulin cover. A further ten men can be seated in the rear cargo area if required. The suspension of the AT-S consists of eight very small road-wheels arranged in pairs with the driving-sprocket at the rear and the idler at the front, there are four small return rollers.

Variants
AT-S with OST Dozer Blade — this is used for general engineer duties such as clearing topsoil. Its working speed is 4km/hr and its maximum work capacity is (for light soil) 80/90m³ per hour, this model retains its load carrying capability. There is also a model with the 240mm BM-24 (12-round) rocket launcher

(multiple) mounted on the rear of the vehicle in place of the cargo body. Some AT-S's have been fitted with various types of radar installation.

The Uragan-8 Snow and Swamp vehicle (8 × 8) uses the complete cab of the AT-S. The SBKh Snow and Swamp vehicle is also based on the AT-S vehicle, this has much wider tracks and features four pneumatic rubber road wheels in place of the standard suspension.

Employment
Warsaw Pact Forces, Finland, United Arab Republic and Yugoslavia.

Above: *The AT-S Medium Tracked Artillery Tractor.*

Heavy Tracked Artillery Tractor AT-T   Soviet Union

Length: 6.99m
Width: 3.17m
Height: 2.845m (o/a)
2.58m (cab)
G/Clearance: .425m
Weight: 25,000kg (loaded)
20,000kg (empty)
G/Pressure: .52kg/cm²
Engine: Model V-401, V-12, water-cooled diesel engine developing 415bhp at 1,600rpm
Crew: 1 + 3
Speed: 35km/hr
Range: 700km

Fuel: 1415 litres
Gradient: 60%
Trench: 2.1m
V/Obstacle: 1m
Fording: .75m

Development
The AT-T is also known as the M-50 or K-10 and is the largest of all the full tracked prime movers in service with the WPF. The cab of the vehicle has seats for four men and a further 14 men can be carried in the rear cargo area. The cargo area is provided with a drop down tailgate, bows and a

tarpaulin cover. Its normal load is 5,000kg and it can also tow a maximum load of 25,000kg. It is often used as a prime mover for the 203mm M-1955 Field Howitzer and was used to tow the 130mm M-1955 (KS-30) Heavy Anti-Aircraft Gun. The suspension system is similar to that employed on the T-34 tank and consists of five road wheels, driving-sprocket at the front and idler at the rear.

Variants

High Speed Ditching Machine BTM — This is basically an AT-T with the ETR-409 ditching machine mounted on the rear of the vehicle in place of the cargo body. In one hour it can dig a trench 1,120m long and .8m in depth, its maximum depth being 1.5m. Its loaded weight is 26,500kg. A later model, the BTM-TMG has been designed for digging trenches in frozen ground, this model has a loaded weight of 30,000kg.

Ditching Machine MDK-2 — This has been designed for digging weapon and vehicle pits. On the front of the vehicle is an OTT hydraulically operated dozer blade, and on the rear, in place on the cargo body, is the excavating machine.

Tractor Dozer BAT — This is used by engineer units for various roles including earth moving, levelling operations and clearing debris. Its maximum working speed is 8km/hr and it has a maximum weight of 25,500kg. As the dozer blade is mounted at the front it retains its load carrying capability. The latest model is the BAT/M, this has a hydraulically operated blade at the front and a small crane with a capacity of 2,000kg mounted at the rear in place of the cargo body. For travelling purposes the blade can be raised to the vertical position. Other models include some fitted with various types of radar (both artillery location and air defence) and crane models.

Employment

Warsaw Pact Forces, United Arab Republic, Yugoslavia.

Below: *The Soviet AT-T Heavy Tracked Artillery Tractor.*

GT-S (GAZ-47) Tracked Amphibious Cargo Carrier   Soviet Union

Length: 4.9m
Width: 2.435m
Height: 1.96m
G/Clearance: .4m
Track: 2.05m
Weight: 4,500kg (loaded)
3,600kg (empty)
Track Width: .3m
G/Pressure: .22kg/cm²
Engine: GAZ-61, 6-cylinder, in-line, water-cooled petrol engine developing 76hp at 3,000rpm. Later models have a 85hp engine.
Crew: 2 + 9

Speed: 35km/hr (road)
4km/hr (water)
Range: 725km
Fuel: 208 litres
Gradient: 60%
Trench: 1.3m
V/Obstacle: .6m
Fording: Amphibious

Development

The GT-S, or GAZ-47 as it is sometimes referred to, is a light, full tracked carrier designed to transport men

and materials over snow, mud or marsh type ground. The Soviet Army use it for both the load carrying and reconnaissance roles. Its maximum payload is 1,000kg and its maximum towed load is 2,000kg. The GT-S is often used to tow light artillery including the 57mm anti-tank gun (ZIS-2) and 120mm mortars. It is fully amphibious being propelled in the water by its tracks at a speed of 4km/hr.

Above: The GT-S Tracked Amphibious Cargo Carrier.

Variants
The LFM-RVD-GPI-66 is essentially a GT-S with its tracks removed and replaced by cylindrical screw-pontoons. This model, which is believed to have entered production, weighs 3,600kg empty and has a maximum payload of 1,200kg. Its water speed of 20km/hr is a vast improvement over the basic vehicle, its speed on snow covered surfaces is about 12km/hr. The United States has built similar vehicles for trials purposes, for example the Chrysler marsh screw and the later RUC (Riverline Utility Craft). A later development of the GT-S is the GT-SM for which there is a separate entry.

Below: The LFM-RVD-GPI-66 is basically a GT-S with its tracks replaced by cylindrical screw-pontoons.

Employment
Soviet Union.

GT-SM Tracked Amphibious Cargo Carrier Soviet Union

Length: 5.365m
Width: 2.582m
Height: 1.74m
G/Clearance: .38m
Track: 2.18m
Weight: 4,850kg (loaded)
3,750kg (empty)
Track Width: .3m
Engine: GAZ-71, 8-cylinder water-cooled petrol engine developing 115hp
Crew: 2 + 10
Speed: 50km/hr (road)
5km/hr (water)
Range: 300km
Gradient: 60%

Development/Variants

The GT-SM, which is also known as the GAZ-71, is the replacement for the earlier GT-S. The GT-SM has a more powerful engine and is slightly longer, it is easily recognisable as it has a total of six road wheels whereas the GT-S has only five. It has a fully enclosed front cab, this has a door either side and two hatches in the roof. The rear cargo area is normally enclosed by a cover with windows in it. A towing hook is provided at the rear and its maximum towed load is 2,000kg.

Employment
Soviet Union.

Above: *GT-SM Tracked Amphibious Cargo Carrier being loaded into a MIL MI-6 Helicopter during exercises in 1972.*

Left: *The GT-T Tracked Amphibious Cargo Tractor.*

GT-T Tracked Amphibious Cargo Tractor Soviet Union

Length: 6.5m
Width: 2.6m
Height: 2.2m
G/Clearance: .45m
Weight: 10,200kg (loaded) 8,000kg (empty)
Track Width: .36m
Engine: 1Z-6, 6-cylinder water-cooled diesel developing 200hp
Crew: 3 + 10
Speed: 45km/hr (road)
Range: 500km
Gradient: 60%
Trench: 1.5m
V/Obstacle: .6m
Fording: Amphibious

Development/Variants
The GT-T is the most recent Soviet tracked amphibious cargo vehicle and is much larger than the earlier vehicles. The above data should be taken as provisional. This unarmoured tracked vehicle can carry 2,000kg of cargo over marshy ground and its maximum towed load is 4,000kg. It is fully amphibious, its method of propulsion in the water is not known, although like the other tracked cargo tractors (GT-S) it probably uses its tracks.

The suspension consists of six road wheels with the drive-sprocket at the front and the idler at the rear. The road wheels are similar to those fitted to the PT-76 light amphibious tank. The driver and commander are seated at the front of the vehicle with the engine between them, the cab is fully enclosed and is provided with a single door each side, there is at least one hatch in the roof. If required the rear cargo area can be fitted with a cover to give some protection to the passengers. Some GT-Ts have been used for towing semi-trailers or SAM-2 anti-aircraft missiles. These vehicles are extensively used in the Soviet Far East and Arctic areas.

Employment
Soviet Union.

Note: *The GT-T is reported to be the basis for the new Soviet M-1970 APC/Multi-Purpose Tracked Vehicle.*

Amphibious Truck
485 (BAV) and 485A (BAV-A) (6 x 6)

Soviet Union

Length: 9.54m
Width: 2.485m
Height: 2.66m
G/Clearance: .28m
Track: 1.62m
Wheelbase: 3.668m + 1.12m
Weight: 9,650kg (loaded)
7,150kg (empty)
Engine: ZIL-123, 6-cylinder in-line water-cooled petrol engine developing 110hp at 2,900rpm
Crew: 2 + 25
Speed: 60km/hr (road)
10km/hr (water)
Range: 480km (land)
Fuel: 240 litres
Gradient: 60%
Trench: .6m
V/Obstacle: .4m
Fording: Amphibious
Tyres: 11.00 × 18 (BAV)
12.00 × 18 (BAV-A)

Development/Variants
During World War II the United States supplied the Soviet Union with a number of DUKWs. After the war the Soviet developed this further, the end result being the 485 (BAV) which first appeared in 1952, for a number of years this was known as the ZIL-485. The main improvement over the American vehicle was that the rear cargo compartment had been extended to the rear of the hull and a tailgate installed, this enabled loads to be loaded more easily. Like the American DUKW, the 485 is fully amphibious, being propelled in the water by a single propeller. Early models were based on the ZIL-151 chassis, these had large tyres with external tyre pressure regulation equipment. Later models used the ZIL-157 chassis with internal airlines for the tyre pressure regulation system.

Typical loads for the 485, both on land and water, would be 2,500kg of cargo, or 25 men, or a GAZ-63 truck or a 85mm anti-tank gun.

Employment
Warsaw Pact Forces.

Below: *A Russian BAV 485 (6 × 6) Amphibious Vehicle leaving the water.*

K-61 (GPT) Tracked Amphibious Cargo Carrier Soviet Union

Length: 9.15m
Width: 3.15m
Height: 2.15m
G/Clearance: .36m
Track: 2.6m
Weight: 12,550kg (loaded)
9,550kg (empty)
Track Width: .3m
G/Pressure: .4kg/cm²
Engine: YaAZ-M204VKr, 4-cylinder, in-line water-cooled diesel developing 135hp at 2,000rpm
Crew: 3
Speed: 36km/hr (road)
10km/hr (water)
Range: 260km
Fuel: 160 litres
Gradient: 60%
Trench: 3m
V/Obstacle: .65m
Fording: Amphibious

Development/Variants
The K-61, which is also known as the GPT, was first seen in 1950 and is currently being replaced by the more recent PTS tracked amphibian. The K-61 can be used to transport men and materials across rivers as well as being used in beach landings. At the rear of the vehicle is a large tailgate which folds down to ground level to facilitate loading. It can carry 3,000kg of cargo on land or 5,000kg of cargo in the water, or 40 fully equipped men, it can carry almost any of the Soviet artillery pieces up to 152mm, and 120mm mortars. The K-61 is propelled in the water by two propellers at the rear.

Employment
Warsaw Pact Forces, Vietnam.

Above: *K-61 Tracked Amphibious Cargo Carrier.*

PTS Tracked Amphibious Load Carrier Soviet Union

Length: 11.6m
Width: 3.5m
Height: 2.9m
G/Clearance: .5m
Track: 2.9m
Weight: 27,700kg (loaded)
17,700kg (empty)
G/Pressure: .6kg/cm²
Engine: A-712P, V-12, water-cooled diesel developing 250hp at 1,800rpm
Crew: 3
Speed: 40km/hr (road)
15km/hr (water)
Range: 300km (road)
Gradient: 60%

Trench: 2.5m
V/Obstacle: .65m

Development/Variants
The PTS (Medium Amphibious Transporter) is the replacement for the older tracked K-61. The PTS is easily distinguishable from the K-61 as it is much longer and larger than the earlier vehicle and has six road wheels whereas the K-61 has seven.

The cab is fully enclosed and is sealed for operation in a NBC environment, infra-red driving and observation equipment is fitted as standard. If required the rear cargo compartment can be fitted with bows and a tarpaulin cover. It can carry 5,000kg of cargo on land and 10,000kg of cargo in the water. The rear cargo compartment is provided with ramps so that vehicles can be easily loaded. Typical loads can include a URAL-375D 6×6 truck or a 100mm anti-tank gun. The PTS is propelled in the water by two propellers at the rear. The vehicle is often used in conjunction with the PKP amphibious trailer.

Employment
Warsaw Pact Forces.

Below: PTS Tracked Amphibious Load Carrier travelling across country.

Pegaso 3045D (4 x 4) 3-Ton Cargo Truck   Spain

Length: 6.47m
Width: 2.48m (w/o rear body)
Height: 2.617m (cab)
G/Clearance: .32m
Track: 1.9m
Wheelbase: 3.7m
Weight: 9,750kg (loaded)
6,750kg (empty)
Fording: 1m
Engine: Pegaso Model 9026/13, 6-cylinder diesel developing 125hp at 2,400rpm
Crew: 1 + 1
Speed: 72km/hr
Range: 650km
Fuel: 260 litres
Gradient: 65%
Angle Approach: 48°
Angle Departure: 34°
T/Radius: 6.96m
Tyres: 12.00 × 20

Development
This vehicle was designed by DAF of the Netherlands (the DAF designation is YA 414), and is similar to the DAF YA 314 vehicle used by the Netherlands Army but uses components of Spanish origin. Production commenced in 1970 and several thousand have been built to date. The first production vehicles were designated Pegaso 3045 and these were powered by a DAF petrol engine developing 134hp at 3,500rpm, it was fitted with a gearbox with 5F and 1R gears and a two-speed transfer case. It is distinguishable from the latter 3045D as it has single rear wheels. The 3045

has a top road speed of 90km/hr and could ford to a depth of .7m; most of these vehicles were issued to the Spanish Foreign Legion and the Air Force.

The second production model was the Pegaso 3045D, this is the more common of the two and is powered by a 6-cylinder diesel engine (built in Spain under licence from British Leyland), it has a gearbox with 6F and 1R gears and a two-speed transfer case, this model is recognisable by its twin rear tyres.

The Pegaso 3045DV has been specially developed for the Spanish Marines and can ford to a depth of 2m.

The Pegaso 3045D can carry 3,000kg of cargo across country or carry 6,000kg of cargo on roads, its towed load being 4,500kg. It has a DAF type cab with a removable canvas roof. The rear body is provided with a tailgate, bows and a tarpaulin cover.

Variants
Various other models are available including vehicle mounted crane, water truck, refueller, dump truck and mobile workshop.

Employment
In service with the Spanish Army, Air Force, Foreign Legion and Marines.

Above right: One of the prototypes of the Pegaso 3045 (4 × 4) 3-Ton Cargo Truck, note the ring mount for a 12.7mm anti-aircraft machine gun.

Pegaso 3050 (6 x 6) 6-Ton Truck

Spain

Length: 7.2m
Width: 2.48m (w/o cargo body)
Height: 2.62m (cab)
G/Clearance: .32m
Track: 1.9m(f)
Wheelbase: 4.05m + 1.39m
Weight: 14,500kg (loaded)
8,500kg (empty)
Engine: Pegaso Model 9101, 6-cylinder in line diesel engine developing 170hp at 2,000rpm
Crew: 1 + 1
Speed: 64km/hr
Fuel: 200 litres
Gradient: 83%

Angle Approach: 48°
Angle Departure: 44°
Fording: 1m
Tyres: 13.00 × 20

Development

The Pegaso 3050 has been developed for the Spanish Army from the earlier Pegaso 3040 (4 × 4) 4-ton truck which is still in service with the Spanish Army. The Pegaso 3050 has a cab similar to that fitted to the Pegaso 3045D (4 × 4) truck and is provided with a cargo body with dropsides, tailgate, bows and a tarpaulin cover. Its gearbox has 6F and 1R gears and a two-speed transfer case is provided.

Right: *The Pegaso 3050 (6 × 6) 6-Ton Cargo Truck.*

Two PTOs are provided, one on the gearbox and another on the transfer case.

The Pegaso 3050 can carry 6,000kg of cargo across country or 10,000kg on roads, its towed load is 12,000kg.

Variants
None in service yet.

Employment
Spanish Army.

Other Pegaso trucks include the Pegaso 3020, this was not used by the Spanish Army although 200 were purchased by Portugal.

Barreiros Series

Spain

	COMANDO (4 × 4)	PANTER 11 (4 × 4)	PANTER 111 (6 × 6)
Length:	4.78m	6.14m	6.74m
Width:	2.25m	2.25m	2.25m
Height:	2.42m (cab)	2.64m (cab)	2.95m (cab)
G/Clearance:	.26m	.34	.38m
Wheelbase:	2.675m	3.92m	—
Angle Approach:	47°	55°	—
Angle Departure:	40°	40°	—
Tyres:	9.00 × 20	11.00 × 20	11.00 × 20
Load Area:	3m × 2.2m	4.3m × 2.2m	—

Development/Variants

Although Barreiros have developed and built many 4 × 4 and 6 × 6 tactical trucks, only a small number have been purchased for the Spanish Army. The majority of Spanish Army trucks being manufactured by Pegaso or are received from the United States under MAP. In most cases both forward control (cab over engine) and standard types have been built.

Comando (4 × 4): This has a forward control-type cab and is powered by a Barreiros 6-cylinder diesel engine, this develops 90hp at 2,400rpm. This vehicle can carry 3,000kg of cargo on roads or 1,500kg of cargo cross-country. Only 25 of these were built for the Spanish Army.

Panter 11 (6 × 6): This is of the forward control-type and is powered by a Barreiros Model B26, 4-cylinder in-line diesel, this develops 115hp at 2,200rpm. Its transmission has 5F and 1R gears, a two speed transfer case is provided. It is used by the Spanish Army under the designation PB-125, Portugal has also purchased a small number of these trucks.

Panter 111 (6 × 6): This is very similar to the United States 5-ton (6 × 6) vehicle. It can carry 10,000kg of cargo on roads or 5,000kg across country. It is powered by a Barreiros Model B26 6-cylinder in-line diesel that develops 170hp at 2,200rpm. One model is called the 6618M, this is distinguished by its louvres on the bonnet side panels, the other model is the PB-185 which has no louvres. The 6618M is also used by Saudi Arabia, who purchased 200 from Spain. Models in service with the Spanish Army include a cargo truck and two types of multiple rocket system, the D-10 (ten rockets) and the E-21 (21 rockets).

Employment
Spanish Army.

Below: *A Barreiros Panter 111 with the E-21 Multiple Rocket System.*

Volvo L 3304 (4 x 4) Reconnaissance Vehicle   Sweden

Length: 4.4m
Width: 1.7m
Height: 1.5m
G/Clearance: .285m
Track: 1.34m
Wheelbase: 2.1m
Weight: 2,200kg (loaded)
1,570kg (empty)
Engine: Volvo B18A, 4-cylinder OHV petrol engine developing 68hp at 4,500rpm (1.78 litres)
Crew: 1 + 4
Speed: 90km/hr
Range: 330km
Fuel: 46 litres
Gradient: 60%
Angle Approach: 35°
Angle Departure: 32°
T/Radius: 5.7m
Fording: .8m
Tyres: 8.90 × 16

Development
The Volvo L3304 is used for both the reconnaissance and anti-tank roles. For the latter role it is fitted with the Bofors 90mm PV-1110 recoilless rifle. The Swedish Army designation for the Volvo L3304 is the Pvpjtgbil 9031. The first prototype was built in 1962. and production was undertaken from 1963 to 1965. It

is based on components of the Volvo 3314 (4 × 4) truck and uses the same engine as the Volvo 3314.

It can carry a maximum of 630kg of cargo, if required. It has a Volvo M-40 gearbox which has 4F and 1R gears and a two-speed transfer box. The front axle is rigid with a banjo of malleable iron with pressed-in tubular steel axles, fully floating drive shafts and Rzeppa universal joints. The rear axle is also rigid with a banjo of malleable iron with pressed in tubular steel axles and semi-floating drive shafts. The springs are of the semi-elliptical leaf type and double-acting hydraulic shock absorbers are provided on all four wheels. Hydraulic brakes are fitted front and rear. A spare wheel is fitted on the front of the vehicle and anti-roll bars are often fitted over the vehicle, the steering is of the cam and roller type.

Variants
Apart from the anti-tank model previously mentioned there are no other variants in service. This vehicle was not available commercially.

Employment
Swedish Army.

Above: *The Volvo L 3304 (4 × 4) reconnaissance vehicle.*

Volvo L 3314 (4 x 4) Laplander Truck   Sweden

Length: 3.985m
Width: 1.66m
Height: 2.09m (o/a)
G/Clearance: .285m
Track: 1.338m
Wheelbase: 2.1m

Weight: 2,450kg (loaded)
1,520kg (empty)
Load Area: 2.3m × 1.535m
Engine: Volvo B18A, 4-cylinder, OHV petrol engine developing 75bhp at 4,500rpm (1.78 litres)
Crew: 1 + 1

Speed: 90km/hr
Range: 330km
Fuel: 46 litres
Gradient: 60%
Angle Approach: 40°
Angle Departure: 40°
T/Radius: 5.4m
Fording: .8m
Tyres: 8.90 × 16

Development

The prototype Laplander was built in 1961, this was followed by the first production models in 1962. Although production has now been completed, Volvo have said that a slightly modified version of this vehicle will enter production again. The Laplander is of the forward control type and was built in two models — the pick-up (PU) and the hard top (HT). The Swedish Army designations are as follows: Pltgbil 903 (soft canvas top above waist line) and Pltgbil 903B which has an all-steel hard top.

The pick-up model is fitted with a two-seat cab and has a large cargo space with a hinged tailgate, a canopy can be fitted over the cargo compartment if required. The hard top model is built with an integral cab and has a total of six seats in the rear.

The gearbox fitted is the type M40, this is fully synchronised and has 4F and 1R gears. The auxiliary gearbox has four gear positions — these being neutral, four wheel drive in high ratio, four wheel drive in low ratio and reverse drive in high ratio.

The chassis is of all-steel, welded construction. The front and rear axles are of the rigid type with banjos made of malleable material and with pressed-in tubular steel axles. The rear axle has a semi-floating drive shaft and the front axle has fully floating drive shafts. The springs are of the semi-elliptical type and are fitted with double acting hydraulic shock absorbers front and rear.

Hydraulic brakes are fitted. The towing hook is of the spring loaded type and optional extras include hitch plate, power take off, speed governor for PTO and Rockinger type towing hook. The winch is mounted on the LHS of the chassis and can be run in both directions, its maximum pulling power is 2,100kg.

Variants

There are numerous variants. Those for military service include an anti-tank missile carrier, ambulance, fire-fighting vehicle and radio vehicle. It is also widely used commercially.

Employment

Norway, Sweden.

Below: *The Volvo L 3314 (4 × 4) Laplander truck.*

Volvo 4140 (4 x 4) 1-2 Ton Truck   Sweden

Length: 4.545m
Width: 1.87m
Height: 2.13m (hard top)
2.25m (soft top)
G/Clearance: .39m
Track: 1.541m
Wheelbase: 2.3m
Weight: 3,300kg (loaded)
2,400kg (empty)
Load Area: 2.49m × 1.67m
Engine: Volvo B-30, 6-cylinder petrol engine developing 145hp at 5,000rpm (2.98 litres)
Crew: 1 + 1
Speed: 100km/hr
Range: 550km
Fuel: 90 litres
Gradient: 60%
Angle Approach: 45°
Angle Departure: 45°
T/Radius: 5.8m
Fording: .9m
Tyres: 8.90 × 16

Development

In 1966 Volvo received a contract to develop a new family of light vehicles to carry 1 to 2.5-tons of cargo. To meet the requirements of larger payloads the chassis could be extended to 6 × 6 and 8 × 8 configurations. The prototype of the Volvo 4140 was built in 1966, this was powered by a B-20 engine which developed 94hp, this was later changed for a B-30 engine. The vehicle entered production late in 1974 and first production vehicles will go to the Swedish Army, civilian models will be available from late 1976. The cargo model, the 4140, has a cab of all-steel construction, the rear cargo body is also of all-steel construction and is provided with a tailgate, bows and a tarpaulin cover. If required the body above the waistline can be removed. The hard top model is called the Volvo 4141 (Swedish Army designation being TGB 11) and has seats for an additional five men.

The gearbox has 4F and 1R gears and a two-speed transfer box, front wheel drive is automatically engaged in low range. The rear axle is a rigid, pressed steel casing with drop-gear hub reduction and differential lock, the front axle is similar with Birfield constant velocity universal joints. The springs are of the semi-elliptical steel type combined with large hollow rubber springs front and rear. There are double-acting shock absorbers on all wheels and hydraulic brakes are provided. The chassis is of all-welded construction and optional extras include a

Below: *One of the prototypes of the Volvo 4140 (4 × 4) cargo trucks.*

side-mounted winch with a capacity of 2,500kg, fuel burning heater installation, 24V electrical system fully suppressed for radio to be installed and a power take off for drive to trailer axle.

Variants
One version of the basic 4140 will be used as an anti-tank vehicle and will replace the Volvo L3304s at present used for this role.

There is also a 6 × 6 model of the Volvo 4140 which is called the 4143, basic data of this is length 5.33m, width 1.9m, height 2.17m, weight empty 2,550kg and weight loaded 4,250kg. It is used as an ambulance or radio/command vehicle, Swedish Army designation is TGB 13. Also built were two prototypes of an amphibious model of the 4143 with a payload of 1,000kg, this did not, however, enter production. An 8 × 8 model has also been tested with a payload of 2,500kg.

There is also a 4 × 4 cargo model with a wheelbase of 2.53m and a payload of 2,000kg, and a 6 × 6 model with a reinforced chassis and springs with a wheelbase of 2.72m + 1.05m and a payload of 2,750kg. Both of these are fitted with a winch and are available either as LHD or RHD.

Employment
In service with the Swedish Army. Also tested by the British Army as Truck, General Service, 1-Tonne (4 × 4) Volvo.

Above: *One of the prototypes of the Volvo 4141 (4 × 4) vehicles.*

Volvo L 2204 (6 x 6) 1 ½ -Ton Truck　　　　　Sweden

Length: 5.86m
Width: 1.9m
Height: 2.56m (overall)
2.14m (cab)
G/Clearance: .27m
Track: 1.55m(f) 1.6m(r)
Wheelbase: 2.65m + 1.06m
Weight: 6,450kg (road loaded)
5,700kg (c/c loaded)
4,200kg (empty)
Load Area: 2.7m × 1.82m
Engine: Volvo Model A6, 6-cylinder OHV petrol engine developing 115bhp at 3,000rpm
Crew: 1 + 2
Speed: 80km/hr

Range: 300km (approximately)
Fuel: 90 litres
Angle Approach: 42°
Angle Departure: 40°
T/Radius: 8.16m
Tyres: 11.00 × 16

Development
This vehicle was designed by Volvo in the late 1940s, and the first prototype, which was called the TL21 was completed in 1950. The Volvo L2204 was in production for the Swedish Army from 1955 to 1959, the Swedish Army designation for the vehicle is Type 912 cross-country cargo vehicle.

It has been designed to carry 1,500kg of cargo for cross-country operations and 2,250kg of cargo for road operations. The cab is of all-steel construction and the windscreen can be lowered to the horizontal position if desired. The rear platform is also of steel construction with a recessed load surface, there are removable seats so that men can be carried if required. The rear platform is covered by a tarpaulin which has a support frame of tubular steel, if required the tarpaulin sides can be rolled up.

The gearbox has 4F and 1R gears and a two-speed transfer case (high and low), it also has a PTO for the winch which is mounted on the RHS of the chassis. This winch is of the worm-gear type and is fitted with an automatically operating check brake. It can be used both front and rear of the vehicle. The winch has a capacity of 4,000kg and is provided with 75m of 12mm cable, speed at 1,500rpm is 30m/min.

The front springs are of the semi-elliptical type and the rear springs are of the double cantilever type. Double acting telescopic hydraulic shock absorbers are fitted to the front axle. All six wheels are provided with hydraulic brakes.

Variants
Fire-fighting, signals and workshop models are in service.

Employment
Used only by the Swedish Army.

Above: *The Volvo L 2204 (6 × 6) 1½-Ton Cargo Truck.*

Volvo L 3154 (6 x 6) 3-Ton Cargo Truck   Sweden

Length: 7.15m
Width: 2.15m
Height: 2.95m (overall)
2.7m (cab)
G/Clearance: .37m
Track: 1.72m
Wheelbase: 3.3m + 1.25m
Weight: 10,320kg (loaded)
7,320kg (empty)
Engine: Volvo Model D96AS, 6-cylinder OHV diesel developing 150hp at 2,200rpm (9.6 litres)
Crew: 1 + 2
Speed: 75km/hr
Range: 300km (approximate)
Fuel: 120 litres

Angle Approach: 40°
Angle Departure: 42°
T/Radius: 9m
Tyres: 11.00 × 20

Development
The Volvo L3154 is used both as a cargo vehicle and a prime mover for artillery, for example the 155mm Model F Field Howitzer or the 150mm m/39 Field Howitzer. The prototype was completed in 1954 and the vehicle was in production from 1956 to 1962, it was not available commercially. The Swedish Army designation for the Volvo 3154 is L934.

The cab is of all steel construction and the rear cargo compartment can be fitted with bows and a

tarpaulin cover if required. It has a Volvo K12 gearbox with 5F and 1R gears and a two-speed transfer case. A winch with a capacity of 8,000kg is fitted as standard. Hydraulic brakes are provided in all wheels.

Variants
These include a fire and crash rescue vehicle which is

designated the 3154S, and the 3164 recovery vehicle. There was also a trials model with a powered trailer.

Employment
Swedish Army only.

Above: *Volvo L 3154 (6 × 6) truck towing 150mm m/39 Field Howitzer.*

SBA 111 (4 x 4) 4½-Ton Truck   Sweden

Length: 6.72m
Width: 2.49m
Height: 2.8m (cab roof)
G/Clearance: .4m
Track: 2.03m
Wheelbase: 4m
Weight: 13,650kg (loaded)
9,150kg (empty)
Load Area: 4.2m × 2.35m
Engine: DS11 LB03, 6-cylinder diesel engine developing 220hp at 2,200rpm (11 litres). If required the DS11 LB02 can be fitted.
Crew: 1 + 2
Speed: 90km/hr
Range: 635km
Fuel: 170 litres
Gradient: 60%
Angle Approach: 43°
Angle Departure: 38°
T/Radius: 8.9m
Fording: .8m
Tyres: 14.00 × 20

Development
The SBA 111 has been designed by the Scania Division of Saab-Scania. The first prototypes were completed in 1971 and the vehicle is scheduled to enter production late in 1975 with deliveries to the Swedish Army commencing early in 1976. The SBA 111 uses many components of the SBAT 111 (6 × 6) truck, such as wheels, axles, cab and gearbox. It has

been designed to carry 4,500kg of cargo both on road and cross-county, it can also tow a trailer with a maximum loaded weight of 6,000kg (cross-country), its climbing ability at gross weight with a trailer is 28%.

The winch is mounted on the right frame side member with differential carrier on the inside of the member and cable drum on the outside of the member, this enables winch operation both forwards and backwards. The winch has a maximum capacity of 5,900kg and is provided with 60m of cable.

The gearbox fitted is the Model GA 763 with a combination of six-speed hydraulic gearbox and mechanical two-speed transfer box with sockets for front and rear wheel drive and winch drive. Double-acting hydraulic telescopic shock absorbers are provided for both front and rear axles.

Details for the cab and cargo body are the same as those for the SBAT 111 truck.

Variants
None announced.

Employment
In production for the Swedish Army.

Above right: *The SBA 111 (4 × 4) 4½-ton cargo truck.*

Volvo L 4854 (4 x 4) 4 ½ - Ton Cargo Truck　　　Sweden

Length: 7.5m
Width: 2.28m
Height: 2.82m
G/Clearance: .25m
Track: 1.83m(f) 1.74m(r)
Wheelbase: 4.4m
Weight: 9,720kg (loaded)
6,720kg (empty)
Engine: Volvo D67C, 6-cylinder, OHV diesel developing 125hp at 2,400rpm (6.7 litres)
Crew: 1 + 2
Speed: 77km/hr
Range: 300km (approximately)
Fuel: 120 litres
Angle Approach: 38°
Angle Departure: 25°
T/Radius: 10m
Tyres: 10.00 × 20

Development
The Volvo L4854 is based on standard commercial components and is designated the Type 939 in the Swedish Army. The first prototype was built in 1960 and the vehicle was in production from 1961 to 1963.

The cargo body is provided with drop sides and a tailgate, and a winch with a capacity of 5,000kg is fitted as standard equipment. Some models have been fitted with a HIAB crane to assist in unloading supplies from the vehicle.

The vehicle has a Volvo K17 gearbox with 5F and 1R gears and a two-speed transfer case. If required twin 7.5mm machine guns can be fitted over the cab.

Variants
There are the following variants: Type 939BF cargo truck with a wheelbase of 5.2m Type 939AF cargo truck with a wheelbase of 4.4m and the Type 939E cargo truck with a wheelbase of 4.4m, this latter model has a longer cab than the other two variants.

Employment
Only in service with the Swedish Army.

The Volvo L 4854 (4 × 4) 4 ½ - Ton Cargo Truck with twin 7.5mm machine guns on the cab roof.

SBAT 111 (6 x 6) 6-Ton Cargo Truck   Sweden

Length: 7.75m
Width: 2.49m
Height: 2.8m (cab)
G/Clearance: .39m
Track: 2.03m
Wheelbase: 3.55m + 1.48m
Weight: 17,300kg (loaded)
11,300kg (empty)
Load Area: 4.72m × 2.35m
Engine: DS11 LB04, 6-cylinder diesel engine
developing 300hp 2,200rpm (11 litres)
Crew: 1 + 2
Speed: 90km/hr
Range: 570km (road)
Fuel: 170 litres
Gradient: 60%
Angle Approach: 43°
Angle Departure: 38°
Turning Radius: 11m
Fording: .8m
Tyres: 14.00 × 20

Development
The first SBAT 111s were delivered by the
manufacturers, Scania Division of Saab-Scania, for
trials, early in 1971. The second batch of vehicles was
delivered during the first quarter of 1972, and
production vehicles are due to be delivered to the
Swedish Army from the first quarter of 1976. The
SBAT 111 was previously known as the LBAT 110.
The vehicle has been designed to carry 6,000kg of
cargo on both road and cross-country and also tow a
trailer with a maximum weight of 12,000kg, it will

also be used to tow the new Bofors FH77 155mm
Field Howitzer.

Many of the components such as the cab, axles,
wheels and gearbox of the SBAT 111 are interchangeable with those of the SBA 111 truck (4 × 4).
The truck has all wheel drive and each axle has a
differential lock. The frame has torsional flexibility
and at maximum lurch it takes up one third of the
suspension travel. All wheels are provided with
hydraulic shock absorbers. The all-steel cab tilts
forward 55° to expose the engine and gearbox, the
cab is provided with a heating and ventilating
system. The engine, which is supercharged, has a
fuel pre-heater and a starter pilot. The batteries are of
the cold-start type and are carried in a heated and
insulated battery box. The hydraulic automatic
gearbox is integrated with the transfer box, this has
six gear positions — three hydraulic positions and low
and high mechanical positions. The transfer box is
also fitted with sockets for front and rear wheel drive,
winch drive and also with an extra PTO for the drive
of, for example, a loading crane. The rear cargo body
is provided with drop sides and a tailgate.

Variants
At the present time there are a number of variants
undergoing trials.

Employment
In production for the Swedish Army.

Below: *The SBAT 111 (6 × 6) 6-Ton Cargo Truck.*

Scania-Vabis (4 x 2) L-36A (L3642) Cargo Truck   Sweden

Length: 6.59m (chassis)
Width: 2.19m
Height: 2.76m
G/Clearance: .355m
Track: 1.85m
Wheelbase: 4.2m
Weight: 10,500kg (loaded)
4,580kg (empty)
Engine: Model D5, 4-cylinder diesel developing
102hp at 2,400rpm
Crew: 1 + 2
Speed: 77km/hr
Range: 450km
Fuel: 100 litres
Angle Approach: 36°
Angle Departure: 30°
T/Radius: 7.3m
Tyres: 8.25 × 20

provided with a heater. The rear cargo body is
provided with drop sides and a tailgate, some
vehicles have been fitted with a HIAB crane behind
the cab.

Variants
These include a shop/van with a fully enclosed rear
body.

Employment
Swedish Army.
   Scania-Vabis have also supplied the Swedish
Army with some 1,500 L50s with various types of
body. This has a wheelbase of 4.2m and is powered
by a D5 4-cylinder diesel engine which develops
110hp at 2,400rpm.

Development
This is basically a commercial model which was built
in two models, one with a wheelbase of 4.2m (L3642)
and the other with a wheelbase of 4.8m (L3648). The
first production vehicle was completed for the
Swedish Army in 1964 and the last in 1967, some 800
were built for the Army. It has a Model S-5-35
transmission with 5F and 1R gears, 2nd to 5th being
synchronised, there is no transfer box. All wheels are
provided with semi-elliptical springs and the front
wheels have double-acting hydraulic shock
absorbers. Air brakes are provided and there are two
circuits, one for the front wheels and the other for the
rear wheels. The cab is of all-steel construction and is

Below: *Scania-Vabis (4 + 2) L-36A (L3642) Cargo
Truck with HIAB crane.*

Scania-Vabis LA 82 (6 x 6) Artillery Tractor   Sweden

Length: 7.6m
Width: 2.61m
Height: 3.35m (inc. mgs)
2.9m (cab roof)
G/Clearance: .3m
Track: 2.01m(f) 1.89(r)
Wheelbase: 3.4m + 1.32m
Weight: 16,000kg (loaded)
11,200kg (empty)
Load Area: 2.45m × 2.45m
Engine: Scania DS-10, 6-cylinder diesel developing 220hp at 2,200rpm (10.26 litres)
Crew: 1 + 2
Speed: 75km/hr
Range: 750km (road)
Fuel: 260 litres
Gradient: 50%
Angle Approach: 41°
Angle Departure: 36°
T/Radius: 10.3m
Fording: .8m
Tyres: 11.00 × 20

Development
The prototype of the LA 82 was built in 1956 and this differed from the production vehicles in that it was powered by an 8-cylinder diesel engine. The LA 82, which is also known as the Ant Eater (*Myrsloken*), was in production from 1960 until 1963 and about 450 vehicles were built. The Swedish Army uses the LA 82 for towing artillery.

It has a gearbox with 5F and 1R gears and a two-speed transfer case. The steering is power-assisted and a winch with a capacity of 10,000kg is fitted, this leads out through the front of the vehicle. The rear body is provided with dropsides and a tailgate, a fully enclosed compartment is provided for the gun crew (ten men) and there is ample space for ammunition and stores. A 7.62mm machine gun is mounted on the roof of the vehicle.

Variants
The following models are in service:
Crane truck fitted with a turntable-mounted crane on the rear, this has a maximum lifting capacity of 20,000kg.
Recovery vehicle with a HIAB crane.

Employment
Used only by the Swedish Army.

Below: *Scania-Vabis LA 62 (6 × 6) Artillery Tractor.*

Right: *Scania-Vabis LA 82 (6 × 6) Crane Truck.*

Scania-Vabis LT 110S

Sweden

This 6 × 4 tractor was in production from 1968 to 1974 and is used by the Swedish Army in conjunction with the DAF YTS 10050 tank trailer (refer to page 107 for details), this is capable of carrying the Centurion and S tanks of the Swedish Army. The vehicle is provided with two 20-ton winches and is powered by a DS11 four-stroke, 6-cylinder, direct-injection diesel with an exhaust-driven turbocharger, this develops 285hp at 2,200rpm. It has a type GR 860 transmission with 5F and 1R gears and a two-speed transfer box, hydraulic power-assisted steering is provided. The Swedish Air Force uses some LS 110s as fuel tankers.

Below: Scania-Vabis LT 110S tractor towing a DAF YTS 10050 trailer with a Centurion MBT of the Swedish Army.

Scania-Vabis L75

Sweden

This 4 × 2 7-ton truck was in production from 1958 until 1963 and is used by the Swedish Army Engineers. It is powered by a D10, 6-cylinder diesel developing 165hp at 2,200rpm, and its transmission has 5F and 1R gears and a two-speed transfer box.

Scania-Vabis L76

Sweden

This 4 × 2 vehicle was in production from 1963 until 1968 and is used by the Swedish Air Force to carry the Bloodhoud 2 SAM. There is also a 6 × 4 model which is used by the Swedish Army to tow the DAF YTS 10050 tank semi-trailer.

Below: Scania-Vabis L T 76A tractor towing a DAF YTS 10050 trailer with a 155mm Bandkanon 1A SPG.

Volvo TP 21, L 2104 (4 x 4) Command Vehicle

Sweden

Length: 4.6m
Width: 1.9m
Height: 3m
G/Clearance: .27m
Track: 1.55m(f) 1.66m(r)
Wheelbase: 2.68m
Weight: 3,200kg (loaded)
2,850kg (empty)
Engine: Volvo ED, 6-cylinder, four-stroke, side-valve petrol engine developing 90hp at 3,600 rpm (3.67 litres)
Crew: 1 + 4
Speed: 105km/hr
Range: 300km (approximately)
Fuel: 76 litres
Angle Approach: 30°
Angle Departure: 30°
T/Radius: 6m
Tyres: 9.00 × 16

Development
The Volvo TP 21, L 2104 was developed by Volvo as a replacement for the earlier Volvo TPV m/43 vehicle which was rather similar in appearance. The prototype was completed in 1952 and the vehicle was in production from 1956 to 1959. The Swedish Army designation of the L 2104 is *Radiopersonterrängbil 915* (radio/command cross-country vehicle 915). It is used as a command and radio vehicle, hence the whip aerials on the roof of the vehicle.

A Volvo type E9 gearbox is fitted, this has 4F and 1R gears and a two-speed transfer case, there is a vacuum-operated differential lock.

Variants
There was a seven-seater model of the L 2104 built for trials purposes.

Employment
Swedish Army, not available commercially.

Above right: The Volvo TP21, L 2104 (4 × 4) Command Vehicle.

Volvo F88 (4 x 4) Recovery Vehicle

Sweden

Length: 7.1m
Width: 2.49m
Height: 3.05m (cab)
G/Clearance: 0.42m
Track: 2.01m(f) 2.07m(r)
Wheelbase: 4.2m
Weight: 12,480kg (unladen)
Engine: Volvo TD 100A, 6-cylinder, four-stroke diesel, OHV, developing 260 hp at 2,200rpm (9.16 litres)
Crew: 1 + 1
Speed: 90km/hr
Fuel: 300 litres
Angle Approach: 35°

Angle Departure: 22 ½ °
T/Radius: 16.8m
Tyres: 14.00 × 20

Development
The prototype of the Volvo F88 (4 × 4) recovery vehicle was completed in 1972 with the first production model following in 1973, approximately 50 of these have been built so far for the Swedish Army. It has a Volvo Type R61 fully-synchronised

Below: *The Volvo F-88 (4 × 4) recovery vehicle from the rear.*

gearbox with 8F and 1F gears. The gear lever has four forward and one reverse positions, changeover between high and low speed is carried out by means of a toggle switch on the gear lever.

The front axle is rigid with a banjo of nodular iron, the differential lock is operated from the vehicle dashboard. The springs are of the semi-elliptical leaf type and the front wheels have double acting hydraulic telescopic shock absorbers. Power steering is of the recirculating ball and nut type with coupled servo unit fitted.

The EKA C/D 10/15 recovery outfit is fitted to the rear. This includes a rear mounted MAL 15.5.3 winch with a maximum pull of 20,000kg and a front mounted winch model MR5 which has a maximum wire pull of 7,000kg. A HIAB 550 hydraulic crane is also fitted. There are earth anchors at the rear of the vehicle and stabilisers either side.

Variants
The F84 (4 × 4) is primarily used as a tow vehicle

although a cargo model has been built, basic data is as follows: length 5.25m, width 2.34m, height 2.65m, wheelbase 2.64, weight 6,070kg and it is powered by a Volvo Model TD50B engine developing 150hp.

The F88 (4 × 4) has also been tested with a cargo platform and canvas top and an F-88 (6 × 6) model with cargo platform will enter production this year, the first prototype F-88 (6 × 6) was completed in 1974. The FB-88 (6 × 4) is a standard vehicle and two of these were tested by the British Army some years ago. The FB-88 (4 × 2) and FB-88 (6 × 4) are in production as standard civlilian trucks.

Employment
In service with the Swedish Army.

Above: The Volvo F-84 (4 × 4) tow vehicle from the front.

Volvo BV.202 Mk 1 Load Carrier

Sweden

Length: 6.172m
Width: 1.759m
Height: 2.21m (overall)
G/Clearance: .3m
Track: 1.118m
Weight: 4,200kg (loaded)
2,900kg (empty)
G/Pressure: .85kg/cm²
Engine: Volvo B18, 4-cylinder petrol engine developing 91bhp at 5,300rpm
Crew: 1 + 1
Speed: 39km/hr
Range: 400km
Fuel: 156 litres
Gradient: 60%
V/Obstacle: .5m
T/Radius: 6.8m
Fording: Amphibious

Development
In 1957 the Swedish Army designed a tracked vehicle for use in snow conditions, two prototypes were built in 1958 and a further ten in 1960. In November, 1961, Volvo was awarded the contract to produce the vehicle and they subcontracted the order to one of their companies at Arvika, called Bolinder-Munktell. Production commenced in 1962.

The BV.202 is designed primarily for the transportation of men and equipment across snow and rough country. It is fully amphibious, water speed being 3.3km/hr. Normal road load is 1,000kg or 800kg across country. It consists of two tracked units connected by a universal coupling, the front units contain the engine, gearbox and steering system as well as the vehicle commander and driver. The rear part carries the load or eight/ten men. The vehicle can tow the Italian 105mm pack howitzer on skies and is used by the British Royal Artillery for this purpose. The gearbox has 4F and 1R gears and a two-speed transfer box. Other features include a body of welded steel, power-steering and heater units fitted in the front and rear units.

Variants
The BV.202 Mk. 2 is similar to the Mk. 1 except that it has a Volvo M-400 transmission in place of the earlier M-42, a different transfer case is also fitted. The Mk. 2 is powered by the Volvo B20 engine which develops 100hp at 5,300rpm. The BV. 203 is the BV.202 but with a 24V electrical system, hard top for the rear unit and is radio suppressed. Some Swedish army BV.202s have 78 litre fuel tanks which give them a range of 200km.

Employment
Used by the armies of Finland, Great Britain, Norway and Sweden. Also available to the civilian market. The British Army has the following special versions of the BV.202 — ambulance, 81mm mortar, Wombat, radio, command, REME, some are fitted with a 7.62mm GPMG on the roof of the front unit.

Note: *The Swedish Defense Material Administration has awarded a contract to Hägglund and Söner of Örnsköldsvik for the development of a new vehicle to replace the BV.202, this will be called the Bandvagn MINY and will consist of two bodies of reinforced plastic. It will be fully amphibious and will have a petrol engine, maximum road speed will be approximately 60/km/hr. It should be in production by 1979.*

Below: *The Volvo BV.202 Mk. 1 Load Carrier.*

Switzerland

Switzerland manufactures very few military trucks but has imported many vehicles from Austria, Britain, Germany and the United States, plus a few other countries. The Mowag company of Kreuzlingen have built a number of trucks for the Swiss Army including a number of 4 × 4 ¾-ton models with various bodies. Also Saurer and Berna have built a number of military trucks which are identical.

SAURER 2DM (AND BERNA 2VM)
Basic data of this 4 × 4 truck is length 7.37m, width 2.3m, height 3.2m, it is powered by a 6-cylinder diesel engine which develops 135hp, this gives it a top road speed of 74km/hr. Its empty weight is 7,100kg and its fully loaded weight is 12,000kg. A total of 160 litres of fuel are carried and its cab has seats for three men including the driver. Gearbox has 8F and 2F gears and a two-speed transfer case.

Wheelbase is 4.2m. This data relates to the models that were built between 1964 and 1973, earlier models were slightly different.

SAURER 2CM (AND BERNA 2UM)
Basic data of this 4 × 4 truck is as follows: length 5.9m, width 2.21m, height 3.14m, wheelbase 3.4m, weight loaded 9,000kg and empty weight of 5,500kg, load area is 4m × 2.04m. It is powered by a 4-cylinder diesel developing 75hp and this gives it a top road speed of 57km/hr. A winch with a capacity of 6,000kg is provided and this has 55m of rope.

SAURER 4CM (AND BERNA 4UM)
Basic data is length 6.39m, width 2.2m, height 3.14m, wheelbase 3.4m, load area 4.27m × 2.06m, weight empty 7,000kg and weight loaded 12,000kg. It is powered by a 6-cylinder diesel which develops 120hp, 160 litres of fuel are carried. The winch has a capacity of 7,000kg and is provided with 50m of

Above left: *The Saurer 2DM (4 × 4) 4½-Ton Truck.*

Centre left: *The Saurer 2CM (4 × 4) Truck.*

Below left: *The Saurer 4CM (4 × 4) Truck.*

Above: *The Saurer M4 (4 × 4) Artillery Tractor.*

Right: *The Saurer M6 (6 × 6) Cargo Truck.*

Below: *The Saurer M8 (8 × 8) Cargo Truck.*

rope. There is a tipper model of the 4CM which can carry 5,000kg and another model which is known as the 5CM tipper which can carry 6,000kg.

TRACTOR, ARTILLERY, 4 × 4 (SAURER M4) (2½-TON)

This 4 × 4 vehicle was in production by Saurer from 1952 to 1955. Basic data is as follows: length 5.2m, width 2m, height 3.14m, wheelbase 2.9m, weight 4,250kg empty and 6,500kg loaded. Powered by a 4-cylinder diesel which develops 75hp. Fuel tank holds 100 litres. Gearbox has 5F and 1R gears and a two-speed transfer case. A winch with a capacity of 2,500kg is fitted and this is provided with 70m of rope.

TRACTOR, ARTILLERY (SAURER M4) (1½-TON)

This was developed in 1946, basic data is length 5.2m, width 1.95, height 2.1m, wheelbase 2.9m, weight empty 4,200kg and weight loaded 5,700kg. It is powered by a 4-cylinder diesel which develops 70hp. Fuel tank holds 70 litres of fuel. Gearbox has

5F and 1R gears and a two-speed transfer case. Winch with a capacity of 2,500kg is provided with 90m of rope.

SAURER M6

This 6 × 6 vehicle was developed in 1939, basic data is length 5.46m, width 2m, height 3.05m, weight empty 6,870kg, weight loaded 9,370kg, load area 3.5m × 1.82m. It is powered by a 6-cylinder diesel engine which develops 85hp at 1900rpm, 90 litres of fuel. Tyres are 9.00 × 20s and the winch has a capacity of 6,000kg and has 55m of rope.

SAURER M8 (8 × 8)

This is a development of the M-6 (6 × 6) truck and was built from 1943 to 1945, basic data is as follows: length 5.88m, width 2m, height 3.05m, weight empty 7,410kg, weight loaded 10,910kg, load area 3.55m × 1.82m. Powered by a 6-cylinder diesel engine developing 100hp at 1,900rpm. Tyres are 9.00 × 20, fuel 150 litres, winch has a capacity of 6,000kg and is provided with 65m of rope.

M-274 Mechanical Mule

United States

Length: 2.98m
Width: 1.178m
1.193m (steering wheel)
.685 (platform)
G/Clearance: .292m
Wheelbase: 1.447m
Track: .95m
Weight: 830kg (loaded)
376kg (empty)
Load Area: 2.413m × 1.168m
Engine: 4-cylinder air-cooled petrol engine developing 25hp at 4,500rpm
Crew: 1
Speed: 40km/hr
Range: 180km

Fuel: 30.3 litres
Gradient: 60%
Angle Approach: 41°
Angle Departure: 36°
T/Radius: 3.048m
Tyres: 7.50 × 10
Fording: .2m

Development

The M-274 Mechanical Mule (full designation is truck platform, ½-ton) was developed in the early 1950s and was officially accepted for production in April, 1956 and since then it has been built by various companies. These companies include Willys, Baifield Industries of Carrollton, Texas (1965) and

One of the prototypes of the DAF Pony which was eventually built in the United States as the Mechanical Mule.

the Brunswick Corporation (1970). The data given left does differ from production, source, especially the engine fitted. Early vehicles were powered by the Willys A O53 4-cylinder petrol engine which developed 15bhp at 3,200rpm.

The vehicle has been designed to transport weapons, stores and ammunition for infantry, airborne and marine units and was extensively used in Vietnam. If required it can be fitted with the M-40 106mm recoilless rifle.

It consists of an aluminium platform mounted on two tubular members, bolted to the front and rear axles. The four aluminium wheels have low pressure tyres and no suspension system is fitted. The engine is at the rear of the vehicle, the steering assembly can be moved forward and lowered, so that the operator, following on foot, can drive from a standing or crouched position while operating the vehicle in reverse.

The gearbox has 3F and 1R gears and a two-speed transfer case. The M-274A4 has a guard for the transmission and transfer gearshift lever, the M-274A5 is powered by a 2-cylinder, horizontally opposed air cooled petrol engine which develops 13.5 HP at 3,000rpm and gives the vehicle a range of about 130km. The M-274A5 has a magnesium, rather than an aluminium chassis.

Employment
In service with the United States Army and Marines. Italy is reported to have some of these vehicles.

Below: *Mules of the United States Army armed with 106mm recoilless rifles.*

M-151 Series (4 x 4) ¼ -Ton Utility Truck   United States

	M-151	M-151A1	M-151A2	M-718A1	M-825
Length:	3.352m	3.371m	3.371m	3.631m	3.4m
Width:	1.58m	1.634m	1.634m	1.818m	1.942m
Height (o/a):	1.803m	1.803m	1.803m	1.94m	1.955m
Height (reduced):	1.332m	1.332m	1.332m	1.314m	—
G/Clearance:	.26m	.24m	.25m	.23m	.28m
Wheelbase:	2.159m	2.159m	2.159m	2.159m	2.159m
Track:	1.346m	1.346m	1.346m	1.346m	1.346m
Weight (loaded):	1,575kg	1,633kg	1,633kg	1,450kg	1,960kg
Weight (empty):	1,012kg	1,088kg	1,088kg	1,246kg	1,174kg
Load Area:	1.04m × .914m	1.04 × .914	1.04 × .914	—	—
Crew:	1+3	1+3	1+3	1+1	1+3
Speed:	106km/hr	104km/hr	104km/hr	106km/hr	80km/hr
Range:	482km	482km	482km	482km	342km
Fuel:	56 litres	56 litres	56 litres	56 litres	56 litres
Gradient:	75%	75%	75%	62%	50%
Angle Approach:	66°	65°	66°	67°	62°
Angle Departure:	37°	37°	37°	38°	33°
T/Radius:	5.486m	5.638m	5.638m	5.638m	5.638m
Fording:	.533m	.533m	.533m	.533m	.533m
Tyres:	7.00 × 16	7.00 × 16	7.00 × 16	7.00 × 16	7.00 × 16

Development

In March, 1951, the Ford Motor Company were awarded a contract to develop a new tactical vehicle. The first prototypes were completed in 1952, and a further six were built in 1954, these were known as XM-151s. In 1956 the XM-151E1 (steel) and XM-151E2 (aluminium) were built. The XM-151E1 was found to be the superior of the two vehicles and Fords were awarded a production contract in June, 1959, the first production models were completed early in 1960, these were known as M-151s. It is sometimes known as the MUTT (Military Utility Tactical Truck). Since 1959 it has been built by Fords (they built 18,000 a year in 1968-71 at their Highland Park plant) and Kaiser Jeep (later AM General Corporation of Wayne, Michigan), and by 1968 over 100,000 M-151s had been completed.

The M-151 is powered by a 4-cylinder petrol engine which develops 71hp at 4,000rpm. It can carry 362kg of cargo across country and 544kg of cargo on the highway, its towed load is 680kg cross-country and 907kg on the highway. Its suspension consists of coil springs with telescopic shock absorbers front and rear. The M-151s gearbox has 4F and 1R gears and a single-speed transfer case. It can be operated in 2 or 4 wheel drive and can be changed from 2 to 4 wheel drive whilst in motion.

There are many kits available for the M-151 and these include M-60 machine gun mount, Xenon searchlight, heater, hard top, 100amp alternator and a deep fording kit which enables it to ford to a depth of 1.524m.

If required the windshield can be folded down and the body can be enclosed with a removable canvas top, side curtains and doors.

Variants

M-151A1 from 1964 had improved suspension.
M-151A2 from 1970 had modified rear suspension, dual brake system, collapsing steering wheel, two speed wipers and modified lights.
M-151A2LC has a gearbox with 3F and 1R gears and a two-speed transfer case.
M-107 and M-108 are communications vehicles.
M-718 ambulance (and M-718A1), this has a crew of two and can carry one litter and three litter patients OR 2 litter and 2 seated patients OR 3 litter patients.
M-825 is fitted with the M-40 106mm recoilless rifle.
Trials versions include the XM-384 which was a 8 × 8 vehicle and the XM-408 which was a 6 × 6 vehicle.

Employment

Israel, Netherlands, United States.

Above left: *M-151 with communications equipment fitted.*

Above right: *M-151 with 7.62mm M-60 machine gun mounted in centre of the vehicle.*

Right: *The M-718 ambulance with rear open.*

M-38 Series (4 x 4) ¼-Ton Utility Truck

United States

	M-38	M-38A1	M-170
Length:	3.377m	3.517m	3.936m
Width:	1.574m	1.539m	1.536m
Height:	1.879m	1.85m	2.032m
Height (reduced):	1.379m	1.428m	—
G/Clearance:	.234m	.234m	.23m
Track:	1.247m	1.247m	1.247m
Wheelbase:	2.032m	2.057m	2.565m
Weight (loaded):	1,791kg	1,753kg	1,706kg
Weight (empty):	1,247kg	1,209kg	1,344kg
Crew:	1 + 3	1 + 3	1 + 1
Speed:	88.5km/hr	88.5km/hr	88.5km/hr
Range:	362km	450km	482km
Fuel:	49 litres	64.3 litres	75.7 litres
Gradient:	65%	69%	71%
Angle Approach:	55°	—	46°
Angle Departure:	35°	—	34°
T/Radius:	6.096m	5.892m	7.467m
Fording:	.939m + 1.879m	.939m + 1.778m	.381m
Tyres:	7.00 × 16	7.00 × 16	7.00 × 16

Development/Variants

Truck, Utility, ¼-Ton (4 × 4) M-38: The M-38 was developed after the end of World War II and was basically the civilian CJ-3A vehicle with modifications to suit it for military operations, these included a 24V electrical system and semi-floating rear axle. It can carry 363kg of cargo cross-country or 544kg of cargo on roads, its maximum towed load cross-country is 680kg and its maximum towed load on roads is 907kg. It is powered by a Willys Model MC 4-cylinder petrol engine which develops 60hbp at 4,000rpm. Its gearbox has 3F and 1R gears and a two-speed transfer box. It has an open body with a folding top, removable canvas doors and side screens, the windscreen folds down flat if required.

Truck, Utility, ¼-Ton, M-38A1: The M-38A1 entered service in 1951/52 and is powered by a Willys Model 4-cylinder engine developing 72bhp at 4,000rpm. It has the same load carrying and towing capability as the earlier M-38. Like the M-38, it can be fitted with a winch if required. Both the M-38 and M-38A1 can be fitted with deep fording equipment. The front axle is a full-floating, single reduction type equipped with a conventional differential with hypoid drive gears, the rear axle is of the semi-floating, single reduction type, with a conventional differential with hypoid gears. The front and rear suspension consists of semi-elliptical leaf springs.

The M-38A1C has a split windshield to provide space for the stowage of a recoilless rifle. There are no rear seats on the M-38A1C and the spare wheel has been moved from the rear to the RHS of the vehicle.

Truck, Ambulance, ¼-Ton (4 × 4), M-170: This has a longer wheelbase than the standard M-38 and in addition to its crew of two it can carry three stretcher patients or six sitting patients. It is powered by a Willys Model MD 4-cylinder petrol engine developing 68bhp at 4,000rpm.

MAP Vehicles: Many Jeeps have been purchased from Willys for overseas armies requirements, these include the CJ-3A, CJ-3B, CJ-5 (81''-2.057m wheelbase) and CJ-6 (101''-2.565m wheelbase). Jeeps built under MAP (i.e. with American money) are the M-606 series, these include the M-606A1, M-606A2 and M-606A3, most of which correspond to a commercial vehicle modified to military requirements. For example, in 1967/69 The Jeep Corporation built 3,579 M-606 for the MAP.

Employment

The M-38 series are used by numerous countries including Belgium, Canada, Denmark, Japan, Netherlands, Spain, Turkey, Israel and Vietnam. In addition it has been, and in some cases still is, being manufactured in a number of countries.

Top: *M-38A1 Jeep in use with the Spanish Army in 1971.*

Centre: *M-170 Ambulance in use with the Spanish Army in 1971.*

Bottom: *Willys jeep being used by the Indian Army in 1971.*

M-37 Series (4 x 4) ¾-Ton Cargo Truck United States

	M-37 Truck	M-43 Ambulance	M-201 Truck Maint.
Length:	4.81m	5.044m	5.174m
Width:	1.784m	1.866m	2.235m
Height:	2.279m	2.333m	2.323m
Wheelbase:	2.844m	3.2m	3.2m
Track:	1.574m	1.574m	1.574m
Weight (loaded):	3,493kg	4,617kg	4,218kg
Weight (empty):	2,585kg	3,952kg	4,218kg
Crew:	1+2	1+1	1+1
Speed:	88.5km/hr	88.5km/hr	88.5km/hr
Range:	362km	362km	362km
Fuel:	91 litres	91 litres	91 litres
Gradient:	68%	68%	68%
Angle Approach:	38°	32°	44°
Angle Departure:	32°	47°	32°
T/Radius:	7.01m	7.62m	8.229m
Fording:	1.066m	1.066m	1.066m
Tyres:	9.00 × 16	9.00 × 16	9.00 × 16

Development
During World War II the United States used large numbers of the ¾-ton T-214 truck which was popularly known as 'The Beep' production of this vehicle was undertaken by Dodge until shortly after the end of the war. It was again placed in production from 1950 to 1955. The M-37 was built by the Dodge Division of the Chrysler Corporation from 1958 until 1964, and was also built in Canada. It has been replaced in some units by the M-715 (4 × 4) 1¼-ton truck.

Variants
Truck, Cargo, ¾-Ton (4 × 4) M-37: This has an open steel body with folding troop seats, removable front rack, seat back and supports. A tarpaulin roof, which is supported by bows, covers the cargo compartment. Canvas front and rear curtain with windows are provided. The M-37 can carry 907kg of cargo on roads or 680kg of cargo across country, its towed allowance is 2,722kg on roads or 1,815kg across country. The basic chassis is designated M-53. The vehicle is powered by a Dodge 4-cylinder petrol engine that develops 78hp at 3,200rpm. Its gearbox has 4F and 1R gears and a two-speed transfer case. If required, a winch with a capacity of 3,402kg can be mounted at the front of the vehicle. Its normal fording depth is 1.066m and with the aid of a special kit it can ford to a depth of 2.133m. Later models were designated M-37B1s.

The M-601 is similar to the M-37 but has a wheelbase of 3.2m and is powered by a 6-cylinder engine that develops 102hp, some of these have been supplied to other countries under MAP, it can carry 1 tonne of cargo.

Truck, Command Post, ¾-Ton (4 × 4) M-42: This is similar to the M-37 but has side curtains with windows and a split-type rear curtain, map light and folding table. Radio and wire communications equipment can be easily installed in the vehicle.

Truck, Ambulance, ¾-Ton (4 × 4) M-43 and M-43B1: This has a panel-type closed steel body consisting of drivers' and patients' compartments which have a connecting door. It can transport four litter patients and an attendant or eight seated patients and an attendant. Some models have a winch with a capacity of 3,402kg. The M-43B1 has an aluminium body instead of a steel body and does not have a winch. The basic chassis is designated M-56 or M-56B1.

Truck, Maintenance, ¾-Ton (4 × 4) M-201 and M-201B1: This is used by the Signal Corps for telephone maintenance. The rear body is of all-steel construction with compartments for the stowage of tools and supplies. The M-201B1 is similar to the M-201 except that it has a winch with a capacity of 3,402kg. Its towed allowance on roads is 2,722kg or 1,815kg across country.

Employment
These are used by many countries including Austria, Canada, Greece, Pakistan, Spain, Vietnam and the United States, and various countries in South America.

Many countries also use the Dodge 'Power Wagon', this 4 × 4 vehicle is very similar in appearance to the M-37 but has a wheelbase of 3.2m and has a 6-cylinder engine.

Top: *Truck, Cargo, ¾-Ton (4 × 4) of the Spanish Army.*

Centre: *Truck, Cargo, ¾-Ton (4 × 4) with front mounted winch.*

Bottom: *Truck, Cargo, ¾-Ton (4 × 4) M-37 of the Canadian Armed Forces adapted to mount and fire the French SS-11B anti-tank guided missile.*

M-705 (4 x 4) 1 ¼ -Ton Truck

United States

Length: 5.327m
Width: 2.159m
Height: 2.413m (overall)
1.498m (lowest)
G/Clearance: .254m (axles)
Track: 1.701m
Wheelbase: 3.2m
Weight: 3,810kg (loaded)
2,494kg (empty)
Engine: Model OHC 6-230, 6-cylinder in-line, liquid-cooled petrol engine developing 132.5bhp at 4,000rpm
Crew: 1 + 1
Speed: 96.6km/hr (road)
Range: 362km
Gradient: 31%
Angle Approach: 45°
Angle Departure: 25°
T/Radius: 8.38m
Fording: .914m
Tyres: 9.00 × 10

Development
The M-715 truck was developed by Kaiser Jeep Corporation (now General Products Division-Jeep Corporation). It was developed from 1965 to replace the M-37 ¾-ton truck, the first contract was awarded on March 31st, 1966. Between January 1967 and May 1969 over 30, 500 M-715s were built. Issues to the Army started early in 1968. In December, 1969, 43 prototypes of an improved M-715 were ordered by the Army, these being in competition with the GM 1 ¼-ton XM-705 which was selected to replace the M-715, development of the XM-705 started in December, 1968.

The basic vehicle is used to transport men or cargo. Its payload on roads is 1,360kg or 1,134kg cross-country, its towed load is 1,288kg cross-country or 1,628kg on roads. The rear part of the vehicle is provided with a longitudinal folding bench seat each side which can seat four fully equipped men, the rear compartment is provided with bows and a canvas top.

The cab has a soft top and the windshield can be folded flat, a winch can be fitted at the front if required. Other kits available include a deep fording kit allowing it to ford to a depth of 1.524m, and an artic kit which includes a cargo and crew compartment enclosure kit, engine heater, crew heater and personnel heater.

The gearbox has 4F and 1R gears and a two-speed transfer case. The suspension consists of horizontal semi-elliptical type leaf springs and direct acting shock absorbers, hydraulic dampers are fitted.

Variants
The basic chassis and cab is designated M-724. The M-725 is the ambulance model and this can seat eight patients and one attendant or five litter patients (this is replacing the M-43 ambulance). The M-726 is a telephone maintenance truck. The M-142 is the M-715 with the S-250 shelter and is used as a communications vehicle.

Employment
United States Army.

Below: *The M-705 (4 × 4) 1 ¼ -Ton Truck.*

M-561 (6 x 6) 1 ¼ -Ton Truck

United States

Length: 5.76m
Width: 2.13m
Height: 2.31m (with cover)
1.65m (w/o cover)
G/Clearance: .38m
Track: 1.83m
Wheelbase: 2.05m + 2.16m
Weight: 4,490kg (loaded)
3,175kg (empty)
Load Area: 2.26m × 1.89m × .79m (maximum)
Engine: GM 3-53, 3-cylinder, in-line, liquid-cooled diesel engine developing 103hp at 2,800rpm
Crew: 1 + 1
Speed: 88km/hr
Range: 840km
Fuel: 151 litres
Gradient: 60%
Angle Approach: 62°
Angle Departure: 45°
T/Radius: 9m
Fording: Amphibious
Tyres: 11.00 × 18

Development
The M-561 (also known as the Gama Goat) was developed by Ling-Tempo-Vought and based on a design by Roger L. Gamaunt, who built prototypes of the vehicle in the late 1950s. The production contract was awarded to the CONDEC Corporation in June, 1968 and the first production vehicles were delivered in 1971.

The M-561 is a dual body configuration with six wheels and selectable two or six wheel drive. The two aluminium bodies are connected by an articulating assembly permitting them to arch vertically (pitch) and rotate (roll) with respect to each other. The vehicle is fully amphibious being propelled in the water by its wheels at a speed of 4km/hr. Its manual gearbox has 4F and 1R gears and a two-speed transfer case. The front and rear wheels have independent coil spring suspension, the centre wheels have a single-leaf spring and swing axle. Its payload is 1,134kg, maximum towed load is 2,721kg. A winch with a capacity of 3,628kg is fitted at the front of the vehicle.

Variants
A wide range of kits have been developed for the M-561 and these include heater kit, M-60 7.62mm machine gun kit, 100amp power source, mortar carrier, mounting a 106mm recoilless rifle, mounting the TOW missile system, radio or command vehicle, and an ambulance model which is designated M-792. The M-561 is also used to mount air defence radars for use with the Vulcan/Chaparral air defence system.

Employment
In service with the United States Army.

Below: *The M-561 (6 × 6) 1 ¼ -Ton Truck with front mounted winch.*

M-34 Series (6 x 6) 2 ½-Ton Cargo Truck   United States

	Cargo M-34 W/W	Cargo M-35 W/W	Dump M-47 W/W	Tractor M-48 W/W	Tractor M-275 W/W
Length:	6.984m	6.978m	6.324m	6.438m	5.791m
Width:	2.235m	2.438m	2.133m	2.375m	2.387m
Height (o/a):	2.819m	2.844m	2.641m	2.469m	2.469m
Height (cab):	2.641m	2.819m	2.082m	—	2.038m
G/Clearance:	.316m	.316m	.352m	.319m	.45m
Track:	1.767m(f)	1.778m(f)	1.767m(f)	1.767m(f)	1.767m(f)
Wheelbase:	3.302m + 1.193m	3.302m + 1.193m	2.997m + 1.193m	3.302m + 1.193m	2.997m + 1.193m
Weight (loaded):	10,223kg	10,537kg ·	10,981kg	8,360kg	8,432kg
Weight (empty):	5,529kg	5,842kg	6,287kg	5,372kg	5,257kg
Crew:	1 + 2	1 + 2	1 + 2	1 + 2	1 + 2
Speed:	93km/hr	96km/hr	93km/hr	93km/hr	93km/hr
Range:	563km	563km	482km	563km	563km
Fuel:	189 litres	189 litres	189 litres	189 litres	189 litres
Gradient:	64%	64%	65%	40%	57%
Angle Approach:	40°	38°	40°	40°	40°
Angle Departure:	43°	44°	76°	74°	84°
T/Radius:	10.972m	10.68m	10.07m	10.971m	10.972m
Fording:	.762m*	.762m*	.762m*	.762m	.762m
Tyres:	11.00 × 20	9.00 × 20	9.00 × 20	9.00 × 20	9.00 × 20

*with kit these can ford to a depth of 1.828m

Development/Variants

Truck, Cargo, 2½-Ton (6 × 6) M-34: This can carry a maximum of 4,693kg of cargo on paved roads. Its chassis is designated M-44 (a latter model is the M44A2 which has a diesel engine developing 140hp at 2,600rpm) and it has single rear wheels. Its rear cargo body is provided with bows, tarpaulin cover and a tailgate. If required, a winch with a capacity of 3,402kg can be fitted. The M-34 is powered by a Reo model OA-331, 6-cylinder petrol engine developing 146hp at 3,400rpm or a Continental model COA-331 engine developing the same hp. It has a gearbox with 5F and 1R gears and a two-speed transfer case. Production of these vehicles has been undertaken by various companies including Reo, Studabaker and more recently by AM General Corporation.

Truck, Cargo, 2½-Ton (6 × 6) M-35: Its basic chassis is designated M-45 and it has dual rear wheels. The M-35 has been designed to carry a maximum of 4,693kg of cargo on roads or 2,426kg of cargo across country, or 14 men. Its maximum towed load is 4,536kg on roads or 2,722kg across country. The rear cargo body is provided with a tailgate, bows and a tarpaulin cover, if required the sides can be removed. The M-35 has a Reo Model OA-331 6-cylinder in-line petrol engine (or a Continental COA-331) developing 146hp at 3,400rpm. The gearbox has 5F and 1R gears and a two-speed transfer box is fitted, if required a winch with a capacity of 4,536kg can be fitted. The M-35A1 has a Continental LDS-427-2 multi-fuel engine developing 140hp at 2,600rpm. The M-35A2 (chassis is M-45A2) has a diesel engine developing 130hp at 2,600rpm. The M-35A2C is similar to the M-35A2 but its dropsides and tailgate are interchangeable with

those of the M-54A2C 5-Ton Truck.

Truck, Cargo, 2½-Ton (6 × 6) M-36: This can carry a maximum of 4,536kg of cargo on roads or 2,268kg of cargo across country, its maximum towed load on roads is 4,536kg or 2,722kg across country. The M-36 has a winch with a capacity of 4,536kg whilst the M-36C has no winch, the basic chassis is the M-46 or M-46C. The cargo body is provided with removable sides, tailgate, bows and a tarpaulin cover. It has the same engine as the M-34 and M-35 vehicles and later models are the M-36A1 and M-36A2.

Truck, Dump, 2½-Ton (6 × 6) M-47: This has single rear wheels and its chassis is designated M-57, it is available with and without a winch. It can carry a maximum of 4,694kg on roads or 2,426kg across country. Same engine as the M-34 cargo truck. Its maximum towed load is 4,536kg on roads or 2,722kg across country.

Truck, Tractor, 2½-Ton (6 × 6) M-48: This is based on a M-45 chassis with dual rear wheels and is designed to tow a semi-trailer with a maximum weight of 7,711kg across country or 16,330kg on roads. It has the same engine as the M-34 cargo truck.

Above right: *Truck, Cargo, 2½-Ton (6 × 6) M-35.*

Right: *Truck, Cargo, 2½-Ton (6 × 6) M-35A2, note the different position of the headlamps.*

Truck, Tank, Gasoline, 2½-Ton (6 × 6) M-49: This is based on a M-45 chassis and carries a total of 4,542 litres of fuel. The M-49 has no rear pintle whereas the M-49C has pintle trailer connections. The M-49C weighs 6,330kg. Later models include the M-49A2C; on this model, bows and a tarpaulin cover can be fitted over the fuel tank.

Truck, Tank, Water, 2¾-Ton (6 × 6) M-50: This holds a total of 3,785 litres of water in two tanks of aluminium construction, insulated by fibre glass. Weight loaded is 8,077kg and weight empty is 6,902kg. Later models include the M-50A2 which can accept bows and a tarpaulin cover.

Truck, Dump, 2½-Ton (6 × 6) M-59: Basic chassis is the M-58 and it can carry 4,536kg of sand, rock, etc or roads or 2,268kg across country. It is available with and without a winch. Same engine as the M-34 and its wheelbase is 2.997m + 1.193m.

Truck, Wrecker, Light, 2½-Ton (6 × 6) M-60: This basically consists of the chassis M-45C with a hydraulically-operated crane mounted on the rear. The crane consists of the crane body, hydraulic pump and relief valve assembly, base plate and pivot post assembly, wing-motor, boom and outriggers. The lifting capacity of the boom with outriggers in position is 3,628kg or 1,814kg with boom fully extended. Maximum towed load is 2,721kg across country and 4,536kg on roads.

Truck, Wrecker, Crane, 2½-Ton, M-108: This is similar to the M-60 Wrecker but has a M-45 chassis.

Truck, Van, Shop, 2½-Ton (6 × 6) M-109: This is basically a M-45 chassis with a van body. Models include the M-109, M-109A1, M-109C, M-109D and M-109A3. The M-132 is a medical van.

Truck, Repair Shop Van, 2½-Ton (6 × 6) M-185A3: This consists of a M-45A2 chassis with a van type body on the rear. This is provided with work bench, tools, power system, etc.

Truck, Tractor, 2½-Ton (6 × 6) M-275: This is designed to tow semi-trailers up to 16,330kg on roads or 7,711kg across country. It is powered by a Reo Model OA-331 6-cylinder petrol engine developing 127hp at 3,400rpm (or a Continental COA-331 developing the same hp). It has a gearbox with 5F and 1R gears and a two-speed transfer case. Later models include the M-275A1 and M-275A2.

Above: *Truck, Cargo, 2½-Ton, M-36 of the Spanish Army.*

Below: *Truck, Tank: Gasoline, 2½-Ton (6 × 6) M-49 of the Spanish Army.*

Truck, Van, Expansible, 2½-Ton (6×6) M-292:
When it is stationary, the sides of the van can be extended to give additional working space, an air conditioning unit is installed. If required it can be equipped with a winch. Its maximum towed load is 2,721kg across country and 4,535kg on roads.

Truck, Cargo, Dump, 2½-Ton (6×6) M-342: The rear body of the M-342 is of welded sheet steel construction and is hydraulically operated, it includes a hinged cab-protector, combination side racks and troop seats. It has the same engine as the M-34 and a Spicer Model 3052 gearbox with 5F and 1R gears and a two-speed transfer case. It is available with and without a winch. Later models include the M-342A1 and M-342A2.

Truck, Maintenance Pipeline, 2½-Ton (6×6) M-756A2: This has a M-45A2 chassis with rear body that is provided with a winch, PTO and rear or side-mounted A frame.

Truck, Maintenance, Earth Boring and Pole Setter, M764: This consists of a modified M-45A2 chassis with PTO and modification of the chassis to accommodate rear winch support brackets, cab protector, out-rigger brackets, boring machine base and controls.

Truck, Maintenance, Earth Boring Machine and Pole Setter, 2½-Ton (6×6) V18A/MTQ: This has a M-44 chassis and a modified M-34 body.

Truck, Maintenance, Telephone Construction and Maintenance, 2½-Ton (6×6) V17A/MTQ: This is based on a M-44 chassis.

MAP Vehicle: This vehicle is built in the United States for foreign sales and includes the following: M-602 Cargo, M-607 Tractor, M-608 Dump, M-609 Shop Van, M-610 Water, M-611 Generator, M-621 Cargo (single rear wheels) and M-623 Shop/Van (single rear wheels). There are numerous other vehicles.

Employment

These are used by the United States and most overseas countries that have received U.S. aid including Spain, Norway, Korea, Greece, Austria and Turkey.

Above: *Truck, Dump: 2½-Ton (6×6) M-59 of the Spanish Army.*

M-211 (6 x 6) 2½-Ton Cargo Truck   United States

Length: 6.527m
Width: 2.438m
Height: 2.847m (o/a)
2.289m
Wheelbase: 3.352m + 1.219m
Track: 1.755m(f) 1.854m(r)
Weight: 10,510kg (loaded)
5,974kg (empty)
Load Area: 3.733m × 2.38m
Engine: General Motors Model 302, 6-cylinder petrol engine developing 130hp at 3,200rpm
Crew: 1 + 1
Speed: 88.5km/hr
Range: 483km
Fuel: 212 litres
Gradient: 60%
Angle Approach: 42°

Angle Departure: 37°
T/Radius: 10.515m
Fording: .762m
Tyres: 9.00 × 20

Note: *data is for vehicle fitted with winch.*

Development

The M-211 has been designed to carry 4,536kg of cargo on highways or 2,268kg of cargo across rough country. The basic chassis is designated M-207 and it has dual rear wheels, if required, a winch with a capacity of 4,536kg can be mounted at the front of the vehicle. The rear cargo body has removable bows, tarpaulin, sideboards and a tailgate. It can be fitted with a deep fording kit which enables it to ford to a depth of 1.981m.

It has a hydramatic transmission with 8F gears, each of the two ranges (high and low), has high, third and low gears.

Variants

Truck, Crane, 2½-Ton (6×6) M-214: This has a crane on the rear and its chassis is designated M-207C.

Truck, Dump, 2½-Ton (6×6) M-215: This has a similar chassis to the above but has a wheelbase of 3.048m + 1.219m. It also has the same engine as the M-211 but has a model 303M hydramatic transmission with 8F gears and a single-speed transfer box. A PTO drives the dump body hoist and the winch, if fitted. It has dual rear wheels and can carry 4,083kg on the highway or 1,700kg across country.

Truck, Tank, Fuel Servicing, 2½-Ton (6×6) M-217 and M-217C: This has three tanks holding a total of 4,542 gallons of fuel. The M-217C has a kit, segregator, aviation, gasoline. It has the same engine as the M-211 and dual rear wheels.

Truck, Light Wrecker, 2½-Ton (6×6) M-218: M-207C chassis, this differs from the M-207 in that it has walking beam suspension on the rear axle.

Truck, Van, Shop, 2½-Ton (6×6) M-220 Series: This has dual rear wheels and the same engine as the M-211. The cab is provided with a hard roof and a van type rear body. Empty weight is 6,842kg and its gross highway weight is 10,450kg. Its maximum towed allowance for highway operation is 3,629kg and for cross-country work, 2,772kg.

Truck, Tractor, 2½-Ton, (6×6) M-221: This has been designed to tow semi-trailers and its maximum load for cross-country operation is 7,711kg or 16,330kg for highway use. It has the same engine as the M-211 and its wheelbase is 3.048m + 1.219m, weight of the basic vehicle is 4,895kg. It can be fitted with a winch if required.

Truck, Tank, Water, 2½-Ton (6×6) M-222: This consists of the M-207 chassis with a tank holding 3,750 litres of water. A rear mounted water pump with a capacity of 265 litres/minute is operated via a propeller shaft from a PTO.

Truck, Cargo, 2½-Ton (6×6) M-135: This is similar to the M-211 but has single rear wheels and its chassis is designated M-133. Like the M-211 it can carry 4,536kg of cargo on highways or 2,268kg of cargo across country. A winch with a capacity of 4,536kg is fitted. Empty weight of the vehicle with winch is 5,778kg. Like other members of this family it can be fitted with a deep fording kit and a winterisation kit.

Employment

No longer in front line service with the United States Army but in service with a number of overseas forces. These have also been built in Canada for the Canadian Armed Forces, and the British Army uses some of these for troops training in Canada.

Above: *The M-215 (6 × 6) 2½-Ton Cargo Truck.*

M-656 (8 x 8) 5-Ton Truck   United States

Length: 7.06m (w/o winch)
Width: 2.438m
Height: 2.946m (overall)
1.981m (reduced)
G/Clearance: .304m
Track: 1.961m
Wheelbase: 1.473m + 3.758m + 1.473m
Weight: 12,564kg (loaded)
7,847kg (empty)
Load Area: 4.572m × 2.235m × .635m
Engine: Model CX-LDS-465-2, 6-cylinder liquid-cooled, turbo-charged multi-fuel diesel developing 200bhp at 2,800rpm
Crew: 1 + 1
Speed: 80.46km/hr
Range: 515km
Fuel: 303 litres

Gradient: 60%
Angle Approach: 55°
Angle Departure: 64°
T/Radius: 12.2m
Fording: Amphibious
Tyres: 16.00 × 20

Above: *The M-656 (8 × 8) 5-Ton Truck with front mounted winch and tarpaulin in position.*

Below: *The M-656 (8 × 8) 5-Ton Truck with drop sides down and ready for loading.*

Development

The M-656 (development designation XM-656) was developed by the Special Military Vehicle Operations Division of the Ford Motor Company from the early 1960s. It was classified as Standard 'A' in April, 1966, although development had not been fully completed. The first production contract was awarded to Ford in January, 1968, for 500 vehicles, most of which were for the Pershing surface-to-surface missile system. First deliveries of the M-656 were made in November, 1968.

It can carry 4,536kg of cargo cross-country or up to 10,160kg on roads, towed load is 5,897kg. The sides and rear of the vehicle fold down for loading purposes and the sides have built in seats which can also assist in loading purposes. It is fully amphibious and special inflatable air seals prevent water seepage at the cab and cargo box openings, it is propelled in the water by its wheels. The cab is of aluminium construction. A winch with a capacity of 9,072kg and 60.9m of cable can be fitted at the front of the vehicle.

The suspension is of the bogie type with parallelogram torque arms and tapered three-leaf springs. Air brakes are fitted and the steering is hydraulic power assisted on the front four wheels. The transmission fitted is the TY-200-6, 6F and 1R gears, fully automatic with a two-speed transfer case.

Special kits developed for the M-656 include a MG mount kit, slave kit, cold weather and artic kits, windshield defogging kit, 100-Amp Alternator kit, slinging kit, air brake hand control kit and cargo box height extension kit.

Variants

The basic vehicle is the M-656 (8 × 8) cargo truck but very few of these have so far been built. The Pershing missile system uses the following vehicles: M-791 van used as the Battery Control Centre, M-656 carrying the Programmer-Test Station/ Power Station and the M-757 tractor towing the Pershing missile which is mounted on an erector/ launcher. Other models projected include a dump truck and a wrecker.

Employment

Used only by the United States Army.

M-809 Series (6 x 6) 5-Ton   United States

	M-814 Cargo W/W	M-817 Dump W/W	M-819 Wrecker W/W	M-820 Van	M-821 Transport
Length:	9.962m	7.237m	9.125m	9.144m	9.892m
Width:	2.438m	2.774m	2.482m	2.482m	2.921m
Height:	2.983m	2.831m	3.352m	3.466m	2.87m
G/Clearance:	.295m	.288m	.295m	.295m	.355m
Wheelbase:	5.46m +1.371m	4.241m +1.371m	5.46m +1.371m	5.46m +1.371m	5.409m +1.422m
Track:	1.869m	1.869m	1.869m	1.879m	1.949m
Weight (loaded):	20,964kg	20,333kg	—	19,462kg	22,353kg
Weight (empty):	11,600kg	11,080kg	15,395kg	12,477kg	13,100kg
Crew:	1+2	1+2	1+2	1+2	1+2
Speed:	84km/hr	84km/hr	84km/hr	84km/hr	84km/hr
Range:	563km	644km	483km	483km	500km
Gradient:	61%	31%	32%	41%	40%
Angle Approach:	35°	35°	36°	46°	37°
Angle Departure:	24°	—	55°	24°	24°
Tyres:	11.00 × 20	11.00 × 20	12.00 × 20	11.00 × 20	14.00 × 20

Development

The M-809 series of 5-ton trucks are now in widespread service with the United States Army, the current manufacturer is AM General Corporation of Michigan.

The basic chassis is designated M-809 and a wide range of bodies are available. A wide range of kits are available, these include deep fording kit, thermal barrier, closure hard top, winterisation personnel heater kit, winterisation power plant kit, 'A' frame and slave receptacle kit. Their normal powerplant is a Cummings diesel engine. They are available with or without a front mounted winch.

Variants

M-813, 5-Ton (6 × 6) Cargo Truck: This can carry a maximum of 4,536kg of cargo cross-country or 9,072kg of cargo on roads, its towed allowance is 6.804kg cross-country or 13,608kg on roads. The rear cargo area has a flat floor, removable side racks, tailgate, troop seats, six bows and a tarpaulin cover. The M-813A1 has dropsides and tailgate that are interchangeable with those of the M-35A2C 2½-Ton Truck.

M-814, 5-Ton (6 × 6) Cargo Truck (LWB): This long wheel base truck has a body of welded steel construction with removable side racks, troop seats,

ten tarpaulin bows, tarpaulin cover. It can carry 9,072kg of cargo on roads or 4,536kg of cargo across country, its towed allowance is 13,608kg on roads and 6,804kg across country.

M-815, 5-Ton (6 × 6) Bolster Truck: Payload on roads is 4,536kg or 9,072kg across country. Towed allowance as M-813.

M-816, 5-Ton (6 × 6) Wrecker: This has a revolving hydraulic crane on the rear with an extending boom, outriggers are provided to stabilise the vehicle when the crane is being operated.

M-817, 5-Ton (6 × 6) Dump Truck: This has an all steel dump body which is hydraulically operated.

Top: *The M-818, 5-Ton (6 × 6) Tractor.*

Above: *The M-817, 5-Ton (6 × 6) Dump Truck.*

M-818, 5-Ton (6 × 6) Tractor: This can tow a semi-trailer with a maximum weight of 11,340kg on roads or 6,804kg across country.

M-819, 5-Ton (6 × 6) Tractor Wrecker: Basic chassis is the M-811A1, the crane has a telescopic boom. Towed allowance is 13,608kg on highways and 9,076kg across country.

M-820, 5-Ton (6 × 6) Van: This consists of chassis M-811A2 with an expanding van body on the rear, this is provided with two hot air heaters. The M-820A2 has a hydraulic tailgate.

M-821, 5-Ton (6 × 6) Bridge Transport: Chassis M-812, this is used for transporting bridge-building equipment.

Employment
United States.

Above: *The M-813, 5-Ton (6 × 6) Cargo Truck.*

M-54 Series (6 x 6) 5-Ton Cargo Truck   United States

	M-51 Dump	**M-52 Tractor**	**M-54 Cargo**	**M-55 Cargo**
Length:	7.146m	6.933m	7.974m	9.797m
Width:	2.463m	2.463m	2.463m	2.463m
Height:	2.809m (o/a)	2.638m (o/a)	2.946m (o/a)	2.98m (o/a)
Height:	2.231m	2.231m	2.231m	2.231m
G/Clearance:	.267m	.267m	.267m	.267m
Track:	1.869m(f) 1.828m(r)	1.869m(f) 1.828m(r)	1.869m(f) 1.828(r)	1.869m(f) 1.828m(r)
Wheelbase:	3.555m + 1.371m	3.555m + 1.371m	3.86m + 1.371m	4.775m + 1.371m
Weight (loaded):	19,351kg	8,616kg	13,582kg	15,451kg
Weight (empty):	10,209kg	—	9,046kg	10,915kg
Crew:	1 + 2	1 + 2	1 + 2	1 + 2
Speed:	84km/hr	80.5km/hr	84km/hr	84km/hr
Range:	785km	483km	344km	344km
Fuel:	416 litres	416 litres	295 litres	295 litres
Gradient:	70%	77%	50%	65%
Angle Approach:	52.5°	52.5°	37°	37°
Angle Departure:	69°	68°	38°	23°
Fording:	.762m + 1.981m	.762m	.762m + 1.981m	.762m + 1.981m
Tyres:	11.00 × 20	11.00 × 20	11.00 × 20	11.00 × 20

Development
The M-54 series of 6 × 6 trucks, which are also known as the M-39 series, this being the designation of the chassis, were developed after the end of World War II. They replaced vehicles in the 4, 5, 6 and 7 ½-ton class. Production commenced in 1950 and, in 1962, the petrol engine was replaced by a diesel engine, in 1963 the diesel engine was replaced by a multi-fuel engine. The M-54 series has been manufactured by a number of companies including

Mack, International and Kaiser Jeep (now AM General Corporation). A wide variety of kits is available for this range including a personnel heater, machine gun mount, deep fording kit, thermal barrier and a hard top closure kit. Similar vehicles have been built in Italy by Fiat, as the OM 6600/CP56 and in Spain by Bairreiros Diesel, as the Panter 11.

Variants

Truck, Cargo, 5-Ton, M-41: This has single rear wheels and can carry a maximum of 6,804kg, its maximum towed load on roads is 13,608kg or 6,804kg across country. A winch with a capacity of 9,072kg is fitted. The M-41 is powered by a Continental 6-cylinder petrol engine developing 196hp at 2,800rpm, this gives it a top speed of 95km/hr and a range of 450km. Its transmission has

5F and 1R gears and a two-speed transfer case is fitted.

Truck, Dump, 5-Ton (6 × 6) M-51: This is powered by a Continental Model R-6602 engine developing 196bhp at 2,800rpm.

Truck, Tractor, 5-Ton (6 × 6) M-52 and M-52A1: Basic chassis is designated M-61. The M-52 is designed to tow semi-trailers, 6,804kg cross-country and 11,340kg on roads. The M-52 is powered by a Continental R-6602, 6-cylinder engine developing 224bhp at 2,800rpm, whilst the M-52A1 is powered by Mack Model ENDT-673, 6-cylinder diesel developing 211bhp at 2,100rpm. Both hard top and

Top: *Truck, Cargo, 5-Ton (6 × 6) M-54A2 with winch.*

Above: *Truck, Wrecker: Medium, 5-Ton (6 × 6) M-543A2.*

179

soft top models are available, as are models with and without a winch. Both models have a gearbox with 5F and 1R gears and a two-speed transfer case.

Truck, Cargo, 5-Ton (6 × 6) M-54: This has dual rear wheels and is designed for general cargo duties and may be seen with a hard or soft top and with or without a winch. It can carry a maximum load of 9,072kg on roads or 4,536kg across country, its maximum towed load is 13,608kg on roads or 6,804kg across country. The M-54 is powered by a Continental Model R-6602 6-cylinder petrol engine developing 196bhp at 2,800rpm and has a Spicer transmission with 5F and 1R gears and a two-speed transfer box. The M-54A1 is powered by a Mack ENDT-673 6-cylinder diesel developing 205bhp at 2,100rpm. The M-54A2 had a multi-fuel engine.

Truck, Cargo, 5-Ton (6 × 6) M-55: This is a LWB cargo truck and can carry 9,072kg of cargo on roads or 4,536kg of cargo across country, its maximum towed load is 6,804kg across country and 13,608kg on roads. It has the same engine and transmission as the M-54. The rear cargo body is of all-steel construction except for the troop seats and the hardwood middle layer in the floor. Later models are the M-55A1 and M-55A2.

Truck, Wrecker, Medium, 5-Ton (6 × 6) M-62: The basic chassis is designated M-40C. The M-62 has been designed to tow, salvage and recover disabled vehicles. On the rear of the chassis, which has dual wheels, is a hydraulically-operated crane, the hydraulic system of which is run off the main engine. The vehicle can tow a maximum 9,072kg cross-country or 13,608kg on roads. It is powered by the same engine as the M-54 and later models include the M-62A1 and M-62A2.

Truck Cargo, Van, 5-Ton (6 × 6) M-64, M-64A1 and M-64A2. Truck, Tractor, Wrecker, 5-Ton (6 × 6) M-246: Basic chassis is the M-63C, on the rear of this is mounted a hydraulic crane with a telescopic boom, boom jacks are provided for the support of the boom when lifting. The crane, which is an Austin-Western has a traverse of 360°, length of boom retracted is 3.504m or 7.924m fully extended.

Truck, Van, Expansible, M-291, M-291A1 and M-291A2. Truck, Stake, Bridging, 5-Ton (6 × 6) M-328. Truck, Wrecker, Medium 5-Ton (6 × 6) M-543: This is essentially a M-40C chassis with a Gar Wood hydraulic crane with a capcity of 4,536kg mounted on the rear, outriggers are provided for support. Later models are the M-543A1 and the M-543A2, this latter was classified in 1963 when the LDS-465 multi-fuel engine was introduced.

Chassis, Truck, 5-Ton (6 × 6) M-139: This chassis is used for a variety of roles such as M-139 for bridge building equipment, M-139C for Honest John missile system and the M-139D which is similar to the M-139C but has high reduction axles to increase tractive effort. Same engine as the M-54 cargo truck.

Truck, Bolster, 5-Ton, M-748, M-748A1 and M-748A2.

Employment

This series of vehicle are in widespread service with United States and Allied Forces.

Above: *Italian CP56 carrying bridge construction equipment.*

M-125 (6 × 6) 10-Ton Cargo Truck

United States

Length: 8.089m
Width: 2.895m
Weight: 3.282m (o/a)
2.819m (cab)
G/Clearance: .523m
Track: 2.006m(f)

Wheelbase: 3.834m + 1.524m
Weight: 22,680kg (loaded)
13,608kg (empty)
Load Area: 4.267m × 2.438m
Engine: Le Roi Model T-H844, 8-cylinder petrol engine developing 297bhp at 2,600rpm

Crew: 1 + 1
Speed: 69km/hr
Range: 531km
Fuel: 736 litres
Gradient: 60%
Angle Approach: 30°
Angle Departure: 45°
T/Radius: 10.97m
Fording: .76m
1.981m (prepared)
Tyres: 14.00 × 24

Development/Variants

The M-125 was developed in the early 1950s, its development designation being XM-125. This vehicle uses many components of the M-123 10-Ton Tractor. The M-125 has been designed to tow the 8'' Howitzer and the 155mm Gun and is still used for this purpose in many parts of the world. It is also used for carrying cargo and the rear body is provided with bows, tarpaulin cover and a tailgate. Hoists are provided for handling the ammunition. When being used in the cargo role this vehicle can carry a maximum of 15,876kg of cargo. It is provided with a gearbox with 5F and 1R gears and a two speed transfer case. A winch with a capacity of 20,412kg is mounted behind the front fender.

Late production models were known as M-125A1s, a long wheel base model was built and this was designated XM-124, this did not however enter service. There was also to have been a dump truck, the M-122, but this did not enter service.

Employment

United States and many overseas countries including Greece and Turkey.

Above: The M-125 10-Ton Cargo Vehicle.

M-123 (6 x 6) 10-Ton Tractor Truck   United States

Length: 7.315m
Width: 2.895m
2.87m (o/a)
Height: 2.87m (o/a)
2.336m (reduced)
G/Clearance: .403m
Track: 2.006m(c)
Wheelbase: 3.834m + 1.524m
Weight: 14,628kg (empty)
15,876kg (empty — late models)
Engine: Le Roi Model T-H844, 8-cylinder petrol engine developing 286bhp at 2,600rpm
Crew: 1 + 1
Speed: 67km/hr
Range: 486km
Fuel: 563 litres
Gradient: 60%
Angle Approach: 52°
Fording: .762m

1.981m (with kit)
Tyres: 14.00 × 24

Development

The M-123 was first manufactured by Mack in 1955 but the vehicle is currently being produced at the Scotia, New York plant of the Condec Corporation. The vehicle is designed to tow semi-trailers carrying armoured fighting vehicles and for the movement of heavy general equipment and cargo, its maximum highway load is 61,235kg and its maximum off-highway load is 36,287kg. Its gearbox has 5F and 1R gears and a two-speed transfer case. Two winches with a capacity of 20,412kg are provided. The M-123 is closely related to the M-125 10-Ton Truck. The M-123 is normally used in conjunction with the Semi-Trailer, Tank Transporter, 45-Ton, 8 Wheel, M-15A1 or the Semi-Trailer, Tank Transporter, 50-ton, 8 Wheel M-15A2. The M-15A1 can carry

vehicles or equipment up to 40,823kg in weight whilst the M-15A2 can carry vehicles up to 45,359kg in weight. The M-15A2 differs from the earlier M-15A1 in that it has a redesigned and reinforced chassis, a wider body to accept heavier tanks, track guides have been installed and the stowage compartment at the forward end of the trailer have been removed. The brakes on the semi-trailer are operated by compressed air from the truck tractor. Basic data of the M-15A2 is as follows: weight empty 19,323kg, length overall 11.721m, width 3.809m and height 2.971m.

Variants
M-123 has dual midship winches and high mounted fifth wheel.

M-123C has a single midship winch and low mounted fifth wheel.
M-123D has dual midship winches and low mounted fifth wheel.
M-123A1C has a diesel engine in place of the petrol engine.

Employment
United States and many overseas countries.

Above: The Truck, Tractor, 10-Ton (6 × 6), M-123 with M-15A2 semi-trailer.

M-520 (4 x 4) 8-Ton Cargo Truck United States

Length: 9.753m
Width: 2.743m
Height: 3.396m
2.438m (reduced)
G/Clearance: .59m
Track: 2.203m
Wheelbase: 5.968m
Weight: 18,500kg (loaded)
10,240kg (empty)
Load Area: 4.977m × 2.482m
Engine: Caterpillar Model D333, 4-cycle, 6-cylinder turbo-charged diesel developing 213hp at 2,200rpm
Crew: 1 + 1
Speed: 48.28km/hr
Range: 650km
Fuel: 416 litres
Gradient: 60%
Angle Approach: 35°
Angle Departure: 41°
T/Radius: 8.3m
Tyres: 18.00 × 33
Fording: Amphibious

Development
In 1958 The Caterpillar Tractor Company started the

development of this range of high mobility amphibious load carriers, usually known as GOER's. The first prototype, designated XM-520 was completed in 1959. A further three were built in 1961, these being followed by a further 23 (13 cargo, 8 tanker and 2 wreckers) GOERs which were completed in 1963/64. Most of these went to Germany for extensive trials, and then, in 1966, to Vietnam. In both cases the vehicles performed very well.

The GOER cargo truck is designed to carry 8,260kg of cargo on both road and cross-country, it is fully amphibious being propelled in the water by its wheels at a speed of 5.3km/hr. The GOER basically consists of two bodies joined together by a hitch, the front body contains the cab, engine and transmission (this has 6F and 1R gears), and the rear body carries the load. A maximum load of 8,260kg can be carried and to facilitate loading the sides and rear of the cargo body can be operated. A winch with a capacity of 4,535kg is mounted at the front of the vehicle.

Variants
M-559 Truck, Tank, Fuel Servicing: This has a similar chassis to the basic M-520 but carries 9,463

litres of fuel. It is provided with three reels, left, right and centre. Space is also provided for two additional drums of fuel, like the M-520, it is fully amphibious. **M-553, Truck, Wrecker:** This has a 5.409m boom with a .914m extension and a total traverse of 360°. Manually operated outriggers are provided and it is fully amphibious.

812 M-520 cargo trucks, 117 M-553 wreckers and 371 M-559 tankers. They are now in service with the United States Army.

Employment

The first production contract for GOERs was awarded to Caterpillar in May, 1971, this being for

Below: *The M-553, Truck, Wrecker is a member of the GOER family of vehicles.*

M-116 Amphibious Cargo Carrier   United States

Length: 4.778m
Width: 2.085m
Height: 2.01m (overall)
1.625m (lowest)
G/Clearance: .355m
Width over Tracks: 1.993m
Wheelbase: 2.616m
Weight: 5,942kg (loaded)
3,574kg (empty)
Engine: Chevrolet 283, 8-cylinder (V-8), liquid cooled petrol engine developing 160hp at 4,600rpm
Crew: 1 + 11
Speed: 59.5km/hr (road)
6.43km/hr (water)
Range: 480km
Fuel: 246 litres
Gradient: 60%
Trench: 1.473m
V/Obstacle: .457m
G/Pressure: .22kg/cm²

Development

The M-116 (also known as the Husky) was developed as a replacement for the World War II

Weasel (M-29C) tracked carrier. Development started in 1956 and in 1957 a contract was awarded to the Pacific Car and Foundry Company of Renton, Washington, to build four prototypes of the T-116, which after further development, became the M-116. Production which has now been completed, was undertaken by Pacific Car and Foundry. The vehicle is capable of operating across rough ground, sand, snow and ice, and inland waterways. It is fully amphibious being propelled in the water by its tracks. It can carry 1,360kg of cargo in the rear compartment and tow a maximum load of 1,088kg. When being used as a personnel carrier the M-116 can carry 11 men in winter gear or 13 in summer gear, in addition to the driver.

A winterisation kit is available which enables the M-116 to be operated in temperatures as low as -65°F. A winch with a capacity of 2,268kg is mounted at the front of the vehicle. Its suspension is of the torsion bar type.

Variants

There are no variants of the basic M-116 in service. The chassis of the M-116 was however used as a basis for the development of the RAMS (Remote

Area Mobility Study) series of armoured vehicles including the XM-729 and XM-733.

Employment
The M-116 is used by the United States Army. The United States Marine Corps have had some for trials purposes.

Above: *M-116 Amphibious Tracked Cargo Carrier undergoing trials with the United States Marine Corps.*

M-548A1 Tracked Cargo Tractor

United States

Length: 5.752m
Width: 2.686m
Height: 2.679m (cab roof)
1.93m (w/o cab)
G/Clearance: .406m
Width over Tracks: 2.54m
Wheelbase: 2.819m
Weight: 12,000kg (loaded)
6,554kg (empty)
Engine: GMC Model 6V53, 6-cylinder liquid-cooled diesel developing 210hp at 2,800rpm
Crew: 1 + 3
Speed: 64.3km/hr
5.6km/hr (water)
Range: 482km
Gradient: 60%
Trench: 1.676m
V/Obstacle: .609m
G/Pressure: .5kg/cm²

Development
The M-548A1 tracked cargo carrier has been developed by the FMC Corporation and is based on components of the M-113 armoured personnel carrier. Production of it commenced in March, 1966.

The M-548A1 has a maximum payload of 5,443kg and a maximum towed load of 6,350kg. It is fully amphibious being propelled in the water by its tracks. A winch with a capacity of 9,072kg is fitted. If required the rear body can be fitted with bows and a tarpaulin cover, the cab roof, sides, front and rear can be removed. A ring mount with a 12.7mm or a 7.62mm machine gun can be fitted over the cab.

The M-548A1 is often used as an ammunition carrier in support of the M-107, M-109 and M-110 self-propelled guns.

Variants
There are a number of variants in service including the M-730 Chaparral anti-aircraft missile system, M-727 Hawk missile launcher vehicle, M-45 flame-thrower fuel carrier which is used to support the M-132A1 flame-thrower, the Lance missile system comprises the loader-transporter M-688 and the self-propelled launcher M-752 (vehicle designation M-667).

Employment
Australia, Canada, Greece, Israel, Italy, Spain, United States.

A M-548A1 Tracked Cargo Carrier of the Australian Army.

M-8A1 and M-8A2 Full Tracked High Speed Tractor   United States

Length: 6.733m
Width: 3.314m
Height: 3.048m
G/Clearance: .488m
Wheelbase: 3.965m
Weight: 24,948kg (loaded)
17,009kg (empty)
Load Area: 3.987m × 2.907m
Track Width: .533m
Engine: Continental AOS-895, 6-cylinder air-cooled petrol engine developing 863bhp at 2,800rpm. M-8A2 has fuel injection.
Crew: 1 + 8
Speed: 64.4km/hr
Range: 290km
Fuel: 852 litres
Gradient: 60%
Trench: 2.133m
V/Obstacle: .762m
G/Pressure: .58kg/cm²
Fording: 1.066m

Development/Variants

This tractor was developed towards the end of World War II and entered service in the late 1940s. It has a hull of welded sheet metal construction and its maximum load is 7,937kg, its maximum towed load is 17,690kg. The rear cargo area is provided with bows and a tarpaulin cover. Many vehicles were fitted with a dozer blade at the front and a hoist at the rear. A winch with a capacity of 20,412kg is provided, and there is a roof mount for a 12.7mm anti-aircraft machine gun. It can tow various types of artillery including 75mm and 90mm anti-aircraft guns and the 155mm Gun M-59.

The suspension of the vehicle consists of torsion bars and there are six double-disc wheels each side, the drive-sprocket is at the front and the idler at the rear, there are four track return rollers. The tracks are steel backed with rubber.

The engine is at the front of the vehicle as is the General Motors Corporation (Allision Division) CD 500-3 cross-drive transmission.

Employment

A number of countries including Japan.

Note: *The Second World War M-4 and M-5 Tractors are still used by a number of countries.*

Below: *M-8A2 High Speed Tractor of the Japanese Self Defence Force towing a 155mm M-59 gun.*

LARC-5 (4 x 4) Amphibious Cargo Carrier   United States

Length: 10.668m
Width: 3.149m
Height: 3.034m (overall)
2.374m (reduced)
G/Clearance: .609m (hull)
Track: 2.565m
Wheelbase: 4.876m
Weight: 14,038kg (loaded)
9,502kg (empty)
Load Area: 4.876m × 2.971m
Engine: Early models had a 8-cylinder petrol engine developing 300hp at 3,000rpm, later models had a

Cummins V-8 diesel developing 300hp.
Crew: 1 + 2
Speed: 48.2km/hr (road)
Range: 400km (road)
Fuel: 545 litres
Gradient: 60%
Angle Approach: 28.5°
Angle Departure: 26.5°
T/Radius: 11.124m
Fording: Amphibious
Tyres: 18.00 × 25

A LARC-5 of the
Australian Army.

Development
The LARC-5 (Lighter, Amphibious, Re-Supply, Cargo, 5-Ton (4 × 4) has been developed to carry 4,536kg of cargo, or 15-20 fully equipped troops, from ships off shore to land and inland areas. Design work on the vehicle was started in 1958 by the Borg-Warner Corporation and seven prototypes were built between 1959 and 1960. The first production contract was awarded on June 6th, 1961 and a total of 950 LARC-5s were built between 1962 and 1968. Manufacturers were Le Tourneau Westinghouse and the Consolidated Diesel Corporation.

The hull of the LARC-5 is of welded aluminium construction, and it is propelled in the water by a propeller, this gives it a top speed of 16km/hr and a range in the water of approximately 60km.

At the front of the vehicle is the operator's cab, in the centre is the load area which is flat, if required fabric curtains, reinforced with standard wire rope can be installed on each side of the cargo deck. The transfer transmission compartment is below the cargo deck and at the rear is the engine compartment. A fixed fire extinguisher is fitted in the engine compartment. Two manual bilge pumps are provided as is an emergency tiller, anchor, anchor line and mooring lines.

Variants
None in service, although various trials versions have existed.

Employment
Argentina, Australia, Germany, United States.

LARC-15 (4 x 4) Amphibious Cargo Carrier   United States

Length: 13.716m
Width: 4.419m
Height: 4.724m
4.165m (reduced)
G/Clearance: .74m
Wheelbase: 6.362m
Weight: 34,100kg (loaded)
20,500kg (empty)
Load Area: 7.315m × 4.114m
Engines: 2 × 4-cycle, V-8 Cummins diesels developing 300hp at 3,000rpm
Crew: 1 + 1
Speed: 50km/hr (road)
Range: 550km (land)
Fuel: 1,363 litres
Gradient: 40%
Angle Approach: 33°
Angle Departure: 22°
T/Radius: 13.716m
Fording: Amphibious
Tyres: 24.00 × 29

Development
The LARC-15 (Lighter, Amphibious, Resupply, Cargo, 15-Ton) was developed by the Ingersoll-Kalamazoo Division of the Borg-Warner Corporation who built a total of three prototypes. The first

production contracts were awarded to the Military Products Division of the Fruehauf Corporation.

The LARC-15 can carry 13,608kg of cargo on both land and water including Conex containers and vehicles such as 6 × 6 trucks and, like the LARC-5 it is designed to transport cargo from ships offshore to beaches or inland areas; it can also operate in marshland and swamp.

Whilst in the water it is propelled at a speed of 15km/hr by a four-bladed propeller and the water range when loaded is 120km, or 142km when unloaded. It is capable of operating in 3.048m surf. Transition from marine drive to land drive, during landing operations is made without loss of momentum.

The hull of the LARC-15 is of welded aluminium construction. The engine room and cab are at the rear, the transmission being below the cargo area. The ramp is at the front of the vehicle and is hydraulically operated, as is the steering and winch. The driver can select two or four-wheel drive as required.

Employment
Germany, United States.

Above right: *LARC-15 of the United States Army approaching land carrying a 6 × 6 truck.*

LARC-60 (4 x 4) Amphibious Cargo Carrier

United States

Length: 19.024m
Width: 8.111m
Height: 6.07m
G/Clearance: .711m
Weight: 97,000kg (loaded)
37,000kg (empty)
Load Area: 12.75m × 4.165m
Engine: 4 × 6-cylinder GM diesel engines developing 165hp (each)
Crew: 8
Speed: 33km/hr (road, unloaded)
Range: 980km (road, unloaded)
Gradient: 40%
T/Radius: 23.774m
Fording: Amphibious
Tyres: 36.00 × 41
Fuel: 2,271 litres

Development

The LARC-60 (Lighter, Amphibious, Resupply, Cargo, 60-Ton) was the first of the post-war amphibious vehicles, and like the LARC-5 and LARC-15, it was developed to transport men, supplies or vehicles from ships offshore to inland areas. The development contract for the LARC-60 (which was originally called the BARC) was awarded to the Pacific Car and Foundry Company in December, 1951.

The LARC-60 can normally carry 60-tons of cargo on both roads or afloat (or 200 men,) although in an emergency it can carry 100-tons of cargo. Cargo is loaded overhead or via the hydraulically operated ramp at the front of the vehicle. Whilst on land each of the four engines drives one of the front wheels and whilst afloat the two starboard engines drive the starboard propeller and the two port engines the port propeller. The two propellers are located in tunnels under the hull.

The wheels are driven through Allison torque converters and torqmatic transmissions. Steering (which is powered) on land is accomplished by turning the entire column-and-wheel assemblies which turn in pairs, both fore and aft.

The water speed of the LARC-60 loaded is 11km/hr or 12km/hr when unloaded.

Variants
None

Employment
United States.

Below: *A LARC-60 (4 × 4) Amphibious Cargo Carrier of the United States Army.*

Yugoslavia

The Yugoslav automotive industry has grown considerably in recent years. Most of the new vehicles are of foreign design and are manufactured under licence in Yugoslavia. Vehicles of this type used by the Yugoslav Army include the following:

FAP 4 GAE-1 (4 × 4): This is made under licence from Saurer of Austria and can carry a maximum of 5,000kg of cargo on roads. It is powered by a FAP E water-cooled diesel engine, this develops 90hp and gives the vehicle a top road speed of 71km/hr.

FAP 6 GAF-L (4 × 4): This is also built under licence from Saurer of Austria and can carry a maximum load of 7,000kg on roads. The FAP 6 is being replaced by the new FAP 10 series of 4 × 2 vehicles which feature a cab of the forward control type.

FAP 1314S (4 × 4): This again is built under licence from Saurer of Austria and can carry a maximum of 8,000kg of cargo on roads. It is powered by a 6-cylinder water-cooled diesel engine which develops 145hp and gives the vehicle a top road speed of 68km/hr.

FAP 2020BS (6 × 6): This forward control type vehicle is used extensively by the Yugoslav Army. It can carry 8,000kg of cargo on both roads and cross-country and, like most current Soviet tactical trucks,

is fitted with a central tyre pressure regulation system. The FAP 2220BDS is similar and is powered by a model 2F/002A 6-cylinder diesel engine which develops 200hp and gives the vehicle a top road speed of 60km/hr.

TAM 1500 (4 × 4): This is one of the more recent Yugoslav vehicles and is intended primarily for military use. It is powered by a TAM 413 4-cylinder diesel engine (built under licence from West Germany), this develops 110hp and gives the vehicle a top road speed of 90km/hr. It can carry 1,500kg of cargo on secondary roads or 2,000kg of cargo on the highway.

TAM 5000 DV: This 4 × 4 military truck is similar to the civilian TAM 4500 series of 4 × 2 vehicles which are manufactured under licence from Klockner-Humbolt-Deutz of Germany. The TAM 5000 DV is powered by a model F4L 514 V-6 air-cooled diesel engine which develops 85hp. The vehicle can carry a maximum cargo of 5,000kg and is fitted with a central tyre pressure regulation system.

Zastava (4 × 4) AR-51: This is essentially the Fiat Campagnola built under licence in Yugoslavia, refer to the Italian section for full details.

China

The first Chinese truck plant was completed in 1956 and by the end of 1959 was turning out about 50,000 vehicles a year, this plant was built under the first five year plan. Under the 2nd five year plan a further seven plants were built. Few details are available at the present time on Chinese vehicles although the

following models have been mentioned: JN-150 Huang Ho 7-Ton dump truck, CA-10 Chieh Fang 3-Ton Truck, CA-10 Chieh Fang 4-Ton Truck, CN-130 3-Ton semi-trailer truck and the Ching Kang Shan 2½-ton truck.

Photo Credits

Aèrospatiale (France) 30(B)
Alvis (Great Britain) 87, 88
Australian Army 7, 9, 69(B), 184(B), 186
Austrian Army 12, 13, 14, 15, 16
Auto-Union (Germany) 50(B)
Berliet (France) 2, 33, 39, 40, 42, 43, 44, 45, 46(T)
Bolinder-Munktell (Sweden) 157
British Leyland (Great Britain) 78
British Ministry of Defence (Army) 85
Canadair (Canada) 21(T)
Caterpillar (United States) 183
Citroen (France) 37, 38(T)
DAF (Netherlands) 100, 101, 102, 103, 104, 105, 106, 107, 108, 141(T)
E.C.P. Armées (France) 30(T), 36, 38(B)
Engesa (Brazil) 20
Faun-Werk (Germany) 50(T), 58(B), 59(T), 60, 63, 64, 65, 66
Finnish Army 26, 27
FN (Belgium) 17, 18, 19
Foden (Great Britain) 82, 83
Ford (Germany and United States) 54, 162, 163, 175
German Army 51, 55, 61, 62
Indian Army 165(B)
Italian Army 90, 91, 92, 93, 94
Japanese Self Defence Force 96(B), 97, 98, 99

Laird (Great Britain) 77(B)
Magirus-Deutz (Germany) 57, 58(T)
Mercedes-Benz (Germany) 52, 53, 56
Pegaso (Spain) 141(B)
Reynolds Boughton (Great Britain) 75(B)
Rover (Great Britain) 67, 68, 69(T), 70, 71(T + C), 73
Saviem (France) 32, 41
Scania-Vabis (Sweden) 149(T), 150, 151, 152, 153, 154
Scammel (Great Britain) 84
Steyr-Daimler-Puch (Austria) 10, 11
Swiss Ministry of Defence 158, 159
Tass 112(T), 137(T)
United States Army 161, 167(C), 168, 169, 171(T), 177, 178, 179(T), 181, 182, 187
United States Marine Corps 184(T)
Valmet (Finland) 28, 29
Vauxhall (Great Britain) 74, 75(T), 76
Volvo (Sweden) 4, 143, 144, 145, 146, 147, 148, 155, 156, 174

T Bell 8
Christopher F Foss 31, 34, 35, 77(T + C), 79, 80, 81
T Gander 72
Col R J Icks 171(B), 179(B)
J I Taibo 71(B), 142, 165(T + C), 167(T), 172, 173

Index